NORTON PROGRAM DESCRIPTIONS

LP	Formats and prints text files.
NCACHE2	Disk cache.
NCC	Controls system options and settings.
NCD	Directory manager.
NDD	Repairs damaged disks.
NDIAGS	Diagnostics.
NDOS	New and improved DOS commands.
NORTON	Norton Utilities shell.
NUCONFIG	Configures the Norton Utilities.
RESCUE	Stores a copy of vital hard disk information.
SFORMAT	Flexible disk formatter.
SMARTCAN	Protects erased data for easy unerasing.
SPEEDISK	Defragments your hard disk.
SYSINFO	System information.
TS	Searches a disk for text.
UNERASE	Recovers erased files.
UNFORMAT	Unformats formatted disks.
WIPEINFO	Destroys specified data.

Computer users are not all alike.
Neither are SYBEX books.

We know our customers have a variety of needs. They've told us so. And because we've listened, we've developed several distinct types of books to meet the needs of each of our customers. What are you looking for in computer help?

If you're looking for the basics, try the **ABC's** series. For a more visual approach, select full-color **Quick & Easy** books.

Running Start books are two books in one: a fast-paced tutorial, followed by a command reference.

Mastering and **Understanding** titles offer you a step-by-step introduction, plus an in-depth examination of intermediate-level features, to use as you progress.

Our **Up & Running** series is designed for computer-literate consumers who want a no-nonsense overview of new programs. Just 20 basic lessons, and you're on your way.

SYBEX **Encyclopedias, Desktop References**, and **A to Z** books provide a *comprehensive reference* and explanation of all of the commands, features, and functions of the subject software.

Sometimes a subject requires a special treatment that our standard series don't provide. So you'll find we have titles like **Advanced Techniques, Handbooks, Tips & Tricks,** and others that are specifically tailored to satisfy a unique need.

You'll find SYBEX publishes a variety of books on every popular software package. Looking for computer help? Help Yourself to SYBEX.

For a complete catalog of our publications:

SYBEX Inc.
2021 Challenger Drive, Alameda, CA 94501
Tel: (510) 523-8233/(800) 227-2346 Telex: 336311
Fax: (510) 523-2373

SYBEX is committed to using natural resources wisely to preserve and improve our environment. This is why we have been printing the text of books like this one on recycled paper since 1982.

This year our use of recycled paper will result in the saving of more than 15,300 trees. We will lower air pollution effluents by 54,000 pounds, save 6,300,000 gallons of water, and reduce landfill by 2,700 cubic yards.

In choosing a SYBEX book you are not only making a choice for the best in skills and information, you are also choosing to enhance the quality of life for all of us.

Norton Utilities 7
Instant Reference

The SYBEX Instant Reference Series

Instant References are available on these topics:

AutoCAD Release 11

AutoCAD Release 12

CorelDRAW 3

dBASE

dBASE IV 1.1 Programmer's

dBASE IV 1.1 User's

DESQview

DOS

DOS 5

DR DOS 6

Excel 4 for Windows

Harvard Graphics 3

Harvard Graphics for Windows

Lotus 1-2-3 Release 2.3 & 2.4 for DOS

Lotus 1-2-3 for Windows

Macintosh Software

Microsoft Access

Norton Desktop for DOS

Norton Desktop for Windows 2.0

Norton Utilities 6

OS/2 2.1

PageMaker 4.0 for the Macintosh

Paradox 3.5 User's

Paradox 4 Programmer's

Paradox 4 User's

PC Tools 7.1

Windows 3.1

Word for Windows, Version 2.0

WordPerfect 5

WordPerfect 5.1 for DOS

WordPerfect 5.1 for Windows

Norton Utilities® 7 Instant Reference

Third Edition

Michael Gross and Linda L. Gaus

SYBEX®

San Francisco • Paris • Düsseldorf • Soest

Acquisitions Editor: Dianne King
Series Editor: James A. Compton
Developmental Editor: Sharon Crawford
Editors: Kathleen Lattinville, Richard Mills, Abby Azrael
Technical Editors: Sharon Crawford, Lillian Chen, Dan Tauber
Word Processors: Susan Trybull, Ann Dunn
Series Book Designer: Ingrid Owen
Production Artists: Charlotte Carter, Lisa Jaffe
Screen Graphics: Cuong Le, John Corrigan
Desktop Publishing Production: Len Gilbert, Stephanie Hollier
Production Assistants: Janet K. MacEachern, David Silva
Indexer: Nancy Guenther
Cover Designer: Archer Design

SYBEX is a registered trademark of SYBEX Inc.

TRADEMARKS: SYBEX has attempted throughout this book to distinguish proprietary trademarks from descriptive terms by following the capitalization style used by the manufacturer.

SYBEX is not affiliated with any manufacturer.
Every effort has been made to supply complete and accurate information. However, SYBEX assumes no responsibility for its use, nor for any infringement of the intellectual property rights of third parties which would result from such use.

The text of this book is printed on recycled paper.

First edition copyright ©1991 SYBEX Inc.
Second edition copyright ©1991 SYBEX Inc.
Copyright ©1993 SYBEX Inc., 2021 Challenger Drive, Alameda, CA 94501.
World rights reserved. No part of this publication may be stored in a retrieval system, transmitted, or reproduced in any way, including but not limited to photocopy, photograph, magnetic or other record, without the prior agreement and written permission of the publisher.

Library of Congress Card Number: 93-83896
ISBN: 0-7821-1212-9

Manufactured in the United States of America
10 9 8 7 6 5 4 3 2 1

*To our grandmothers,
Irma Gaus (1902-1987),
Regina Gross,
Mary Kamens,
and Dorothy S. White.*

Acknowledgments

We would like to thank all those who contributed to this book as it would not have been possible without them. We apologize in advance to anyone inadvertently omitted. The following people deserve special mention:

- To Dianne King, Acquisitions Editor, who provided the opportunity once again.

- To Sharon Crawford, Developmental Editor, for her good counsel, humor, and attitude (as always).

- To Abby Azrael, for her careful and attentive editing and for making an unwieldy project manageable.

- To Nancy Stevenson and Dave Hicks at Symantec for making the program available and for invaluable technical help, respectively.

- To the SYBEX production team: Lisa Jaffe, chapter artist; John Corrigan, graphic artist; Stephanie Hollier, typesetter; and David Silva, production assistant.

Table of Contents

Introduction

xvii

BE	1
ASK	1
BEEP	3
BOX	3
CLS	4
DELAY	4
EXIT	5
GOTO	5
JUMP	5
MONTHDAY	6
PRINTCHAR	6
REBOOT	7
ROWCOL	7
SA	8
SHIFTSTATE	8
TRIGGER	9
WEEKDAY	9
WINDOW	9
CALIBRAT	13
DISKEDIT	17
Edit/Object Functions	17
Window Functions	32
Info Functions	36
Tools Functions	37
DISKMON	47
DISKREET 6	50

DISKREET 7	**64**
DISKTOOL	**78**
DS	**84**
DUPDISK	**86**
EP	**88**
FA	**91**
FD	**93**
FILEFIND	**94**
FILEFIX	**107**
FL	**114**
FS	**115**
IMAGE	**116**
INSTDOS	**117**
LP	**118**
NCACHE2/NCACHE	**121**
NCC	**125**
NCD	**133**
NDD	**142**
NDIAGS	**150**
NDOS	**155**
ALIAS	**156**
ATTRIB	**157**
BEEP	**158**
CANCEL	**158**
CD	**158**
CHDIR	**159**
CDD	**159**
CLS	**160**
COLOR	**160**
COPY	**161**
DEL	**162**

DELAY	163
DESCRIBE	164
DIR	164
DIRS	166
DRAWBOX	167
DRAWHLINE	168
DRAWVLINE	169
ECHOS	170
ENDLOCAL	170
ERASE	171
ESET	171
EXCEPT	171
EXIT	172
FOR	172
FREE	173
GLOBAL	173
GOSUB	174
HELP	175
HISTORY	175
IF	176
IFF	178
INKEY	179
INPUT	180
KEYSTACK	181
LH	181
LIST	182
LOADBTM	183
LOADHIGH	183
LOG	183
MEMORY	184
MOVE	184

POPD	**185**
PROMPT	**186**
PUSHD	**187**
QUIT	**188**
RD	**188**
REBOOT	**188**
REN	**189**
RENAME	**190**
RETURN	**190**
RMDIR	**190**
SCREEN	**191**
SCRPUT	**191**
SELECT	**192**
SET	**194**
SETDOS	**195**
SETLOCAL	**196**
SWAPPING	**197**
TEE	**197**
TEXT/ENDTEXT	**197**
TIMER	**198**
TRUENAME	**198**
TYPE	**199**
UNALIAS	**199**
UNSET	**200**
VOL	**200**
VSCRPUT	**201**
Y	**201**
NORTON	**203**
NUCONFIG	**222**
RESCUE	**226**
SFORMAT	**229**
SPEEDISK	**237**

SYSINFO	**247**
TS	**253**
UNERASE	**256**
UNFORMAT	**268**
WIPEINFO	**270**

Index

Introduction

The intent of this book is simple. It is designed to help users of the Norton Utilities find information about the package quickly and easily. It will be the most helpful to users who have some familiarity with the software and need information on something in particular that is eluding them or want to try out aspects of a program unfamiliar to them. PC users who are new to the package will also find the book sufficient to give them a working knowledge of the programs.

NEW FEATURES

There are a number of new features in the Norton Utilities 7, which are detailed in the Upgrade Information sections throughout the book. Worthy of particular mention, however, is the ability to support compressed drives. The Norton Utilities 7 works with a compressed drive like any other drive (for example, you can unerase files on a compressed drive in the same way you unerase files on a normal drive). The Norton Utilities 7 supports compressed drives created with the following programs: Stacker 2.0 and 3.0, SuperStore 2.0, SuperStore Pro, DR DOS 6's SuperStore, and MS DOS 6's DoubleSpace.

HOW THIS BOOK IS ORGANIZED

There is one section devoted to each of the programs that make up the package. Within each section you will find a summary description of the program and its capabilities, upgrade information detailing any differences between version 6 and version 7, if any, an annotated sequence of steps detailing each of the program's functions, and complete command-line syntax. The sections are ordered alphabetically, as are the program functions within each section (with the exception of DISKEDIT where, because of the size of the program, functions are grouped first by type and then alphabetically within each type).

NAVIGATING THE INTERFACE

Most of the programs in the Norton Utilities have an interactive interface, replete with pull-down menus, dialog boxes, lists, and options of various sorts. For the sake of economy and clarity, the sequences of steps throughout the book tell you only to "select" this or that option. What "select" means in any particular case depends entirely upon what you are selecting where. The following sections detail the different parts of the interactive interface and how to navigate each of them.

Using Pull-Down Menus

You can pull down a menu in one of three ways:

- Press the **Alt** key alone or **F10**. This highlights the first menu on the left of the menu bar. You can then access the menu you want by pressing ← and → as needed, and then pressing ↵.

- Hold down the **Alt** key and press the highlighted letter in the menu's name—to pull down the File menu, for example, hold down the Alt key and press F.

- Place the mouse pointer on the menu name and click the left button.

Once the menu you want is pulled down, there are four ways to select an option:

- Use ↑ and ↓ to highlight the option, and press ↵.

- Press the highlighted letter in the option's name.

- Place the mouse pointer on the option and click the left button.

- Press the **Ctrl** or **Alt** key combination listed next to the option. Such a combination is not available for all options.

Using List Boxes

Often you will be required to select an item from a list of items within a box (usually files or directories). If the list contains more items than can be displayed at once, you can display different parts of the list as follows:

- Press ↑ and ↓ as needed.
- Press the Home key to go to the beginning of the list.
- Press the End key to go to the end of the list.
- Place the mouse pointer on the scroll box (the solid rectangular block) on the scroll bar, found on the right-hand edge of the list box. Click the left button and hold it down. Drag the box up or down as needed and release the button when you're finished.

You can select an item from a list in one of the following ways:

- Highlight the item with a combination of ↑, ↓, Home, and End, and press ↵ or select the accompanying OK option.
- Place the mouse pointer on the item, and double-click the left button or click the right button once.
- Place the mouse pointer on the item, click the left button once, and then select the accompanying OK option.

Some lists in version 7 require you to select multiple items. You select each item in one of two ways:

- Highlight the item with a combination of ↑, ↓, Home, and End, and press the spacebar.
- Place the mouse pointer on the item and double-click the left button or click the right button once.

Using Drop Down Lists (Version 7 Only)

A drop down list contains a set of options from which you are required to select one. The location of the list is marked by a down arrow next to the currently selected option and is "folded up" like a window blind until you pull it down. You can pull down a drop down list in one of the following ways:

- Move the highlight bar to the list by pressing the Tab key or the Alt key in combination with the list's highlighted hot key and then press Alt-↓.

- Move the mouse pointer to the list's down arrow and click the left button once.

Once the list is down, select an option in one of two ways:

- Use the ↑ and ↓ to highlight the option and press ↵.

- Move the mouse pointer to the option and click the left button once.

Using Dialog Box Buttons

Dialog box buttons usually appear in groups horizontally across the bottom of a dialog box, though there are other configurations. You can select a button in one of the following ways:

- Use the cursor keys to highlight a button and press ↵.

- Press the capitalized letter of the button.

- Move the mouse pointer to the button and click the left button.

Using Toggle Options and Radio Buttons

A *toggle option* appears as a box in graphics mode or as square brackets in non-graphics mode. When activated, it is marked with a check mark or with an *x*. A *radio button* appears as a circle in graphics mode or as parentheses in non-graphics mode. When activated, it is marked with a filled circle.

When you activate one radio button, it automatically turns off the others in the group. Toggle options are independent of one another and can be turned on or off regardless of the state of neighboring toggle options.

You can turn toggle options and buttons on or off in either of the following ways:

- Use ↑, ↓, ←, or → to move the cursor to the option and press the spacebar. The spacebar also cycles you through a group of radio buttons.

- Move the mouse pointer to the option and click the left button.

Using Prompts

Prompts are those sections of a dialog box in which you are required to enter text. The standard editing keys are available when typing text at a prompt:

- The Home key moves you to the beginning of the line, and the End key moves you to the end.

- The ← and → keys move the cursor one space to the left and right, respectively.

- The Backspace key deletes the character to the left of the cursor. The Delete key deletes the character at the cursor position.

To move the cursor with the mouse, position the mouse pointer at the new location and click the left button.

Navigating within Dialog Boxes

Dialog boxes are often crowded with many different kinds of options; similar options tend to be grouped together. You can move among these discrete groups in the following ways:

- Press the Tab key to move from one group to the next—for example, from a prompt to the first button in a buttons area to the first option in a dialog box menu.

- Press one of the arrow keys to move to the next option, regardless of the group.

- Move the mouse pointer to the option you want. (Click the left button to select the option.)

The mouse is the most efficient means of selecting an option. If, however, you do not have a mouse or simply prefer the keyboard, some combination of the Tab key and the arrow keys works best.

Moving Dialog Boxes (Version 7 Only)

Many dialog boxes can be moved around on the screen, allowing you to see information behind (or beneath) them. You can move those dialog boxes that have a control box in their upper left corner and that do not occupy the entire screen. (Some programs have such a control box, but occupy the entire screen. These cannot be moved.) You can move a dialog box in one of two ways:

- Place the mouse pointer on the dialog box's title bar, click and hold the left mouse button, drag the box to a new location, and release the button when finished.

OR

1. Pull down the control box menu by placing the mouse pointer on the control box in the upper left corner of the dialog box and clicking the left button or by pressing **Alt-Spacebar**.

2. From the control box menu, select **Move.**

3. Move the box using ↑, ↓, ←, and → and press ↵ when you are finished.

Quitting Norton Programs (Version 7 Only)

You can quit most programs in one or more of the following ways:

- Select the Exit option from the program's first pull down menu (whatever it is called) or press Alt-X.

- Press Escape.

- Select Quit (or sometimes Cancel) from the program's main dialog box.

- Press Alt-F4.

- Pull down the control box menu and select Close.

You can quit most programs in at least three of these ways. A few programs (FA, FD, FL, FS, IMAGE, LP, TS) do not use dialog boxes and quit automatically when they finish running.

GETTING HELP (Version 7)

Help is available for each of the programs that constitute the Norton Utilities. To get help, follow these steps:

1. Pull down the Help menu and select **Index** or press **F1**.

2. In the Help dialog box, read the help information.

3. Use the Tab key to highlight any related topic about which you wish further information (related topics appear in a different color or shade of gray) and select **Go To**.

4. Repeat step 3 as necessary. Alternatively, select **Go Back** to return to the previous help screen or **Index** to return to the first screen you saw. These options allow you to retrace your steps and examine different related topics.

5. When you are finished, select **Cancel** to return to the program.

Help information in the Norton Utilities is extensive, but, more importantly, context-sensitive. If you are in the middle of an operation or sequence of steps, pressing **F1** (the Help menu may not be accessible when you are in the middle of something) brings up a description of that function. This is a good way to get an explanation of an option on a pull-down menu, for example (pull down the menu, highlight the option, press **F1**).

Some programs do not have Help menus, but context-sensitive help is available anyway via **F1**. A few programs (FA, FD, FL, FS, IMAGE, LP, TS) do not have dialog boxes, etc. and are used only from the command line. Context-sensitive help is not available for these programs. Command-line help is available for these (and all other) programs: Simply type the program name, followed by a space and a ?, at the command line, and press ↵. You will see a listing of command-line syntax and options.

GETTING HELP (Version 6)

Help is available for each of the programs that constitute the Norton Utilities. To get help on a topic, follow these steps:

1. Click the left mouse button on **F1=Help** in the upper-right corner of the screen, or press **F1**.

2. In the Help dialog box, highlight a topic and select **Help**. You can select **Cancel** at this point to return to the program.

3. When you've finished reading, select **Cancel** to return to the program. Alternatively, select **Next** to see help on the next topic in the list, select **Previous** to see help on the previous topic, or select **Topics** to go back to the list of topics. Selecting Topics returns you to step 2.

Help is context-sensitive—that is, if you are in the middle of an operation or a sequence of steps, selecting Help takes you directly to the description of that function.

The sequence of steps above requires that the program you are working in have an interactive mode (interactive help, therefore, is unavailable in those programs that are only used from the command line). Command-line help is available for these and all other programs: Simply enter the program name, followed by a space and a ?, at the command line, and press ↵. You will see a listing of command-line syntax and options.

BE
The Batch Enhancer

BE allows you to add the following enhancements to your batch files: custom menus or prompts, sound, boxes, windows, timed delays, timed execution, color, conditional branching, cursor control, and rebooting.

- **UPGRADE INFORMATION**   BE 7 is identical to BE 6.

- **SYNTAX**

    BE *datafile* [[GOTO] *label*]

OR

   BE *command*

datafile is the name of a file containing a list of BE commands. Each command must be on its own line, and the last line must end with a carriage return. Normal DOS commands within *datafile* are ignored. Commands within *datafile* can be grouped into subroutines marked off by a label and executed selectively. (See "GOTO.")

command is one of seventeen possible BE commands, each having its own options and switches. Descriptions of these commands follow.

label is the label within *datafile* at which you wish execution to begin.

ASK

Puts custom menus or prompts in batch files.

Syntax

   BE ASK "*prompt*", [*keys*] [default=*key*] [timeout=*secs*] [adjust=*#*] [*textcolor*][ON *background*][/debug]

"prompt" is the text of the menu or prompt to be displayed. *Prompt* must be enclosed in quotation marks.

keys are the keys that are valid responses to *prompt*. Pressing a key other than the one listed causes a warning beep to sound. ASK provides conditional branching by returning a different DOS ERRORLEVEL code for each key in *keys*. The first key returns ERRORLEVEL 1, the second ERRORLEVEL 2, etc.

default=key specifies the key returned if no key is pressed before timeout or if you press enter.

timeout=secs specifies the number of seconds ASK waits before automatically assuming the default. If no timeout is specified, ASK will wait forever.

adjust=# adds a specified number (integer) to the DOS ERRORLEVEL code returned by each key in *keys*. ASK provides conditional branching by returning a different DOS ERRORLEVEL code for each key in *keys*. The first key returns the code ERRORLEVEL 1, the second ERRORLEVEL 2, etc. If, then, one of the menu choices calls up another menu, its first key will also return ERRORLEVEL 1 and its second key ERRORLEVEL 2. To prevent a conflict, use adjust=# to change the value of the ERRORLEVEL codes returned by one of the two menus. The maximum value for # is 254.

textcolor specifies the text color of *prompt*. Valid colors are black, blue, green, cyan, red, magenta, yellow, white, bright blue, bright green, bright cyan, bright red, bright magenta, bright yellow, and bright white. For colors to work reliably, the ANSI.SYS driver should be loaded.

background specifies the background color of *prompt*. Valid colors are black, blue, green, cyan, red, magenta, yellow, and white. For colors to work reliably, the ANSI.SYS driver should be loaded.

debug displays the DOS ERRORLEVEL code returned by the *key* pressed.

Example See the comprehensive example that shows BE ASK in context at the end of the BE section.

BEEP

Plays tones for a specified duration and of a specified pitch. Tones can be specified on the command line or grouped together in a file.

Syntax

BE BEEP [/D#] [/F#] [/R#] [/W#]

Or

BE BEEP *filename* [/E]

/D# specifies the duration of a tone in eighteenths of a second; # must be positive.

/F# specifies the frequency of a tone in hertz; # must be positive.

/R# specifies the number of times a tone is repeated; # must be positive.

/W# specifies the interval between tones in eighteenths of a second; # must be positive.

filename specifies the name of a file containing tones to be played. Tones are specified in *filename* just as they are on the command line by using the switches listed above.

/E echoes comments in *filename* to the screen. Comments are set off from commands by a semicolon. To be echoed, they must be enclosed in quotation marks (for example, /f440; "Play this note").

Example See the comprehensive example that shows BE BEEP in context at the end of the BE section.

BOX

Draws a box at specified screen coordinates.

Syntax

BE BOX *TLCrow TLCcol BRCrow BRCcol*
[Single | Double] [*textcolor*][**ON** *background*]

4 BE

TLCrow TLCcol are the screen coordinates of the top-left corner of the box. *TLCrow* is the row in which this corner sits, and *TLCcol* is the column.

BRCrow BRCcol are the screen coordinates of the bottom-right corner of the box. *BRCrow* is the row in which this corner sits, and *BRCcol* is the column.

Single ¦ **Double** specifies whether the box is drawn with single or double lines.

textcolor specifies the foreground color of the box. Valid colors are listed under the ASK command.

background sets the background color of the bo ⸱. Valid colors are listed under the ASK command.

Example   See the comprehensive example that shows BE BOX in context at the end of the BE section.

CLS

Clears the screen.

Syntax

BE CLS [textcolor][ON *background*]

textcolor sets the foreground color after the screen is cleared. Valid colors are listed under the ASK command.

background sets the background color after the screen is cleared. Valid colors are listed under the ASK command.

Example   See the comprehensive example that shows BE CLS in context at the end of the BE section.

DELAY

Pauses batch-file execution for a specified length of time.

Syntax

BE DELAY #

specifies the duration of the pause in eighteenths of a second; *#* must be positive.

Example See the comprehensive example that shows BE DELAY in context at the end of the BE section.

EXIT

Quits a BE *datafile* and returns you to the DOS prompt. This command can only be used within BE *datafiles*.

Syntax

BE EXIT

Example See the comprehensive example that shows BE EXIT in context at the end of the BE section.

GOTO

Allows for selective execution of BE commands within *datafile*. BE essentially supports the DOS GOTO batch file command, but within BE *datafiles*.

Syntax

BE *datafile* **[[GOTO]***#label*]

datafile is the file containing BE commands.

label is the name of the label within *datafile* marking the group of commands you want to execute. Labels in *datafile* are functionally identical to labels in DOS batch files.

JUMP

Provides conditional branching with BE *datafiles*. This command can only be used within BE *datafiles*.

Syntax

BE JUMP *label1* [, *label2* , ... , *label#*] [/default:*label*]

labels is a list of label names within *datafile* marking different groups of commands. JUMP uses the DOS ERRORLEVEL code returned by the command immediately prior to it (such as MONTHDAY or WEEKDAY). If ERRORLEVEL is 1, execution jumps to *label1*; if ERRORLEVEL is 2, execution jumps to *label2*; and so on.

/default:*label* is the label to which execution jumps if the DOS ERRORLEVEL code is 0 or if there is no corresponding label in the list (i.e. ERRORLEVEL = 3 and there are only two listed labels). If these conditions apply and the default label is not specified, execution simply moves on to the next command.

Example   See the comprehensive example that shows BE JUMP in context at the end of the BE section.

MONTHDAY

Provides the current day of the month as a DOS ERRORLEVEL code.

Syntax

BE MONTHDAY [/debug]

debug displays the DOS ERRORLEVEL code returned by MONTHDAY.

PRINTCHAR

Writes a character to the screen a specified number of times.

Syntax

BE PRINTCHAR *char* # [*textcolor*][**ON background**]

char is the character to be written.

specifies the number of times the character is to be written up to a maximum of 80.

textcolor specifies the color of the character. Valid colors are listed under the ASK command.

background sets the background color on which characters are written. Valid colors are listed under the ASK command.

Example See the comprehensive example that shows BE PRINTCHAR in context at the end of the BE section.

REBOOT

Reboots your machine.

Syntax

BE REBOOT [/verify]

verify prompts you for confirmation. Press Y to reboot. Press any other key not to reboot.

Example See the comprehensive example that shows BE REBOOT in context at the end of the BE section.

ROWCOL

Positions the cursor and optionally writes text at specified screen coordinates.

Syntax

BE ROWCOL *row col* **[***text***] [***textcolor***][ON** *background***]**

row is the row in which the cursor is positioned.

col is the column in which the cursor is positioned.

text is the text to be written at the new cursor position. Text must be enclosed in quotes if it contains spaces or commas.

textcolor specifies the color of *text*. Valid colors are listed under the ASK command.

background specifies the background color of *text*. Valid colors are listed under the ASK command.

Example See the comprehensive example that shows BE ROW-COL in context at the end of the BE section.

SA

The Screen Attributes command. Sets text, background, and border colors. For SA to be used, the ANSI.SYS driver must be loaded.

Syntax

BE SA *default* **[/N] [/CLS]**

OR

BE SA [*intensity*] [*textcolor*] [**ON** *background*] **[/N] [/CLS]**

default manipulates the default display colors (white on black). The three valid settings are Normal, Reverse, and Underline.

intensity specifies the intensity of the foreground text. Can be set to Bright or Blinking, or, in version 7 only, Bold.

textcolor specifies the color of the foreground text. Valid colors are listed under the ASK command.

background specifies the background color. Valid colors are listed under the ASK command.

/N leaves the border color unchanged. (Normally, the border color is automatically set to the background color.) Use this switch to change the background color but not the border color.

/CLS clears the screen after colors are changed.

Example See the comprehensive example that shows BE SA in context at the end of the BE section.

SHIFTSTATE

Provides the current state of the Shift, Ctrl, and Alt keys as DOS ERRORLEVEL codes.

Syntax

BE SHIFTSTATE [/debug]

debug displays the DOS ERRORLEVEL codes returned by SHIFTSTATE. When the right Shift key is down, a code of 1 is returned. Left Shift returns 2, Ctrl returns 4, and Alt returns 8. Moreover, the codes are additive. If, for example, both Shift keys are being pressed, SHIFTSTATE will return 3.

TRIGGER

Pauses execution and causes the remainder of the batch file to run at a specified time.

Syntax

BE TRIGGER *hh:mm* **[AM ¦ PM]**

hh:mm is the time of batch-file execution. Use 24-hour format unless the AM or PM options are included.

AM ¦ PM specifies the time of execution in 12-hour format.

WEEKDAY

Provides the current day of the week as a DOS ERRORLEVEL code.

Syntax

BE WEEKDAY [/debug]

debug displays the DOS ERRORLEVEL code returned by WEEKDAY. Sunday = 1, Monday = 2, Saturday = 7, etc.

Example   See the comprehensive example that shows BE WEEKDAY in context at the end of the BE section.

WINDOW

Draws a window at specified screen coordinates.

Syntax

BE WINDOW *TLCrow TLCcol BRCrow BRCcol* [explode | zoom] [shadow] [*textcolor*][ON *background*]

TLCrow TLCcol are the screen coordinates (row and column) of the top-left corner of the window.

BRCrow BRCcol are the screen coordinates (row and column) of the bottom-right corner of the window.

explode causes the window to expand from its center to its final position when it is drawn.

zoom is the same as explode.

shadow gives the window a three-dimensional look by drawing a shadow along the right and bottom edges of the window. The shadow does not obscure text underneath it.

textcolor specifies the color of the window. Valid colors are listed under the ASK command.

background specifies the background color of the window. Valid colors are listed under the ASK command.

Example   See the comprehensive example that shows BE WINDOW in context at the end of the BE section.

- **EXAMPLE**   The following examples illustrate most of the BE commands.

The first file demonstrates the BOX, CLS, DELAY, EXIT, JUMP, ROWCOL, and WEEKDAY commands. It displays the day of the week by jumping to the label indicated by the WEEKDAY command. Given the presence of the EXIT command, this example should be used as a BE *datafile*.

```
be weekday
be jump sun, mon, tue, wed, thu, fri, sat
:sat
   be cls
   be box 10 30 14 50 double green on black
   be rowcol 12 37 "Saturday" bright white on black
   be delay 36
   be exit
```

BE 11

```
:fri
    be cls
    be box 10 30 14 50 double green on black
    be rowcol 12 38 "Friday" bright white on black
    be delay 36
    be exit
:thu
    be cls
    be box 10 30 14 50 double green on black
    be rowcol 12 37 "Thursday" bright white on black
    be delay 36
    be exit
:wed
    be cls
    be box 10 30 14 50 double green on black
    be rowcol 12 36 "Wednesday" bright white on black
    be delay 36
    be exit
:tue
    be cls
    be box 10 30 14 50 double green on black
    be rowcol 12 37 "Tuesday" bright white on black
    be delay 36
    be exit
:mon
    be cls
    be box 10 30 14 50 double green on black
    be rowcol 12 38 "Monday" bright white on black
    be delay 36
    be exit
:sun
    be cls
    be box 10 30 14 50 double green on black
    be rowcol 12 38 "Sunday" bright white on black
    be delay 36
    be exit
```

This example demonstrates the ASK, BEEP, GOTO, PRINT-CHAR, REBOOT, SA, and WINDOW commands. It displays a small sample menu from which you may choose one of four functions.

BE

```
be cls
be ask "will you (e)xclaim, (b)eep, (c)hange colors,
(r)eboot, or (q)uit?", ebcrq
    if errorlevel 5 goto: quit
    if errorlevel 4 goto: boot
    if errorlevel 3 goto: color
    if errorlevel 2 goto: sound
    if errorlevel 1 goto: rats
:rats
    be cls
    be window 10 30 14 49 green on black zoom
    be rowcol 12 37
    be printchar ! 6 red
    goto quit
:sound
    be beep /d9 /f800 /r3
    goto quit
:color
    be cls
    be sa bright white on blue
    goto quit
:boot
    be reboot
:quit
```

CALIBRAT

CALIBRAT optimizes the performance of your hard disk by checking and optionally changing your hard-disk interleave and by testing the integrity of every byte on the disk. Optimizing the interleave maximizes the speed at which data is read from and written to your hard disk. Checking every byte ensures the integrity of your data by moving data from questionable or corrupted areas on the disk to safe areas.

- **UPGRADE INFORMATION** CALIBRAT 7 is indentical to CALIBRAT 6.

To Use the Disk Calibrator

1. After starting CALIBRAT, an introductory screen appears. Select **Continue** when you are finished reading.

2. Select a target drive. (This step is omitted if you have only one logical drive or if the drive is specified on the command line.)

3. You will see two information screens. Select **Continue** when you are finished reading them.

4. After System Integrity Testing and Seek Testing, select **Continue**.

5. After Data Encoding Testing, select **Continue**.

6. Select an interleave and then select **Continue**.

7. Select a level for Pattern Testing.

8. On the Report for Drive screen, select **Done** if you do not wish to keep CALIBRAT's report of its results. Select **Print** to print the report or select **Save As** to save it in a file. If you choose **Save As**, enter the name of the report file in the Save Report dialog box.

9. On the Select Drive window, you may select another drive to calibrate (this takes you back to step 3) or select **Cancel** to quit.

In step 4, System Integrity Testing checks to make sure that various components and functions integral to the working of your hard disk do, in fact, work properly. The computer's RAM, the hard-disk controller, the hard-disk controller's RAM, and the FATs (file allocation tables) are checked, among others. CALIBRAT cannot correct any errors it finds in these tests.

Seek Testing tests various aspects of the performance of your harddisk. BIOS Seek Overhead measures how long it takes for the relevant ROM BIOS instructions to be executed when the hard disk is accessed. Track-to-Track measures how long it takes for the disk heads to move from one track to the next. Full Stroke measures how long it takes for the disk heads to move from the first track to the last. Average Seek measures how long it takes, on average, for the heads to find a randomly selected track. This is the most common measure of hard- disk speed.

In step 5, Data Encoding Testing checks your hard disk and harddisk controller to determine the method by which data is written to the hard disk. Results are displayed in the Encoding Test box.

In step 6, you select an *interleave;* For "bookkeeping" purposes, DOS numbers each sector on a hard disk. When consecutively numbered sectors are located next to one another on your disk, the disk has a 1:1 interleave; when they are located every other sector, the disk has a 2:1 interleave; when they are located every third sector, the disk has a 3:1 interleave; and so on.

CALIBRAT determines your current interleave and checks other possible settings to determine which will allow your computer to read and write data the fastest. This setting, at which your hard disk makes the fewest revolutions when reading or writing some given amount of data, is said to be the *optimal interleave.*

CALIBRAT can alter the interleave of your hard disk by doing a nondestructive low-level format. This format, executed during Pattern Testing, is different from the format you normally do to prepare a disk for use and does not destroy any of your data.

CALIBRAT cannot adjust the interleave on every hard disk (see NOTES, below). If CALIBRAT cannot adjust your hard disk's interleave, it will present a message to this effect. Select OK to acknowledge the message and continue on to Pattern Testing in Step 7.

In step 7, Pattern Testing checks every sector on your hard disk to make sure data can be written to it and read from it accurately. CALIBRAT writes and reads patterns of bits (0's and 1's)—if it finds an error in any byte, it marks the cluster containing that byte as bad, thus removing it from use by DOS. If there is any data on that cluster, it is moved to an errorless cluster.

Pattern Testing can take a number of hours, depending on the level you choose. It can be safely interrupted at any time by pressing Esc or by clicking either mouse button and can be resumed in a later session.

• SYNTAX

CALIBRAT [drive:] [/options]

drive: specifies the drive you want to calibrate.

The options are the following:

/BATCH omits introductory screens, information screens, and "Continue" prompts. It runs all tests consecutively and exits to DOS when finished.

/BLANK turns off the display during Pattern Testing.

/NOCOPY omits track copying during Pattern Testing.

16 CALIBRAT

/NOFORMAT omits the nondestructive low-level format (i.e., testing and changing the interleave).

/NOSEEK omits Seek Testing.

/PATTERN:*n* sets the Pattern Testing level; *n* can be 0, 5, 40, or 80.

/R:*filename* writes CALIBRAT's report to *filename*. If you use this switch, you must also use /BATCH.

/RA:*filename* appends CALIBRAT's report to *filename*. If you use this switch, you must also use /BATCH.

/X:*drives* excludes drives you specify from any testing. For Zenith DOS users only.

- **NOTES** CALIBRAT cannot do a low-level format (i.e., adjust the interleave), but it can do pattern testing on the following:

  - Hard disks with SCSI or IDE controllers. The kind of controller you have is shown in Data Encoding Testing.

  - Hard-disk controllers that use *sector translation;* that is, controllers that cause DOS to think that the number of sectors per track is different from what it actually is.

  - Hard-disk controllers that have built-in disk caches.

CALIBRAT does not work on the following:

- Floppy drives
- Network drives or volumes
- RAM disks or Ndisks
- Drives created with the ASSIGN and SUBST commands in DOS
- File servers

DISKEDIT

DISKEDIT is perhaps the most powerful program in the Norton Utilities. Essentially a data editor, it allows you to edit (or simply view) any part of a disk. You can access data in files, directories, boot records, file allocation tables (FATs), partition tables, and in unused space. Be careful when you use DISKEDIT, as it is possible to damage files or drives, sometimes irrevocably.

- **UPGRADE INFORMATION** DISKEDIT 7 has the same functions as DISKEDIT 6 and adds a few other features. It provides a programmer's calculator, an advanced recovery mode for recovering data from severely damaged disks, and it allows you to confine data searches to certain areas of the disk or to certain kinds of objects.

EDIT/OBJECT FUNCTIONS

To Copy Marked Data

1. Mark data as a block (see "To Mark Data").
2. Pull down the Edit menu and select the **Copy** option, or press **Ctrl-C**.
3. Move to the area where the data is to be copied.
4. Pull down the Edit menu and select the **Paste Over** option, or press **Ctrl-V**.
5. Save your changes to disk: Pull down the Edit menu and select the **Write Changes** option, or press **Ctrl-W**.
6. Select **Write** in the Write Changes dialog box to confirm saving your changes to disk, or select **Review** to review your changes (this takes you back to where you were after step 4).

When you issue the Copy command, a copy of the marked data is placed in the clipboard. The Paste Over command then copies the data in the clipboard to the current cursor location. Once placed in the clipboard, data remains there until it is replaced (by copying another marked block). You can, therefore, paste the same data any number of times in different locations.

To Dump Memory

1. Pull down the Object menu and select the **Memory Dump** option or press **Alt-M**.
2. In the Memory Dump dialog box, enter the starting address of the memory segment you want to see.
3. Enter the ending address of the memory segment and select **OK**. (In steps 2 and 3, memory addresses must be specified in hex.)

This option gives you access to a copy of all or part of the first megabyte of conventional memory. You can simply look or, if you wish, you can edit and copy it. (See "To Copy Marked Data," "To Edit the Clipboard," or "To Use Write To.")

To Edit the Boot Record

Warning: Since the boot record contains critical disk information, it is recommended that you do not make any changes to it.

1. Pull down the Object menu and select the **Boot Record** option, or press **Alt-B**.
2. Make your changes.
3. Save your changes to disk: Pull down the Edit menu and select the **Write Changes** option, or press **Ctrl-W**.
4. Select **Write** in the Write Changes dialog box to confirm saving your changes to disk, or select **Review** to review your changes (this takes you back to step 2).

The boot record contains both booting instructions and information about the physical layout of a disk, such as the version of DOS under which the disk was formatted, the number of sectors on the disk, and the number of sectors in a cluster, in a track, and in the FAT. Since this information is used by both DOS and device drivers, the boot record's integrity is essential to the proper functioning of some software. **Do not edit the boot record without a very good reason**.

Information that can be edited is displayed in a single column under the header Boot Record Data. To edit, move the highlighter to the appropriate cell by using the mouse or ↑ and ↓, and enter your change.

To Edit the Clipboard

1. Pull down the Object menu, and select the **Clipboard** option.
2. Make your changes.

When you copy data, a copy of the marked data is placed in the clipboard. When you paste data, the contents of the clipboard are inserted at the cursor. Thus, editing the contents of the clipboard allows you to copy one thing and paste something else (see "To Copy Marked Data").

The clipboard has a capacity of 4K (4096 bytes). Though you can mark a block larger than this, you cannot copy it to the Clipboard.

To Edit Clusters

1. Pull down the Object menu and select the **Cluster** option, or press **Alt-C**.
2. In the Select Cluster Range dialog box that appears, type the number of the first cluster in the range you want to edit.
3. Type the number of the last cluster in the range you want to edit and select **OK**.
4. Make your changes.
5. Save your changes to disk: Pull down the Edit menu and select the **Write Changes** option, or press **Ctrl-W**.
6. Select **Write** in the Write Changes dialog box to confirm saving your changes to disk, or select **Review** to review your changes (this takes you back to step 4).

20 DISKEDIT

The Cluster option and Alt-C are not available when the current drive-type setting is Physical. To edit a cluster, the drive type must be set to Logical. Since the drive type can only be set when selecting a drive, reselect the current drive and start the step sequence again. (See "To Select a Drive.")

The Select Cluster Range dialog box displays the current drive and valid cluster numbers for that drive. You can only select clusters on the current drive. To edit clusters located on another drive, you must first select that drive. (See "To Select a Drive.")

To edit clusters, you must be in hex view. To change to hex view, pull down the View menu and select the As Hex option, or press F2. (See "To Select a Different View.")

Once in hex view, you can make changes either to the hex values or to their ASCII equivalents. Changes are entered at the cursor. Move the cursor between the hex values area and the ASCII values area by clicking either mouse button or by pressing the Tab key. Make sure to enter hex values in the hex values area and ASCII values in the ASCII values area.

To Edit a Directory

1. Pull down the Object menu and select the **Directory** option, or press **Alt-R**.
2. In the Change Directory dialog box, select a directory.
3. Make your changes.
4. Save your changes to disk: Pull down the Edit menu and select the **Write Changes** option, or press **Ctrl-W**.
5. Select **Write** in the Write Changes dialog box to confirm saving your changes to disk, or select **Review** to review your changes (this takes you back to step 3).

The Directory option and Alt-R are available only when the current drive-type setting is Logical, not Physical. Since the drive type can only be set when selecting a drive, reselect the current drive and start the step sequence again. (See "To Select a Drive.")

DISKEDIT **21**

Only the directories on the currently selected drive appear in the Change Directory dialog box. To select a directory located on another drive, you must first select that drive. (See "To Select a Drive.")

A directory can be highlighted for selection in any of the usual ways (scrolling with the mouse or arrow keys) or by using Speed Search. To use Speed Search, type the first letter or letters of the directory you want to highlight. Each time you type a letter, the highlight bar jumps to the next directory name beginning with the letter(s) typed. Pressing Ctrl-↵ cycles the highlight bar through all directories that match the current search string.

Once you have selected a directory, its structure is displayed on the screen, and you can edit any file's name, extension, size, creation date and time, starting cluster, and attributes. Altering a file's starting cluster is potentially dangerous, as DOS may no longer be able to find the entire file when needed. A file's attributes can also be changed with the Set Attributes option on the Tools menu or the File Attributes program.

The directory is laid out in columns and rows. To edit it, move the highlighter to the appropriate cell by using the mouse or the Tab and arrow keys, and enter your change.

To Edit the FAT (1st Copy)

Warning: Since the FAT contains critical information about the file structure of your disk, it is recommended that you do not edit it except as a last resort.

1. Pull down the Object menu and select the **1st FAT** option, or press **Alt-F1**. (In version 6, this option is called **1st Copy of FAT**.)
2. Make your changes.
3. Save your changes to disk: Pull down the Edit menu and select the **Write Changes** option, or press **Ctrl-W**.
4. In the Write Changes dialog box, make sure that the **Synchronize FATs** option is toggled on. This updates your changes on both copies of the FAT.

5. Select **Write** in the Write Changes dialog box to confirm saving your changes to disk, or select **Review** to review your changes (this takes you back to step 2).

6. Select **Rescan** in the Rescan dialog box to display the changes you have just made.

RAM disks have only one FAT. If you are editing a RAM disk, skip step 4. The FAT is the means by which DOS keeps track of all the files on a disk. Every cluster on a disk has a corresponding entry in the FAT indicating whether the cluster is in use and, if so, by what file.

As displayed by DISKEDIT, the first position shown in the table is the entry for cluster 2, the next is for cluster 3, and so on from left to right and top to bottom. Clusters 0 and 1 are not represented, as they contain the boot record, partition table, and the FATs, not files. If a cluster's entry shows **0**, the cluster is not in use. If it shows <BAD>, the cluster has been marked as bad and will not be used by DOS. If it shows a number other than 0, this is the number of the *next* cluster used by the file. If an entry shows <EOF>, this is the *last* cluster used by the file.

To help you navigate, the name of the file containing the highlighted cluster entry is displayed in the lower-left corner of the screen. If Quick Move is off (see "To Configure DISKEDIT"), all entries belonging to a file are highlighted when the cursor is placed on one of them.

To make changes, type over the current entry:

- Type a number to enter a number.
- Type **E** to enter an <EOF> marker.
- Type **B** to mark a cluster as <BAD>.

The highlight is moved by clicking either mouse button on an entry or by using the arrow keys. On some displays, the highlight contains a cursor. Moving left and right to other entries when the cursor is present requires multiple keystrokes.

Because editing the FAT carries with it the risk of scrambling your file structure beyond recognition, **it is recommended that you do not edit the FAT unless absolutely necessary**.

To Edit the FAT (2nd Copy)

1. Pull down the Object menu and select the **2nd FAT** option, or press **Alt-F2**. (In version 6, this option is called **2nd Copy of FAT**).

2. Follow the same steps under "To Edit the FAT (1st Copy)."

DOS creates two copies of the FAT, as there is some security in redundancy. Should the first FAT become corrupted, the second is used. (See "To Edit the FAT (1st Copy).")

To Edit a File

1. Pull down the Object menu and select the **File** option, or press **Alt-F**.

2. Select a file in the Select File dialog box.

3. Make your changes.

4. Save your changes to disk: Pull down the Edit menu and select the **Write Changes** option, or press **Ctrl-W**.

5. Select **Write** in the Write Changes dialog box to confirm saving your changes to disk, or select **Review** to review your changes (this takes you back to step 3).

This function allows you to edit the contents of a file.

In version 7, you can select a file by typing a complete file name and path (if necessary) at the File: prompt and selecting OK. Or, you may select a file by double-clicking in the Directories and Files list boxes. (You may select a file on a drive other than the current one by first selecting a drive from the Drive: drop-down list.)

In version 6, type a complete file name and path (if necessary) in the text box at the top of the Select File dialog box or select a file by double-clicking on the Drives, Dirs, and Files list boxes. Any file on your system can be selected.

To edit a file, you must be in hex view. To change to hex view, pull down the View menu and select the As Hex option, or press F2 (see "To Select a Different View").

Once in hex view, you can make changes either to the hex values or to their ASCII equivalents. Changes are entered at the cursor (as opposed to the highlight). Move the cursor between the hex values area and the ASCII values area by clicking either mouse button or by pressing the Tab key. Make sure to enter hex and ASCII values in the appropriate areas.

To Edit the Partition Table

Warning: As you stand to lose all the data in a partition you edit, it is recommended that you do not edit a partition unless absolutely necessary.

1. Pull down the Object menu and select the **Partition Table** option, or press **Alt-A**.
2. Make your changes.
3. Save your changes to disk: Pull down the Edit menu and select the **Write Changes** option, or press **Ctrl-W**.
4. Select **Write** in the Write Changes dialog box to confirm saving your changes to disk, or select **Review** to review your changes (this takes you back to step 2).

In the partition table, DOS keeps track of the boundaries of the various partitions on your hard disk. In general, you should make changes to the partition table with the FDISK command in DOS. However, since FDISK does not recognize non-DOS partitions or partitions created by other partitioning software, using DISKEDIT can be a good way to remove such partitions. Keep in mind, however, that when you *resize* a partition, you generally have to reformat it, thereby erasing all data in it.

DISKEDIT displays the partition table in rows and columns. Each row represents one partition. There are six columns.

System: the operating system under which the partition was created. Valid entries in this column are listed in Table 1.

Boot: the active partition (i.e., the partition from which an operating system boots).

Starting and Ending Locations: the first and last physical sectors of a partition; that is, the starting and ending sectors described in terms of their physical location on the disk—a particular sector on a particular cylinder (track) on a particular side of the disk.

Table 1: Valid System Entries in the Partition

ENTRY	EXPLANATION
BBT	UNIX–Bad Block Table partition
BIGDOS	Primary DOS partition larger than 32Mb (created by Compaq DOS 3.31 and MS-DOS 4.0,4.01,5.0)
BTMGR	Partition created by OS/2 Boot Manager
CP/M	CP/M partition
DM	Partition created by Disk Manager
DOS12	DOS partition with a 16-bit FAT (created by DOS versions 3.0 and later)
DOS-16	DOS partition with a 12-bit FAT (created by DOS versions 3.0 through 6 inclusive)
EXTEND	Extended DOS partition. The partition table should have no more than two DOS partitions: the main and the extended
GB	Partition created by GoldenBow VFeature
HPFS	OS/2 partition
NET286	Novell Partition
NET386	Novell Partition
PCIX	PCIX partition
Speed	Partition created by SpeedStor
Split	Partition created by SplitDrive
386-ix	UNIX partition
Unused	Unused partition
XENIX	XENIX (IBM UNIX) partition
?	Unknown partition

Relative Sectors: the "logical" location of the starting sector; that is, the number assigned to the starting sector by the partitioning software.

Number of Sectors: the total number of sectors in the partition.

Since both the number of the starting sector and the total number of sectors in a partition may be difficult to calculate, DISKEDIT can do this for you with the Recalculate Partition option in the Tools pull-down menu:

1. In the partitions to be recalculated, set Relative Sectors and Number of Sectors to 0.

2. Highlight the entire row with the mouse or cursor keys.

3. Pull down the Tools menu, and select the **Recalculate Partition** option.

Since the partition table is laid out in rows and columns, editing the table is simply a matter of highlighting the appropriate cell or entry and entering a new value. The highlight can be moved either by clicking with the mouse or by pressing Tab and the arrow keys.

To Edit Physical Sectors

1. Pull down the Object menu and select the **Physical Sector** option, or press **Alt-P**.

2. In the Select Physical Sector Range dialog box that appears, type the number of the cylinder containing the first sector in the range you want to edit.

3. Type the number of the side containing the first sector in the range you want to edit.

4. Type the number of the first sector in the range you want to edit.

5. Enter the total number of sectors in the range you want to view.

6. Make your changes in the View window that appears.

7. Save your changes to disk: Pull down the Edit menu and select the **Write Changes** option, or press **Ctrl-W**.

8. Select **Write** in the Write Changes dialog box to confirm saving your changes to disk, or select **Review** to review your changes (this takes you back to step 6).

The essential difference between editing physical and logical sectors is one of identification. Physical sectors are addressed in terms of their physical location on the disk rather than by an integer assigned by DOS for bookkeeping purposes (i.e., a logical location). So, in steps 2, 3, and 4, you identify the first sector in the range you want to edit as a particular sector on a particular track on a particular side of the disk. In step 5, you then specify the size of the range you want to edit.

Since you access sectors by physical, rather than by logical, location, you can use the steps above to view the contents of non-DOS partitions or disks with damaged file or directory structures.

Other than sector identification, editing physical sectors is identical to editing "regular" sectors. (See "To Edit Sectors.")

To Edit Sectors

1. Pull down the Object menu and select the **Sector** option, or press **Alt-S**.

2. In the Select Sector Range dialog box that appears, type the number of the first sector in the range you want to edit.

3. Enter the number of the last sector in the range you want to edit.

4. Make your changes in the View window that appears.

5. Save your changes to disk: Pull down the Edit menu and select the **Write Changes** option, or press **Ctrl-W**.

6. Select **Write** in the Write Changes dialog box to confirm saving your changes to disk, or select **Review** to review your changes (this takes you back to step 4).

The Sector option and Alt-S are available only when the current drive-type setting is Logical, not Physical. Since the drive type can only be set when selecting a drive, reselect the current drive and start the step sequence again. (See "To Select a Drive.")

The Select Sector Range dialog box displays the current drive and the valid sector numbers for that drive. You can only select sectors on the current drive. To edit sectors located on another drive, you must first select that drive. (See "To Select a Drive.")

To edit sectors, you must be in hex view. To change to hex view, pull down the View menu and select the As Hex option, or press F2 (see "To Select a Different View").

Once in hex view, you can make changes either to the hex values or to their ASCII equivalents. Changes are entered at the cursor. Move the cursor between hex values and ASCII values by clicking either mouse button or by pressing Tab. Make sure to enter hex and ASCII values in the appropriate areas.

To Fill Data

1. Mark the block to be filled (see "To Mark Data").
2. Pull down the Edit menu, and select the **Fill** command.
3. Select a fill character from the list box and select **OK**.

Data fill allows you to overwrite a marked block from beginning to end with one character.

Some fills cannot be undone. **If the block to be filled spans a sector boundary, you cannot undo the fill**. You receive a warning to this effect when you are prompted for the fill character. Sector boundaries are marked on the screen; just look for the "mile marker": for example, you might see a sector boundary marked **Cluster 103, Sector 208, or Sector 76**.

The procedure for filling in the FAT differs slightly from filling anywhere else. In step 3, instead of merely choosing the fill character, you have a choice of five ways to fill the block: You can mark the clusters in the block as Unused, as Bad, or as End-of-File marks, or you can overwrite them with a decimal or hex character of your choosing.

To Link to Corresponding Data

- Pull down the Link menu, and select an appropriate link option (file, directory, cluster chain, or partition). These options have Ctrl-key equivalents:

File	Ctrl-F
Directory	Ctrl-D
Cluster Chain (FAT)	Ctrl-T

With the link functions, you can move directly from a file to its entry in the directory or to its entries in the FAT, or vice versa. Although you can make such moves by using the Object menu, linking is faster, as the highlight will always be positioned on the corresponding file, directory entry, or cluster chain.

The link commands are only available after a file, directory, cluster, or FAT has first been selected for editing from the Object menu. The links are unavailable (and are grayed out on the Link menu) if a sector, physical sector, or boot record has been selected for editing.

An object cannot be linked to itself, so while a file is selected, File is grayed out on the Link menu.

Selecting Partition while the partition table is being edited establishes a link to the boot record corresponding to the highlighted partition. Unused partitions have no corresponding boot record, so selecting Partition has no effect.

To Mark Data (Mark Block)

1. Position the highlight at the beginning of the block to be marked.

30 DISKEDIT

2. To turn marking on, pull down the Edit menu and select the **Mark** option, or press **Ctrl-B**.
3. Using the arrow keys, move the cursor to the end of the block.
4. Repeat step 2 to turn marking off.

Or if you have a mouse,

- Click and hold the left mouse button at the beginning of the block, and drag to the end of the block.

When editing with DISKEDIT, data can be manipulated in blocks as well as in discrete units. Data marked as a block can be copied from one place to another, deleted, or overwritten.

To Print Data

1. Pull down the Tools menu and select the **Print Object As** option, or press **Ctrl-P**. (In version 6, this option is called **Print As.**)
2. In the Where To Print box in the Print As dialog box, select the print destination.
3. If you selected **File** in step 2, type the file name and path in the box next to the **File** option.
4. In the Format box, select the format in which you would like the data to be printed.
5. Select **OK**.

This function allows you to print the currently selected object in a coherent form, that is, a format that matches the kind of data you are printing.

In step 2, you have two options: you may send output to your printer or to a file.

In step 4, you may choose from five formats: Hex, Directory, FAT, Boot Record, and Partition Table. Chances are the best or most useful format is already selected (i.e., if the current object is the Boot Record, the Boot Record option will be selected).

To Select a Drive

1. Pull down the Object menu and select the **Drive** option, or press **Alt-D**.
2. In the dialog box that appears, specify the drive type in the Type box (Logical or Physical).
3. Select a drive from the drive list.

This function selects a drive (either Logical or Physical) whose contents you want to edit or view.

Selecting the Logical drive type makes all drives available by drive letter. The drive list includes all floppy drives, hard-disk partitions (D:, E:, etc.), and drives created with device drivers (RAM disks or encrypted disks created with DISKREET).

Selecting the Physical drive type makes only physical drives (for example, Floppy Disk A:, Floppy Disk B:, and Hard Disk 1) available in the drive list. It does not list logical partitions on a hard disk or drives created with device drivers.

To Undo Edits

- Pull down the Edit menu and select the **Undo** command, or press **Ctrl-U**.

This command undoes edits in reverse order—the last edit made is the first one undone.

When using Undo, keep in mind that it has important limitations:

- If you are going to undo a change, you must do it before changes are written to the disk. Once changes are saved, you cannot undo them.
- Changes written across sector boundaries cannot be undone. Sector boundaries are marked on the screen; just look for the "mile marker": **Cluster 1273, Sector 56, or Sector 76**, etc.
- The size of the undo buffer is only 512 bytes. Therefore, if you make an edit larger than this, only the last 512 bytes of the edit can be recovered.

To Write an Object

1. Pull down the Tools menu, and select the **Write Object To** option or press **Alt-W**. (In version 6, this option is called **Write To**.)

2. In the Write dialog box, select how you want to write out the current selection and select **OK.**

3. If you chose **File** in step 2, enter the name and path of the file to create. Otherwise, select the disk on which to write.

4. Specify the starting cluster, starting sector, or starting physical sector, and select **OK**. If you chose **File** in step 2, skip this step.

5. Select **Yes** to confirm writing.

The Write Object To command creates a new object by writing out a copy of the currently selected object to a destination you specify: a new file or specific clusters, sectors, or physical sectors.

DISKEDIT's Copy command, Paste Over command, and clipboard are adequate for most data-copying situations, but they do have limitations. The clipboard has a 4K capacity, and Copy and Paste Over can only copy data between existing objects. It is occasionally necessary to create *new* objects larger than 4K, such as when you move data from a damaged floppy disk to a new file on your hard disk.

WINDOW FUNCTIONS

To Close a Split Window

- Pull down the View menu and select the **Unsplit Window** option, or press **Shift-F5**.

Or if you have a mouse,

- Click either mouse button inside the Close Window box on the status bar for the window you want to close (see Figure 1).

Using the mouse allows you to close the window of your choice. The Unsplit Window command, issued either from the menu or

DISKEDIT 33

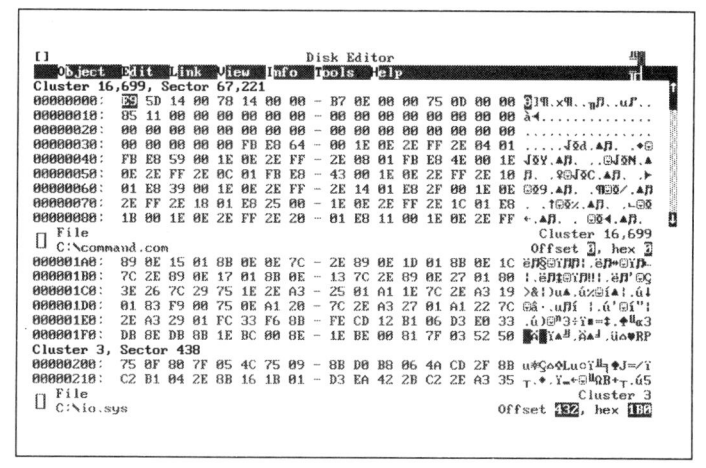

Figure 1: Hex Files

with Shift-F5, closes only the *inactive* window. The cursor and highlight appear only in the active window.

To Compare Windows

1. With split windows on the screen, pull down the Tools menu, and select the **Compare Windows** option.
2. Repeat as necessary.

The Compare Windows command enables you to compare, byte by byte, the contents of the inactive window with the contents of the active window. It is most useful when the two windows are supposed to hold identical things.

The comparison stops when a mismatch is found. Lengthy comparisons can be terminated by selecting Stop.

To Link Windows

- With split windows on the screen, pull down the Link menu, and select the **Window** option.

34 DISKEDIT

When windows are linked, highlighting an entry in a FAT in one window displays the corresponding sector in the other window, highlighting a directory entry in one window displays the corresponding file or directory in the other window, and so on.

The Window option is not available when both windows display non-System Area data (files, clusters, sectors, or physical sectors).

Linked windows are turned off the same way they are turned on: Pull down the Link menu, and select the Window option. Closing one window does not turn off linked windows. If you resplit the window, the two resulting windows will once again be linked.

To Resize Split Windows

- Pull down the View menu and select the **Grow Window** command, or press **Shift-F6**.

OR

- Pull down the View menu and select the **Shrink Window** command, or press **Shift-F7**.

Or if you have a mouse,

- Click and hold either mouse button on the status bar dividing the two windows, and drag to a new location.

The most efficient way to resize split windows is to use the mouse. Whether issued through the View menu or by using the function-key combinations, the Grow Window and Shrink Window commands resize the windows only one line at a time.

To Select a Different View

- Pull down the View menu, and select the appropriate view option:

Option	Key
As Hex	F2
As Text	F3
As Directory	F4

Option	Key
As FAT	F5
As Partition Table	F6
As Boot Record	F7

If the Auto View option is turned on (See "To Configure DISK-EDIT"), the program automatically selects the best view. ASCII text files appear in text view, binary files in hex view, FATs in FAT view, and so on. If Auto View is turned off, the view is determined by your data selection. Directories, FATs, partition tables, and boot records come up in their appropriate views. Data selected as files, clusters, sectors, or physical sectors always comes up in hex view.

You can change from one view to another at any time. However, some views are incompatible with some selections. The FAT, partition, boot record, and directory views, for example, display garbage when used to view data on the disk outside of these areas.

You can edit in every view except ASCII text view. Though text files are easier to see in text view, they should be edited in hex view.

To Split a Window

- Pull down the View menu and select the **Split Window** option, or press **Shift-F5**.

Or if you have a mouse,

- Click either mouse button anywhere on the status bar, and drag until the window is sized to your liking.

With two windows open, you can edit two different objects in two different views, though you can work in only one at a time (the active window). The cursor and the highlight appear only in the active window.

To Switch Active/Inactive Windows

- Pull down the View menu and select the **Switch Windows** command, or press **Shift-F8**.

Or if you have a mouse,

- Click either mouse button when the pointer is in the window you want to make active.

INFO FUNCTIONS

To Display Information about the Current Drive

1. Pull down the Info menu, and select the **Drive Info** option.
2. Select **OK**, or press **Esc** or ↵ when finished.

The Drive Info option gives information on the currently selected drive. This is the drive selected by the Drive option or the File option on the Object pull-down menu. In addition to the drive name and type, both logical and physical information are displayed. The logical information given is the number of bytes that make up a sector, the number of sectors in a cluster, the number of clusters on the disk, and the type of FAT on the disk. The physical information given is the number of sides and tracks on the disk, the number of sectors in a track, and the number of the drive.

To Display Information about the Current Object

1. Pull down the Info menu, and select the **Object Info** option.
2. Select **OK**, or press **Esc** or ↵ when finished.

The Object Info option provides information about the currently selected object: file, cluster, FAT, directory, etc.

Such information can be useful in many instances. For example, if a cluster containing data goes bad, it is possible to identify the endangered file. If it suddenly is not possible to save a file in the root directory, you can check to see whether the directory already contains its maximum number of files. Or, if you attempt to delete a file and get a message that says "Access denied," you can check to see whether the file is read-only.

To Map the Current Selection

1. Pull down the Info menu, and select the **Map of Object** option.
2. Select **OK**, or press **Esc** or ↵ when finished.

This function maps the amount of used and unused space on the disk and shows the relative size of the current selection.

The Map of Object option is not available for all possible selections. When the current selection is a FAT, boot record, partition table, or physical sector, the option is unavailable and grayed out on the Info menu. When the current selection is a directory, file, cluster, or sector, the option is available.

TOOLS FUNCTIONS

To Configure DISKEDIT

1. Pull down the Tools menu, and select the **Configuration** option.
2. Toggle selections.
3. Select **OK** or **Save**.

The DISKEDIT Configuration menu is a dialog box with six possible settings. The Read Only setting enables and disables editing. When it is on, editing is off; changes cannot be entered or written to disk. Every option on the Edit pull-down menu, except the Mark option, is grayed out and unavailable.

The Quick Move setting affects how quickly DISKEDIT can move from object to selected object. When it is off, 1) the name of the file that contains the displayed data appears on the status bar, and 2) in FAT view, when one cluster of a file is highlighted, all other clusters making up that file are highlighted as well. DISKEDIT requires a little time to constantly track the current file name, so switching is slowed down. Switching is faster when Quick Move is on.

The Auto View setting determines how DISKEDIT chooses a view. If it is turned on, the program automatically selects the best view. ASCII text files appear in text view, binary files in hex view, FATs in FAT view, and so on. If Auto View is off, the view is determined by your data selection. Directories, FATs, partition tables, and boot records, when selected from the Object pull-down menu or by using equivalent keystrokes, come up in their appropriate views. Data selected as files, clusters, sectors, or physical sectors always comes up in hex view.

The Quick Links setting enables linking much like what is available from the Link pull-down menu (see "To Link to Corresponding Data"), though Quick Links is faster. When this setting is on, you can link to corresponding data simply by double-clicking on an entry or by pressing ↵ when an entry is highlighted. Specifically, double-clicking on a cluster in the FAT takes you to the file containing that cluster in directory view. Double-clicking on a file name in directory view takes you to the hex view of that file. Double-clicking in hex view on any byte in use by a file takes you to that file in directory view or to the corresponding cluster in the FAT, depending on a number of different conditions.

The Exit Prompt setting enables or disables a confirmation dialog box that will appear when you quit DISKEDIT with the Escape key. (This setting is called Quit Prompt in version 6.)

The Character Filters setting essentially determines how DISKEDIT displays files in WordStar format. If Show All Characters is selected, such files appear as they do when viewed with the TYPE command in DOS, full of "ASCII noise." If View WordStar Files is selected, such files are readable as if they were regular ASCII text.

Selecting OK puts your settings in effect for the current session only. Selecting Save writes your settings to disk.

To Consult a Built-In ASCII Table

1. Pull down the Tools menu, and select the **ASCII Table** command.
2. Scroll to see the complete list of characters.
3. Select **OK**, or press **Esc** or ↵ when finished.

DISKEDIT has a built-in ASCII table for reference, showing all 256 ASCII characters and their decimal and hex equivalents. You can scroll the list up and down or jump directly to a character. To jump to a character that appears on the keyboard, simply type the character. To jump to a character not on the keyboard, hold down the Alt key and type the character's decimal equivalent on your keyboard's numeric keypad. (See also "To Convert Numeric Bases.")

To Convert Numeric Bases (Version 6 Only)

1. Pull down the Tools menu, and select the **Hex Converter** option.
2. In the Converter dialog box, enter a number, a hex number, or an ASCII character in the appropriate text box.
3. Select **OK**, or press **Esc** or ↵ when finished.

This function converts between hex numbers, decimal numbers (positive integers), and ASCII characters. Entering a value of any type produces equivalents in the other two types. For example, entering the hex value 91 produces its decimal equivalent, 145, and its ASCII character equivalent, æ. You are not limited to the 256 ASCII characters and their equivalents, because you can enter decimal numbers ten digits long and hex numbers eight digits long.

The Converter dialog box has three component text boxes: Hex, Decimal, and Character (ASCII). Be sure to enter values in the appropriate box. ASCII characters that appear on the keyboard can be entered simply by typing their keys. To enter an ASCII character that does not appear on the keyboard, hold down the Alt key and type the character's decimal equivalent on your keyboard's numeric keypad.

To Search for Data

1. Pull down the Tools menu and select the **Find** option, or press **Ctrl-S**.
2. Type the search string in ASCII or hex.
3. Optionally toggle the **Ignore Case** option on or off.

4. Version 7 only. Optionally toggle the **Search at Specified Sector Offset** option on and then enter the number of the sector offset at which you wish to begin the search.
5. Select **Find**.
6. To search for another occurrence of the string, pull down the Tools menu and select the **Find Again** option, or press **Ctrl-G**.

The Find command searches the current selection for the specified string; it is particularly useful for finding misplaced data. The search string can be entered in either ASCII or hex and can be no longer than 48 ASCII characters.

Ignore Case instructs Find to disregard capitalization in its search. Searching for "Linda," for example, will find every consecutive occurrence of the letters l-i-n-d-a without regard to case: "Linda," "LINDA," "LiNdA," and so on. If Ignore Case is turned off, searching for "Linda" will find "Linda" only.

The Search at Specified Sector Offset option allows you to restrict your search by specifying the sector offset at which to search. This option allows you to avoid searching areas of the disk where your search string could not possibly be located. It searches every sector only at the specified offset.

While DISKEDIT is searching, you can interrupt the search by selecting Stop.

After one occurrence of the search has been located, the Find Again option becomes available on the Tools menu.

To Search for System Area Objects (Version 7 Only)

1. Pull down the Tools menu and select the **Find Object** option.
2. On the submenu that appears, select **Partition/Boot**, **FAT**, or **Subdirectory**.

This option is best used on severely damaged disks, i.e., those disks in which all or some parts of the System Area have been lost or corrupted. For example, if you are trying to reconstruct a disk's directory structure, this function will find a lost subdirectory.

Note that the Find Again option on the Tools menu works in conjuction with the Find Object option just as it works with the Find option. (See "To Search for Data".)

To Set File Attributes

1. If you aren't currently editing a directory, pull down the Object menu and select the **Directory** option, or press **Alt-R**. Then highlight the directory you want and select **OK.**
2. Highlight the file or files whose attributes you want to set.
3. Pull down the Tools menu, and select the **Set Attributes** command.
4. In the Change Attributes dialog box, mark each attribute you want to set or clear.
5. Select **OK** when you're finished.
6. To make your changes permanent, pull down the Edit menu and select the **Write Changes** option, or press **Ctrl-W**.

This function is also available in the FA (File Attributes) and FILEFIND programs.

To set file attributes, you must be editing a directory in directory view. The file or files whose attributes you want to change must have their entries completely highlighted, from left to right across the screen. If only part of the complete entry is highlighted, the Set Attributes command will be grayed out and unavailable.

Under DOS, there are four file attributes:

System: DOS has two system files, named IBMBIO.COM and IBMDOS.COM in PC-DOS and IO.SYS and MSDOS.SYS in MS-DOS. These files make a disk bootable but do not appear in a normal directory listing. If you have formatted a bootable disk and want to recover the space used by the system files (for example, for data storage), remove the system attribute (and the hidden attribute) first. IBMBIO.COM and IBMDOS.COM will then be visible in the directory listing and can be deleted with the DEL command.

Hidden: Like the system files, hidden files do not appear in normal directory listings. Turning on the hidden attribute can give you an added measure of security. Similarly, some copy protection schemes write hidden files to your hard disk, which can remain behind after the program has been removed.

Read-Only: Files that have the read-only attribute set cannot be altered or deleted.

Archive: Used exclusively by backup programs (particularly BACKUP.COM, which comes with DOS) as follows: Only files with the archive attribute set can be backed up. Every time a file is created or modified, its archive attribute is turned on. When a file is backed up, the archive attribute is turned off. Therefore, BACKUP.COM is able to back up only files that have been added or changed since your last backup.

In step 4, setting and clearing attributes differs between versions 6 and 7. In version 7, each attribute is set or cleared with one toggle box that has three settings instead of the usual two. When the Change Attributes dialog box appears, all toggles appear in a "neutral" state, neither set nor cleared, regardless of whether any individual attribute is actually on or off. This "neutral" state appears as a box within a box. To clear an attribute, toggle its box once by clicking on it once with the mouse or moving the cursor to the toggle box and pressing the spacebar once. A newly cleared attribute has an empty toggle box. To set an attribute, toggle its box twice. A newly set attribute has a checked toggle box.

In version 6, each attribute has two toggle boxes, one marked "Set" and one marked "Clear." Toggle on the "Set" toggle box to set an attribute; toggle on the "Clear" toggle box to clear an attribute.

To Set File Date and Time

1. If you aren't currently editing a directory, pull down the Object menu and select the **Directory** option, or press **Alt-R**. Then highlight the directory you want to view and select **OK**.

2. Highlight completely (from left to right) the file or files whose date and/or time you want to set.

3. Pull down the Tools menu, and select the **Set Date/Time** option.
4. In the Set Date/Time dialog box, enter the new date and/or time if you do not want to accept the suggested system date and time.
5. Toggle on the **Set Date** and/or **Set Time** options.
6. Select **OK**.
7. To make your changes permanent, pull down the Edit menu and select the **Write Changes** option, or press **Ctrl-W**.

This function is also available in the FD (File Date) and FILEFIND programs.

To set file dates or times, you must be editing a directory in directory view. The file or files whose dates or times you want to change must have their entries completely highlighted, from left to right across the screen. If only part of the complete entry is highlighted, the Set Date/Time command will be grayed out and unavailable.

After specifying the date and/or time to which the target file(s) are to be set, you must still toggle on the adjacent switches if you want to make the change. This extra step enables you to change the date and not the time, or vice versa.

To Use 2nd FAT Table

1. Pull down the Tools menu and select the **Use 2nd FAT Table** option.

Because there is safety in redundancy, DOS creates two copies of the FAT table on every disk. Normally, DISKEDIT looks to the first FAT when you select a drive. If, however, the first FAT is damaged beyond recognition, you can tell DISKEDIT to use the 2nd, hopefully undamaged, FAT. If the second FAT is not damaged, this can make data recovery easier.

When DISKEDIT is using the 2nd FAT, the option on the Tools menu changes to **Use 1st FAT Table**. Select this option to work with the first FAT once again.

To Use the Calculator

1. Pull down the Tools menu and select the **Calculator** option.
2. Calculate.
3. Pull down the Control menu from the Calculator's Control Menu Box and select **Close** or press **Alt-F4** or **Esc**.

DISKEDIT contains a handy programmer's calculator with basic mathematical functions and the capability to work with binary, decimal, and hexidecimal numbers. These functions and their corresponding buttons are listed in Table 2.

Table 2: DISKEDIT Calculator Functions

BUTTON	FUNCTION
Clear	Clears the calculator's memory
Swap	Swaps the values in the first two registers of the memory stack.
2Comp	Gives the 2's complement of the displayed number.
~	Gives the 1's complement of the displayed number.
Backspace	Clears the last digit entered.
/	Division
*	Multiplication
−	Subtraction
	Addition
BIN	Sets calculator to work in binary numbers. Converts any displayed hexidecimal or decimal number to binary.
DECI	Sets calculator to work in decimal numbers. Converts any displayed binary or hexidecimal number to decimal.
HEX	Sets calculator to work in hexidecimal numbers. Converts any displayed binary or decimal number to hexidecimal.

To Use Advanced Recovery Mode (Version 7 Only)

1. Pull down the Tools menu and select **Advanced Recovery Mode**.
2. On the Advanced Recovery dialog box, select **Drive** and then, in the dialog box that appears, select the drive you wish to work on.
3. Select **Test**.
4. If all five tests on the Test Drive dialog box come up "Valid," select **OK**. If not, select **Search Up** or **Search Down** until they do.
5. Select **Virtual**.
6. View, copy, or recover data.

Advanced Recovery Mode (ARM) is used to recover data from severely damaged disks, specifically those disks that are unreadable under DOS. To some extent, this is already possible with DISKEDIT's Maintenance Mode and by editing physical sectors. While these methods allow you to work with a damaged disk sectors at a time, ARM allows you to work with a damaged disk the same way you would work with a healthy one. It does so by imposing a virtual logical structure on the disk in place of the one that was damaged. The practical upshot of this, for example, is that you can copy entire files from the damaged disk in one operation, even though pieces of the file may be on different locations on the disk. Such a recovey under Maintenance Mode, by contrast, would be piecemeal—only one piece of the file could be recovered at a time.

In step 2, ARM presents the logical information it thinks is proper for the disk you specify. If it is correct, all tests in step 3 will show "valid."

In step 4, if the tests from step 3 do not show "valid," select Search Up or Search Down until all tests pass. These searches cause ARM to look for the probable beginning of a partition. If you are working on a damaged hard disk that had multiple partitions, you should search for each one (stopping to look for and recover data from one before going on to the next). If the tests in this step never all read valid, you can enter the proper values in the Advanced Recovery dialog box yourself. This information, on a healthy disk, is available by viewing the Boot Record, Partition Table(s), and Drive Info.

To Shell to DOS (Version 6 Only)

- Pull down the Quit menu, and select the **Shell to DOS** option.

This function allows you to exit temporarily to the DOS prompt. Type **EXIT** and press ↵ to return to DISKEDIT.

● SYNTAX

DISKEDIT [*drive*:] [*filespec*] [/*options*]

drive: is the drive to be edited. If *drive*: is not specified, the current drive is used.

filespec starts DISKEDIT with *filespec* selected as the current object.

The options are the following:

/M starts DISKEDIT in Maintenance Mode. Looks at data by file or physical sector (without regard to the operating system's data organization).

/SKIPHIGH disables DISKEDIT's use of High Memory.

/W starts DISKEDIT with Read Only mode turned off.

/X:[*drive*] excludes the drive you specify from use. For Zenith DOS users only.

See Also FILEFIND, FA, FD

DISKMON

DISKMON enables you to park the heads on your hard disk, display a disk activity light, and write-protect your disks so that you are prompted for confirmation each time a program attempts to write to a protected file or area of a disk.

- **UPGRADE INFORMATION**   DISKMON 7 is identical to DISKMON 6.

To Park Your Hard Disk

1. Start DISKMON.
2. Select **Disk Park** in the Disk Monitor dialog box.
3. Shut off your machine.

Disk Park positions the read/write heads over an unused area of the disk. This helps guard against damage and data loss in the event of a head crash. If you do not have a hard disk whose heads park automatically when the power is shut off, be sure to use Disk Park before you move your machine.

To Turn the Disk Light On or Off

1. Start DISKMON.
2. Select **Disk Light** in the Disk Monitor dialog box.
3. Select **On** or **Off**.

Disk Light enables (or disables) a drive activity indicator that monitors the activity of all drives on your system. When a drive on your system is accessed, the drive letter flashes in the upper-right corner of your screen. This is particularly useful for monitoring RAM disks and network drives, and for users who place their machines on the floor.

48 DISKMON

To Use Disk Protect

1. Start DISKMON.
2. Select **Disk Protect** in the Disk Monitor dialog box.
3. In the Disk Protect dialog box, select an area to protect.
4. In the Files list, specify the files you want to protect.
5. In the Exceptions list, specify any exempted files.
6. Toggle **Allow Floppy Access** on.
7. Select **On** or **Off**.

Disk Protect write-protects files and selected areas of all drives on your system. Whenever a program (DOS or any application) attempts to write to a protected file or area, the user is asked to allow or disallow the action. This is particularly useful as protection against accidental deletion of important files and as protection against many viruses (for example, those that attempt to modify your COMMAND.COM file or write hidden files to your hard disk).

In step 3, selecting System Areas protects all partition tables, boot records, and DOS system files (COMAND.COM, IBMBIO.COM, and IBMDOS.COM or COMMAND.COM, IO.SYS, and MSDOS.SYS).

Selecting files protects all files specified in the Files list. Selecting Entire Disk protects empty disk space on every drive, all partition tables, boot records, DOS system files, FATs, and directories, as well as the specified files.

In step 4, specify the files to be protected by extension only (i.e., *.* to protect all files). By default, all .COM, .EXE, .OVL, .BIN, and .SYS files will be protected.

In step 5, the Excepted Files list specifies files that are not protected. You may specify up to 20 file names as exceptions. Wildcards are allowed.

In step 6, toggling Allow Floppy Access on allows you to format a floppy without DISKMON asking for confirmation. If this option is toggled off and you attempt to format a disk, you will be prompted for confirmation often, which will annoy you.

If you choose to protect only the system areas, skip steps 4 and 5.

• SYNTAX

DISKMON [/*options***]**

The options are the following:

/STATUS displays the current state of DISKMON.

/PROTECT+ turns on Disk Protect. Since DISKMON always remembers your selections for protected areas, file lists, etc., the last active settings are used.

/PROTECT– turns off Disk Protect.

/LIGHT+ turns on Disk Light.

/LIGHT– turns off Disk Light.

/PARK parks the read/write heads on all hard drives.

/UNINSTALL removes DISKMON from memory.

/SKIPHIGH loads DISKMON into the main 640K of memory instead of High Memory. This option can be used with the /PROTECT and /LIGHT options above.

• **NOTES** DISKMON is a Terminate-and-Stay Resident (TSR) program that occupies less than 10K of memory. It can be removed from memory by using the /UNINSTALL option at the command line or by turning off both Disk Light and Disk Protect. Keep in mind, though, that you will not be able to remove DISKMON if you load another TSR while DISKMON is resident.

DISKREET 6
The File Encryption Program

DISKREET offers two forms of file encryption to protect confidential data; it can encrypt files individually or create encrypted drives called NDisks. A password is required to access all encrypted data.

To use NDisks, the DISKREET.SYS driver must be placed in your CONFIG.SYS file:

device=path**\DISKREET.SYS**

where *path* is the location of the DISKREET.SYS driver on your disk.

To Adjust the Size of an NDisk

1. Start DISKREET.
2. In the Diskreet dialog box, select **Disks**.
3. In the Diskreet Disks dialog box, highlight the NDisk you want to resize.
4. Pull down the Disk menu, and select the **Adjust Size** option.
5. Enter the NDisk's password.
6. In the Adjust NDisk Size dialog box, select **Expand** or **Shrink** to size the NDisk accordingly.
7. Select **Proceed** after you read the warning.
8. Select the amount of disk space to add to or subtract from the NDisk.

This function adjusts the amount of space an NDisk occupies on its host drive.

In step 8, you have four options:

- Select the Maximum adjustment to increase the size of the NDisk so that it occupies all remaining disk space on its host drive or to decrease it so that it is as small as possible (approximately 2K).

- Select the Half adjustment to add to the NDisk half of the remaining disk space on the host drive or to cut the NDisk approximately in half.
- Select the Quick adjustment to increase or decrease the NDisk by an amount suggested by DISKREET.
- Select the Specific Size adjustment to increase or decrease the NDisk by a specific number of kilobytes.

To Change the Main Password

1. Start DISKREET.
2. In the Diskreet dialog box, select **Disks**.
3. Pull down the Options menu, and select the **Change Main Password** option.
4. Select **OK** to acknowledge the Change Main Password dialog box.
5. Enter the current main password.
6. Enter a new main password.
7. Reenter this password to validate your entry in the previous step.

The main password is used to set DISKREET program options and is different from the ones used to encrypt individual files. Specifically, the main password is needed to set start-up options and auto-close timeouts, and to lock the keyboard and display.

When you first use DISKREET, there is no main password. When prompted for it, simply press ↵. The main password remains "null" until you change it. This new password remains, even in different DISKREET sessions, until you change it again.

Unlike passwords assigned to encrypted files, all is not lost if you forget the main password. To reset the password to "null," delete the DISKREET.INI file found in the Norton Utilities directory and reboot the machine. This also resets all DISKREET options to their original defaults.

To Change an NDisk's Password or Description

1. Start DISKREET.
2. In the Diskreet dialog box, select **Disks**.
3. In the Diskreet Disks dialog box, highlight the NDisk whose password or description you want to change.
4. Pull down the Disk menu, and select the **Change Disk Password** option.
5. In the Change NDisk Password dialog box, select **Proceed**.
6. Enter the NDisk's current password.
7. In the Change NDisk Password dialog box, select **Change** to change the NDisk's *description*.
8. In the Change NDisk Description dialog box, enter a new description or press ↵ to leave the description unchanged.
9. Enter a new password for the NDisk.
10. Reenter the password for verification.
11. In the Change NDisk Password dialog box, select **Full** to change the password and rewrite the NDisk, or select **Quick** to change the password only.

In step 11, the Full option assigns the new password to the NDisk and, for maximum security, reencrypts it. The Quick option, by contrast, only assigns the new password. It is unlikely that you run any risk by using the Quick option, though if security is a major concern, use Full instead. Keep in mind that reencrypting a large NDisk can be time consuming.

To Change System Settings

1. Start DISKREET.
2. In the Diskreet dialog box, select **Disks**.
3. Pull down the Options menu, and select the **System Settings** Option.

4. If prompted, enter the main password.
5. In the System Settings dialog box, optionally toggle the **Do Not Load the NDisk Manager** option on.
6. Select the number of drive letters to assign to NDisks.
7. Select **OK**.
8. Select **Reset** to reboot the computer and to put the new options into effect.

In step 5, the Do Not Load the NDisk Manager option is off by default and should remain that way unless memory is tight. Toggling this option on saves approximately 50K by deactivating the DISKREET.SYS driver loaded in your CONFIG.SYS file. However, it prevents you from using any of DISKREET's NDisk functions.

In step 6, you are effectively selecting the number of NDisks that can be opened simultaneously, since each open NDisk must be assigned a drive letter. (See "To Create an NDisk" and "To Open an NDisk.")

To Close All Open NDisks

- Pull down the Disk menu and select the **Close All** option, or press **Alt-C**.

OR

1. Pull down the Options menu, and select the **Keyboard & Screen Lock** option.
2. If prompted, enter the main password.
3. In the Keyboard and Screen Lock Settings dialog box, toggle the **Enable Quick-Close** option on.
4. In the Quick Close/Lock Hot Key box, select a hotkey combination and then select **OK**.
5. Exit DISKREET and press the hotkey combination selected in step 4.

All NDisks are automatically closed if the machine loses power or is rebooted. (See "To Open an NDisk.")

To Close an NDisk

- In the Diskreet Disks dialog box, highlight the NDisk you want to close and select **Close**.

To Create an NDisk

1. Start DISKREET.
2. In the Diskreet dialog box, select **Disks**.
3. In the Diskreet Disks dialog box, select the **Make** option.
4. Select the drive on which data in the NDisk is to be stored, and select **OK**.
5. In the Make NDisk on Drive dialog box and at the File Name prompt, enter the name of the NDisk.
6. At the **Description** prompt, enter a description of the NDisk.
7. In the Audit box, choose when you want to see audit information.
8. In the Encryption box, choose a method of encryption.
9. In the Password Prompting box, choose how you want to be prompted for the NDisk's password when the NDisk is opened.
10. Select **OK**.
11. In the Select NDisk Size dialog box, specify the size of the NDisk.
12. In the Enter New Password dialog box, enter a password six or more characters long.
13. Reenter the password for verification.
14. Select **OK** after you read the caution.
15. In the Make an NDisk dialog box, select a drive letter for the NDisk.

To use any of DISKREET's NDisk functions, the driver DISKREET-
.SYS must be loaded in your CONFIG.SYS file.

An NDisk is an encrypted logical disk drive. As it is assigned a drive letter, an NDisk can be addressed like any other logical or physical drive installed on your system. The difference is that all data written to an NDisk is encrypted, and the NDisk itself is secured with a password. To be accessed, an NDisk must be "opened" (see the section "To Open an NDisk"). When "closed," data in an NDisk cannot be accessed and is secure. **Do not forget the password that you have assigned an NDisk**! Without the password, all data in the NDisk is inaccessible.

NDisks use space on other drives installed on your system to store data. In step 4, you specify the drive on which NDisk data is stored.

The first time you run DISKREET, you will be asked, "Do you wish to define a new DISKREET Drive?" Select No and follow the above steps.

An NDisk is treated as a file by DOS. The name you enter for the NDisk in step 5, therefore, must conform to DOS file-name conventions (a maximum of eight characters, with no spaces). The file is hidden, and DISKREET automatically appends the extension .@#! to the file name.

In step 7, there is one option in the Audit box: Show Audit Info When Opened. When it is toggled on and you open an NDisk, DISKREET displays the number of times the NDisk has been opened, when the NDisk was last opened, when the NDisk password was last changed, and the number of failed attempts to open the NDisk.

In step 8, there are two methods of encryption you can choose from. The Fast proprietary method is adequate for any normal use. The DES encryption method is more secure and is slower than the proprietary method.

In step 9, there are four options you can choose from:

- Select Beep Only if you want to be beeped for a password only when an NDisk is opened.

- Select Pop-Up Prompt Only if you always want to enter an NDisk's password in a dialog box. Dialog boxes, however, may conflict with graphical interfaces or screens.

- Select Choose Automatically to have DISKREET choose whether to prompt you for a password with a dialog box or with just a beep. This prevents conflicts with graphical screens.
- Select Manually Open Only if you want to disable automatic opening of NDisks (in AUTOEXEC.BAT files or when NDisks are accessed for the first time, for example). (See "To Open an NDisk" and "To Set Start-up Options.")

In step 12, there are three options: An NDisk can occupy all the available space on the disk on which it resides, it can occupy half the available space, or you can specify an NDisk's size in kilobytes.

In step 15, select a drive letter for the NDisk. By default, only one drive letter is available (the next in the sequence on your system). This means that, although you can create more than one NDisk, only one can be open at a time. To have multiple NDisks open simultaneously, more drive letters have to be made available, and different drive letters must be assigned to different NDisks. To make more drive letters available, see "To Change System Settings."

Once an NDisk is created, it is automatically opened and appears in the list in the Diskreet Disks dialog box.

To Decrypt a File

1. Start DISKREET.
2. In the Diskreet dialog box, select **Files** or **Disks**.
3. Pull down the File menu, and select the **Decrypt** option.
4. In the Select File to Decrypt dialog box, select a file you want to decrypt.
5. Enter the password for this file.
6. Select **OK** to confirm completion.

If you select Files in step 2, you do not have to select the File pull-down menu in step 3, as it is selected for you. In any DISKREET session, steps 1 and 2 are unnecessary after you have encrypted or decrypted one file or performed one NDisk operation.

In step 4, select a file by entering a file name at the File Name: prompt or by selecting from the Drives, Dirs, and Files lists.

To Delete an NDisk

1. Start DISKREET.
2. In the Diskreet dialog box, select **Disks**.
3. In the Diskreet Disks dialog box, highlight the NDisk you want to delete.
4. Pull down the Disk menu, and select the **Delete** option.
5. Enter the main password, if prompted.
6. If you are certain you want to delete the NDisk, select **Delete** in the Warning dialog box.

To Edit an NDisk

1. Start DISKREET.
2. In the Diskreet dialog box, select **Disks**.
3. In the Diskreet Disks dialog box, highlight the NDisk you want to edit and select **Edit**.
4. Enter the password for this NDisk.
5. Follow the steps in the section "To Create an NDisk" to change the NDisk's file name, description, method of encryption, audit information, and password prompting.
6. In the Options box, optionally toggle the **Write Protection** option on.
7. Select **OK** after you have made your changes.

Editing an NDisk, as explained in step 5, allows you to change the configuration you entered when you created the NDisk.

In addition, in step 6, you can write-protect your NDisk, thereby protecting its data from accidental deletion or alteration.

To Encrypt a File

1. Start DISKREET.
2. In the Diskreet dialog box, select **Files** or **Disks**.
3. Pull down the File menu and select the **Encrypt** option, or press **Alt-E**.
4. In the Select Files to Encrypt dialog box, select the file(s) to be encrypted and then select **OK**.
5. In the File Encryption dialog box, type the name of the new, encrypted file and select **OK**, or just select **OK** to accept the suggested file name.
6. Enter a password of six or more characters.
7. Reenter this password to confirm it.
8. Select **OK** to confirm completion of the encryption.

Do not forget the password you assign to an encrypted file! If you do, the file's data cannot be accessed.

If you select Files in step 2, you do not have to select the File pull-down menu in step 3, as it is selected for you. In any DISKREET session, steps 1 and 2 are unnecessary after you have encrypted or decrypted one file or performed one NDisk operation.

In step 4, select file(s) by entering a file name (wildcards are OK) at the File Name: prompt or by selecting from the Drives, Dirs, and Files lists. Although you can select more than one file at a time (for example, *.DOC), the files are not encrypted into separate files but all together into one file.

To Lock the Keyboard and Blank the Display

1. Pull down the Options menu, and select the **Keyboard & Screen Lock** option.
2. Enter the main password if prompted to do so.
3. In the Keyboard & Screen Lock Settings dialog box, toggle the **Enable Locking** option on.

4. In the Quick Close/Lock Hot Key box, select a hotkey combination.
5. Select **OK**.
6. To blank the screen and lock the keyboard, hit the hotkey combination.
7. To unblank and unlock, enter the main password.

Steps 1 through 5 are only necessary once. After you go through them once, the keyboard can be locked and the screen blanked at any time and in any application by hitting the hotkey combination.

To Open an NDisk

1. Start DISKREET.
2. In the Diskreet dialog box, select **Disks**.
3. In the Diskreet Disks dialog box, highlight the NDisk you want to open and select **Open**.
4. In the Open an NDisk dialog box, select a drive letter for the NDisk.
5. Enter the password for the NDisk.

Skip steps 1 and 2 if you are already in a DISKREET session and the Diskreet Disks dialog box is already on the screen.

To access data within an NDisk or to add data to an NDisk, the NDisk must be open. Data in an open NDisk is still encrypted, though accessible.

An NDisk can be opened automatically when the machine is booted or the first time its drive letter is called. In both cases, you still have to enter the NDisk's password. (See "To Set Start-up Options.")

Open NDisks appear with check marks beside them on the Diskreet Disks list of NDisks.

To Search Floppy Disks for NDisks

1. Pull down the Disk menu and select the **Search Floppies** option, or press **Alt-S**.
2. In the Search Floppies dialog box, select the floppy drive you want to search for.

When DISKREET first starts, only NDisks that are on a hard disk are displayed in the Diskreet Disks dialog box. To work with NDisks that are on floppies (i.e., to complete the list), follow the procedure above.

To Set Auto-Close Timeouts

1. Pull down the Options menu, and select the **Auto-Close Timeouts** option.
2. Enter the main password.
3. In the Set Auto-Close Timeouts dialog box, toggle the **Enable** option on, and specify the duration of the auto-close timeout.
4. Select **OK**.

This function automatically closes all NDisks if no keyboard activity is detected in the specified amount of time. This is not a usual closure, however. When you reopen an NDisk, all other NDisks closed by the timeout are also reopened. (See "To Close an NDisk" and "To Open an NDisk.")

In step 3, the duration of the timeout may be set anywhere from 0 to 59 minutes.

To Set File Encryption Options

1. Start DISKREET.
2. In the Diskreet dialog box, select **Files** or **Disks**.
3. Pull down the File menu, and select the **File Options** option.

4. In the File Encryption Options dialog box and in the Encryption Method box, select a method of encryption.

5. Optionally toggle on any of the four encryption options.

6. Select **OK** to set these options for the current session only, or select **Save** to set options for both current and future sessions.

If you select Files in step 2, you do not have to select the File pull-down menu in step 3, as it is selected for you. Steps 1 and 2 are unnecessary if setting file encryption options is not the first thing you do in a DISKREET session.

In step 4, there are two methods of encryption you can choose from. The Fast proprietary method is quite fast and is adequate for any normal use. The DES encryption method is more secure and is slower than the proprietary method.

In step 5, there are four options you can choose from; the meaning of the first three is fairly self-evident: Wipe/Delete Original Files after Encryption, Set Encrypted File to Hidden, and Set Encrypted File to Read-Only. Select the fourth option, Use the same password for the Entire Session, if you are going to encrypt more than one file and want to use the same password for each. (See "To Encrypt a File"; you will skip steps 6 and 7 for every file you encrypt after the first.)

To Set Security Options

1. Pull down the Options menu, and select the **Security** option.

2. In the Security Options dialog box, select how you want to dispose of discarded NDisk data.

In step 2, you must choose what to do with NDisk data after an NDisk is deleted. There are three options:

- Select Quick Clear to leave encrypted data on the disk where it will eventually be overwritten.
- Select Overwrite to have data overwritten once.
- Select Security Wipe to have data overwritten according to Department of Defense specifications.

To Set Start-Up (Automatic Open) Options

1. Pull down the Options menu, and select the **Startup Disks** option.
2. If prompted to do so, in the Startup NDisks box, highlight the NDisk you want to be opened automatically and select **Edit**.
3. In the All NDisks dialog box, highlight the NDisk you want to be opened automatically and select **OK**.
4. If prompted to do so, in the Startup NDisks dialog box, choose whether you want to have the NDisk opened when the machine is booted or when the NDisk is first accessed.
5. Select **OK**.
6. In the Startup NDisks dialog box, select **OK**.

NDisks can always be opened manually (see "To Open an NDisk"). They can be opened automatically when the computer is (re)booted or when the drive letter of a closed NDisk is addressed.

- SYNTAX

    DISKREET [/*options*]

The options are the following:

/ENCRYPT:*filespec* encrypts the file or files specified by *filespec*.

/DECRYPT:*file* decrypts the specified file.

/PASSWORD:*password* supplies the necessary password. Use this option in combination with /ENCRYPT and /DECRYPT.

/SHOW:*drive* unhides all NDisks on the specified drive.

/HIDE:*drive* hides all NDisks on the specified drive.

/CLOSE closes all open NDisks.

/OFF deactivates the DISKREET.SYS device driver.

/ON reactivates the DISKREET.SYS device driver.

• SYNTAX

device=path\DISKREET.SYS[/options]

DISKREET.SYS will load into Upper Memory or High Memory if a driver enabling this memory (HIMEM.SYS, for example) appears before the above statement in your CONFIG.SYS.

The options are the following:

/A20ON may eliminate problems when using DISKREET on a network.

/NOHMA tells DISKREET.SYS not to load in the High Memory Area. Use this option if you are using DISKREET with DOS 5 or Windows.

/Q "quiets" the message telling you of disabled features when you start Windows.

/SKIPHIGH tells DISKREET.SYS not to load in Upper Memory.

• **NOTES** If you are running Windows 3.0 or 3.1, a number of DISKREET's functions will not work—specifically, Auto-open, Quick-close, and Auto-close Timeouts—which means you must actually run DISKREET to open or close NDisks.

If you are using a RAM disk, such as VDISK, the DISKREET.SYS driver should be placed *after* the RAM disk driver in your CONFIG.SYS file. Placing DISKREET.SYS before a RAM disk driver will probably cause a conflict in which the RAM disk and NDisk try to use the same drive letter.

DISKREET 7
The File Encryption Program

DISKREET offers two forms of file encryption to protect confidential data; it can encrypt files individually or create encrypted drives called NDisks. A password is required to access all encrypted data.

To use NDisks, the DISKREET.SYS driver must be placed in your CONFIG.SYS file:

device=path\DISKREET.SYS

Where *path* is the location of the DISKREET.SYS driver on your disk. If this driver is not loaded, only the functions for encrypting and decrypting individual files are available.

- **UPGRADE INFORMATION** DISKREET 7 is functionally equivalent to DISKREET 6. However, differences in interface make the two programs procedurally distinct, the steps required to perform any given function in one program differ from the steps required to perform the same function in the other.

To Blank the Screen and Lock the Keyboard

1. Pull down the Options menu and select the **Driver** option.
2. If prompted, type the master password and select **OK**.
3. Toggle on the **Keyboard/Screen Lock** option.
4. From the Hot Key drop-down list, select a key combination to use. The default selection is both SHIFT keys.
5. Select **OK**.
6. Press the hot key combination selected in step 4 to blank the screen and lock the keyboard.
7. Enter the master password to unblank the screen and unlock the keyboard.

Steps 1 through 5 must be performed only once. When you have performed them, the screen can be blanked and the keyboard locked at any time simply by pressing the selected hot key combination.

In step 2, you will be prompted for the master password only if you have changed it from its default (the Enter key). (See "To Change the Master Password.") DISKREET cannot blank the screen while Windows is running.

In step 4, the hot key combination you select is also used to close all NDisks. Therefore, if the option to Quick Close NDisks is on, blanking the screen and locking the keyboard also closes all NDisks. (See "To Close All NDisks.")

To Change an NDisk's Password

1. From the NDisk list box on the DISKREET program window, highlight the NDisk whose password you wish to change.

2. Pull down the NDisks menu and select the **Password** option.

3. If the NDisk is open, you will be prompted to close it. Select **Close** to do so.

4. Pull down the Re-Encryption Type drop down list and select **Secure** to change the password and rewrite the NDisk, or select **Quick** to change the password only.

5. At the **Enter Old Password** prompt, type the old NDisk password (the one you wish to change).

6. At the **Enter New Password** prompt, type the new password you wish to assign to the NDisk.

7. At the **Re-Enter New Password** prompt, retype the new password for verification.

8. Select **OK**.

In step 4, the Secure option assigns the new password to the NDisk and, for maximum security, reencrypts it. The Quick option, by contrast, only assigns the new password. It is unlikely that you run any risk by using the Quick option, though if you are concerned about security, use Secure instead.

To Change the Master Password

1. Pull down the Options menu and select the **Master Password** option.
2. At the **Enter Old Password** prompt, type the current master password (the one you wish to change).
3. At the **Enter New Password** prompt, type the new master password.
4. Retype the new master password at the **Re-Enter New Password** prompt for verification.
5. Select **OK**.

The master password is needed to access any option available from the Driver option on the Options menu (reserving drive letters, Auto-Close timeouts, blanking the screen and locking the keyboard, and closing all NDisks with a hot key combination).

When you first use DISKREET, the master password is set to the Enter key. If you change it, your new password remains, even in different DISKREET sessions, until you change it again. It is possible to change the master password back to the Enter key by entering nothing in steps 3 and 4.

Skip step 2 if the master password is set to the Enter key.

To Close all NDisks

- Pull down the NDisks menu and select the **Close All** option.

OR

1. Pull down the Options menu and and select the **Driver** option.
2. If prompted, type the Master Password and select **OK**.

3. Toggle on the **Quick Close All** option (if it is not already on).
4. From the Hot Key drop down list, select a hot key combination. The default selection is both SHIFT keys.
5. Select **OK**.
6. Press the key combination you selected in step 4.

Steps 1 through 5 must be performed only once. When you have performed them, you can close all open NDisks by pressing the chosen hot key combination.

In step 2, you will only be prompted for the master password if you have changed it from its default (the Enter key). (See "To Change the Master Password".)

In step 4, the hot key combination you select is also used to blank the screen and lock the keyboard. Therefore, if the option to blank and lock is on, closing all NDisks in this manner also blanks the screen and locks the keyboard. (See "To Blank the Screen and Lock the Keyboard".)

To Close One NDisk

1. From the NDisk list box on the DISKREET program window, highlight the NDisk you wish to close.
2. Pull down the NDisks menu and select the **Close** option or press **Ctrl-C**.

To Create an NDisk

1. Pull down the NDisks menu and select the **Create** option or press **Ins**.
2. At the **Name:** prompt, on the Create an NDisk dialog box, give the NDisk a file name.
3. From the Location drop down list, select the drive on which the NDisk will be located.

4. At the **Description:** prompt, type a unique description of the NDisk.

5. At the **Size:** prompt, type the size of the NDisk in kilobytes.

6. From the Encryption Method drop down list, select the method by which data in the NDisk will be encrypted.

7. Optionally toggle on the **Show Audit Info** option.

8. Select **OK**.

9. On the Set Password dialog box that appears, select the drive letter you want to give the NDisk from the Assigned Drive Letter drop down list.

10. At the **Enter Password** prompt, type the password you will use to access the NDisk.

11. At the **Re-Enter Password** prompt, retype the password for verification.

12. Select **OK**.

To use any of DISKREET's NDisk functions, the driver DISKREET.SYS must be loaded in your CONFIG.SYS file.

An NDisk is an encrypted logical disk drive. As it is assigned a drive letter, an NDisk is addressed like any other logical or physical drive installed on your system. The difference is that all data written to an NDisk is encrypted, and the NDisk itself is secured with a password. To access an NDisk, you must first open it (see "To Open an NDisk"). When closed, data in an NDisk cannot be accessed, and it is secure. **Do not forget the password you assigned to an NDisk!** Without the password, all data in the NDisk is inaccessible.

At the level of DOS, an NDisk is actually a file located on a specified drive. The name you give the NDisk in step 2, therefore, must conform to DOS file-name conventions (a maximum of eight characters, no spaces). DISKREET automatically appends the extension .@#! to the file. You choose the location of this NDisk file in step 3. Note that it is possible to put NDisks on floppy drives.

In step 3, NDISK should be placed only on uncompressed drives (i.e., the DOS 6 host drive).

In step 4, an NDisk description may be up to 30 characters long. Make sure to enter a distinct description that will enable you to tell your NDisks apart.

In step 5, an NDisk may be as small as 32K and as large as the available space you have remaining. Note that you will not be able to store quite as much data in an NDisk as the size you specify here because DISKREET uses some of the NDisk for "overhead."

In step 6, you choose the method by which the NDisk is encrypted. There are two encryption methods from which to choose: Fast Proprietary Method and Government Standard (DES). The former is faster and adequate for any normal use. If you are concerned about data security, however, use the latter method. If you are using an export version of the Norton Utilities, DES encryption may not be available.

In step 7, toggling on Audit Info will display information about each NDisk when that NDisk is opened (when the NDisk was last opened, how many times it has been opened, when the password was last changed, etc.).

In step 9, you select a drive letter for the NDisk. By default, only one drive letter is available (the next in sequence on your system). This means that although you can create more than one NDisk, only one can be open at a time. To have multiple NDisks open simultaneously, more drive letters must be made available and different drive letters must be assigned to different NDisks. To make more drive letters available, see "To Reserve NDisk Drive Letters."

In steps 10 and 11, an NDisk password must be six or more characters long. For security, asterisks appear on the screen as you type.

When you have successfully created an NDisk, it is automatically opened and it appears in the NDisk list on the DISKREET program window, together with a detailed description of its essential characteristics.

To Decrypt a File

1. Pull down the File menu and select the **Decrypt** option.

2. In the Browse for a File to Decrypt dialog box, specify the file to decrypt.
3. In the Password dialog box, type the password for the file you chose to decrypt.
4. Select **OK**.
5. Select **OK** again to acknowledge decryption.

In step 2, you may specify a file to decrypt by typing its name and path (if necessary) at the File prompt or you may specify it from the Drive drop down list and the Directories and Files list boxes.

You may eliminate step 5 by turning off the Confirm Successful Encryption/Decryption option. See "To Set File Encryption Options."

To Delete an NDisk

1. From the NDisk list on the DISKREET program window, select the NDisk you wish to delete.
2. Pull down the NDisks menu and select the **Delete** option, or press **Del**.
3. On the warning dialog box that appears, type the password of the NDisk you wish to delete.
4. Select **Delete**.

Deleting an NDisk irretrievably destroys all data contained therein. Make sure there is nothing in the NDisk you need before you delete it.

You may delete an NDisk regardless of whether it is open or closed.

To Encrypt a File (or Files)

1. Pull down the File menu and select the **Encrypt** option.
2. In the Browse for Files to Encrypt dialog box, specify the file or files to encrypt.
3. At the **TO**: prompt in the Encrypt a File dialog box, specify the name you wish to give the encrypted file.

4. At the **Enter Password** prompt, type a password for the encrypted file.
5. At the **Re-Enter Password** prompt, retype the password for verification.
6. Select **OK**.
7. Select **OK** again to acknowledge encryption.
8. In the Wipe Original Files dialog box, select **Delete**.

In step 2, you may specify a file to encrypt by typing its name and path (if necessary) at the File prompt or you may specify it from the Drive drop down list and the Directories and Files list boxes. If you wish to encrypt multiple files into one encrypted file, type a filespec at the File prompt. For example, to encrypt all .DOC files in the C:\word directory, type C:\WORD*.DOC at the File prompt. Whether you type a file name or select from lists, click OK to proceed.

You may skip step 3 if you wish to accept DISKREET's suggested file name for the encrypted file.

In steps 4 and 5, the password you type must be at least six characters long. For security, asterisks will appear on the screen when you type the password.

You may eliminate step 7 by turning off the Confirm Successful Encryption/Decryption option. See "To Set File Encryption Options."

In step 8, by default, DISKREET encrypts a copy of the file(s) you select for encryption, leaving the original(s) untouched. This defeats the purpose of encrypting them in the first place. Selecting Delete here tells DISKREET to dispose of the original file(s). You may eliminate this step and automatically delete the original files by turning on the Delete Original Files after Encryption option *and* turning off the Ask Whether To Delete Original Files option. See "To Set File Encryption Options." (Note that if you toggle on the Disable This Message option on the Wipe Original Files dialog box, this is equivalent to turning off the Ask Whether To Delete Original Files option. If you toggle on the Disable This Message option, therefore, you should then go and turn on the option. Otherwise, the original file(s) will remain after encryption.)

To Modify an NDisk

1. From the NDisk list on the DISKREET program window, highlight the NDisk you wish to modify.

2. Pull down the NDisks menu and select the **Edit** option, or press **Ctrl-E**.

3. If the NDisk is open, you will be prompted to close it. Select **Close** to do so.

4. At the Enter Password prompt, type the NDisk's password and select **OK**.

5. On the Edit an NDisk dialog box, you may automatically assign a drive letter to the NDisk from the Auto Drive drop down list.

6. At the **Description** prompt, you can change the NDisk's description.

7. At the **Size** prompt, you can change the NDisk's size in kilobytes.

8. Optionally toggle the **Show Audit Info** option.

9. Optionally toggle the **Read-Only** option.

10. Select **OK**.

In step 5, the Auto Drive drop down list allows you to assign a particular drive letter to an NDisk. By default, Auto Drive is set to None, meaning that an NDisk has no particular drive letter associated with it. That is, when opened, an NDisk is simply given the next available drive letter. If, however, you wish to always address an NDisk by a particular drive letter, D: for example, select D: from the Auto Drive list.

Note that by default, only one drive letter is available on the Auto Drive list. To make more drive letters available, you must reserve them for NDisk use. See "To Reserve NDisk Drive Letters."

In step 7, you may increase or decrease the size of an NDisk. Keep in mind, though, that an NDisk cannot be made smaller than 32K or the amount of data stored in it, whichever is larger.

In step 8, toggling on the Show Audit Info option displays information about the NDisk whenever the NDisk is opened (when the NDisk was last opened, how many times it has been opened, when the password was last changed, etc.)

In step 9, making an NDisk read-only freezes the contents of the NDisk; data can neither be deleted from it nor written to it.

To Open an NDisk

1. From the NDisk list on the DISKREET program window, highlight the NDisk you wish to open.
2. Pull down the NDisks menu and select the **Open** option, or press **Ctrl-O**.
3. From the Assigned Drive Letter drop down list, select a drive letter for the NDisk.
4. At the **Enter Password** prompt, type the NDisk's password.
5. Select **OK**.

Skip step 3 if an Auto Drive letter has been assigned to this NDisk. See "To Modify an NDisk."

To Reserve NDisk Drive Letters

1. Pull down the Options menu and select the **Driver** option.
2. If prompted, type the master password and select **OK**.
3. From the Drive Letters to Reserve drop down list, select the number of drive letters you wish to reserve for NDisk use.
4. Select **OK**.
5. Select **OK** to acknowledge the change.

While you can create as many NDisks as disk space will allow, at any one time you can only use as many NDisks as there are drive letters reserved. For example, if you have created three NDisks but have only reserved two drive letters for them, you can only open two NDisks simultaneously. To open the third, you must first close one of the two already open.

By default, one drive letter is reserved for NDisk use. This function allows you to reserve as many as five drive letters.

In step 2, you will only be prompted for the master password if you have changed it from its default (the Enter key). (See "To Change the Master Password.")

Note that you must quit DISKREET and reboot your machine for the new number of reserved drive letters to take effect.

To Search for NDisks

1. Pull down the NDisks menu and select the **Search** option, or press **Ctrl-S**.
2. On the dialog box that appears, select the drive on which to search.
3. Select **OK**.

When you start DISKREET, only those NDisks located on the drive where DISKREET itself is located appear on DISKREET's program window. If you have put NDisks on other hard disks or floppies, they will not appear on the NDisk list until you search for them.

In step 2, you can select the drive on which to search in two ways. You can select one specific drive from the Drives list. Or, you can search all drives of a type (i.e., all floppy drives, all hard drives, etc.) by choosing the appropriate option from the Drive Types dialog box. Note that the All Other Drives option searches all drives that are not floppy drives, not hard drives, and not network drives.

To Set Auto-Close Timeouts

1. Pull down the Options menu and select the **Driver** option.
2. If prompted, type the master password and select **OK**.

In step 3, the duration may be set from 1 to 59 minutes.

To Set File Encryption Options

1. Pull down the Options menu and select the **File** option.
2. In the Encryption Options dialog box, select the method of file encryption from the Encryption Method drop down list.
3. Optionally select any of the six encryption options.
4. Select **OK** to set the options for the current session only. Select **Save** to set the options for the current session and all future sessions.

In step 2, you choose the default method for encrypting files. There are two encryption methods from which to choose: Fast Proprietary Method and Government Standard (DES). The former is faster and adequate for any normal use. If you are concerned about data security, however, use the latter method.

In step 3, the available options are as follows:

Delete Original Files after Encryption, when toggled on, causes DISKREET to automatically delete original, unencrypted files after encryption. This option should always be set on. See "To Encrypt a File (or Files)."

Ask Whether to Delete Original Files, when toggled on, prompts you to delete original, unencrypted files after encryption. This option should be off. See "To Encrypt a File (or Files)."

Hide Encrypted File, when toggled on, hides all encrypted files.

Make Encrypted File Read-Only, when toggled on, makes all encrypted files read-only, thereby preventing their deletion.

Use Same Password For Entire Session. Use this option if you are going to encrypt more than one file in any session and want to use the same password for each.

Confirm Successful Encryption/Decryption, when toggled on, causes the user to acknowledge the completion of every encryption and decryption.

To Set Global NDisk Options

1. Pull down the Options menu and select the **Global** option.
2. If prompted, type the master password and select **OK**.
3. From the Data Clearing Method drop down list, select a method for deleting data from your disk when NDisks are deleted or are reduced in size.
4. Optionally toggle the **Warn If Driver Not Loaded** option.
5. Select **OK**.

In step 2, you will be prompted for the master password only if you have changed it from its default (the Enter key). (See "To Change the Master Password.")

In step 3, when an NDisk is deleted, the data it contained will still exist on your disk. When you delete files from an NDisk and then reduce the NDisk's size, the deleted data also still exists on your disk. Though all such data is encrypted, you may still wish to dispose of it permanently. This step provides three options for disposal. Select None if you do not wish to dispose of this data and do not mind it remaining on your disk. In time, it will be overwritten anyway. Select Overwrite Once to destroy this data by overwriting it one time. If you are concerned about data security, select Government Wipe to have data overwritten in accordance with Department of Defense specifications. This thoroughly destroys the data. See WIPEINFO for more details about overwriting data and Goverment Wipe.

In step 4, when toggled on, this option warns you that NDisk functions are not available if you start DISKREET without the DISKREET.SYS driver loaded.

- **SYNTAX (Command Line)**

    DISKREET [/options]

The options are the following:

/**CLOSE** closes all open NDisks.

/**D:**filename decrypts the specified file. Use with the /P option.

/E:*filespec* encrypts the file or files specified by *filespec*. Use with the /P and /T options.

/HIDE:*driveletter* hides all NDisks on the specified drive.

/OFF deactivates DISKREET.SYS device driver.

/ON activates DISKREET.SYS device driver.

/P:*password* supplies the password necessary to encrypt or decrypt a file. Use with the /D and /E options.

/SHOW:*driveletter* unhides all NDisks on the specified drive.

/T:*filename* supplies the name of the encrypted file created by /E. Use with the /E option.

● **SYNTAX (Device Driver)**

device = *path*\DISKREET.SYS [*/options*]

The options are the following:

/A200N may eliminate problems when using DISKREET on a network.

/NOHMA tells DISKREET.SYS not to load in the High Memory Area. Use this option if you are using DISKREET with Windows 3.0 or 3.1 or if you have loaded DOS high.

/QUIET "quiets" the message telling you of disabled features when you start Windows.

/SKIPHIGH tells DISKREET not to load in Upper Memory.

If you are using DOS 6's DoubleSpace, make sure of two things: 1) NDISK should be placed only on uncompressed volumes, and 2) the **DBLSPACE.SYS** driver is loaded before the DISKREET.SYS driver in your CONFIG.SYS file.

● **NOTES** If you are using a RAM disk, the DISKREET.SYS driver should be placed after the RAM disk driver in your CONFIG.SYS file. Placing DISKREET.SYS before a RAM disk driver may cause the RAM disk and an NDisk to try to use the same drive letter.

DISKTOOL

DISKTOOL is a collection of four functions (six in version 6) that can fix problems ranging from the fairly common to the catastrophic. Specifically, you can make a nonbootable disk bootable, restore the damage done by the DOS RECOVER program, reformat an error-laden disk without loss of data, and mark specific clusters as bad (or good). Version 6 also allows you to save and restore critical system information to and from a separate disk.

- **UPGRADE INFORMATION** All four DISKTOOL 7 functions are contained in DISKTOOL 6. DISKTOOL 6 has two additional functions. Create Rescue Diskette and Restore Rescue Diskette exist in version 7 as the separate program RESCUE.

To Create a Rescue Disk (Version 6 Only)

1. Start DISKTOOL.
2. Select **Continue** after reading the introductory screen.
3. Highlight **Create Rescue Diskette** on the Procedures list.
4. Select **Proceed**.
5. Select **OK** after you read the information screen.
6. Select the disk on which you will store rescue information. (Insert a disk in the drive before selecting **OK**.)
7. When the operation is complete, select **OK** to return to the Disk Tools main screen.

Create Rescue Diskette stores vital disk information on a separate floppy. Specifically, it stores a copy of the boot record, partition table, and CMOS (Complementary Metal Oxide Semiconductor, a special kind of chip) information. Your system's internal hardware configuration, number and kind of drives installed, kind of graphics installed, amount of memory, etc., are stored in a CMOS. This information is retained even when your computer's power is off, as it is backed up by a battery. Only

DISKTOOL 79

286, 386, and 486 machines store setup information in CMOS; XTs do not. If you lose any of this information, it can be restored to your machine from the rescue disk. (See "To Restore the Rescue Disk.")

To Make a Disk Bootable

1. Start DISKTOOL.
2. Select **Continue** after reading the introductory screen. (Version 6 only.)
3. Highlight **Make a Disk Bootable** on the Procedures list.
4. Select **Proceed**.
5. Select the drive you want to make bootable.
6. If you select a hard disk, select **Yes** to proceed. If you select a floppy drive, insert the disk to be made bootable in the drive indicated and select **OK**.
7. If necessary, insert a DOS system disk in the drive indicated and select **OK**. (If you are working on a floppy drive, reinsert the disk to be made bootable in the drive indicated and select **OK**.)
8. Select **OK** when the operation is complete to return to the Disk Tools main screen.

This funtion transfers the DOS system files (IO.SYS, MSDOS.SYS, and COMMAND.COM) To a selected drive, thereby making it bootable.

To Mark a Cluster (as Good or Bad)

1. Start DISKTOOL.
2. Select **Continue** after reading the introductory screen. (Version 6 only.)
3. Highlight **Mark a Cluster** on the Procedures list.
4. Select **Proceed**.
5. Select **OK** after you read the information screen.

80 DISKTOOL

6. Select the drive on which to mark clusters. (If you've selected a floppy drive, insert the target disk in the indicated drive and select **OK**.)
7. In the Mark Cluster dialog box, enter the number of the cluster you want to mark.
8. Select **Good** or **Bad** in the Mark As: box.
9. Select **OK**.
10. When the operation is complete, select **OK** to return to the Disk Tools main screen.

If you are able to identify a cluster that has gone bad, you can remove it from use by DOS with the Mark a Cluster function. If, however, the cluster in question contains data, use the Norton Disk Doctor's Surface Test instead. This moves the data from the damaged cluster to a healthy one. (See also the NDD section.)

Mark a Cluster can also mark bad clusters as good, thereby returning them to use. Since casually reinstating a cluster marked as bad by DOS or some other disk utility may be hazardous to your data, use this function with care. Do not mark custers (either as good or as bad) on the compressed volumes.

To Recover from DOS's Recover

1. Start DISKTOOL.
2. Select **Continue** after reading the introductory screen. (Version 6 only.)
3. Highlight **Recover from DOS's Recover** on the Procedures list.
4. Select **Proceed**.
5. Select **OK** when you are finished reading the information screen.
6. Select the drive you want to "fix." (If you choose a floppy drive, insert the "damaged" floppy in the indicated drive and select **OK**.)
7. Select **Yes** after you read the warning screen.

8. Select **Yes** if you are absolutely sure you want to continue.

9. When the operation is complete, select **OK** to return to the Disk Tools main screen.

The RECOVER program in DOS is intended to recover data on disks whose directory structure has been corrupted. It ends up doing more harm than good, though, because it eliminates all subdirectories and renames all files, numbering them sequentially beginning with 0.

Recover from DOS's Recover has two uses:

- Use it *after* you have run DOS's RECOVER to return your disk to its pre-RECOVER condition (or at least a good approximation thereof).

- Use it *instead* of DOS's RECOVER to repair a disk with a damaged directory structure.

To Restore a Rescue Disk (Version 6 Only)

1. Start DISKTOOL.

2. Select **Continue** after reading the introductory screen.

3. Highlight **Restore Rescue Diskette** on the Procedures list.

4. Select **Proceed**.

5. Select **Yes** when you are absolutely sure you want to proceed.

6. Select the kind of information you want to restore (boot record, partition table, CMOS), and select **OK**.

7. Select the drive from which to restore information.

8. Select **Yes** when you are sure you wish to restore boot record, partition table, or CMOS information.

9. When the operation is complete, select **OK** to return to the Disk Tools main screen.

If you lose all or part of your boot record or partition table because of disk failure or careless meddling with the DISKEDIT program,

82 DISKTOOL

you can restore this critical information and perhaps prevent the loss of most or all of your data.

If your CMOS information is lost (probably because of the death of the battery supplying power to the CMOS), you can restore this information instead of running your Setup program.

To Revive a Defective Disk

1. Start DISKTOOL.
2. Select **Continue** after reading the introductory screen. (Version 6 only.)
3. Highlight **Revive a Defective Diskette** on the Procedures list.
4. Select **Proceed**.
5. Select the drive you want to revive.
6. Insert the damaged disk in the indicated drive and select **OK**.
7. When the operation is complete, select **OK** to return to the Disk Tools main screen.

The Revive a Defective Diskette function can repair the bad clusters or sectors that may appear on your disks after they have been in use for a while. It reformats your disks *but without destroying any data*. Use this function if you get data-read errors on a floppy that had been in good working order. You may also want to use the Norton Disk Doctor's Surface Test. (See also the NDD section.)

- **SYNTAX**

    DISKTOOL [/*options*]

    The options are as follows:

    /DEVICEDRIVEN runs with the REVIVE function if you are using a device driven floppy.

    /DOSRECOVER runs the Recover from DOS's RECOVER function.

    /MAKEBOOT runs the Make a Disk Bootable function.

/MARKCLUSTER runs the Mark a Cluster function.

/RESTORE runs the Restore Rescue Diskette function. (Version 6 only.)

/REVIVE runs the Revive a Defective Diskette function.

/SAVERESCUE runs the Create Rescue Diskette function. (Version 6 only.)

/SKIPHIGH runs DISKTOOL in the main 640K, rather than High Memory. This option can be used with any of the options above.

- **SEE ALSO** RESCUE

DS
Directory Sort

DS sorts your directory listings by file name, extension, date, time, or size, or in any combination thereof.

- **UPGRADE INFORMATION**   DS 7 is identical to DS 6.

To Reposition Individual Files

1. In the file list, highlight the file you wish to reposition.
2. Press the spacebar and then press ↑ or ↓ and ↵ to relocate the file, or click the right mouse button and drag the file to its new location.
3. Select the **Write** option to write the new file arragement to disk.

If there are files you wish to keep an eye on, you can, for example, use this function to move them to the beginning of your directory.

To Sort a Directory

1. On the Sorting dialog box, select the **Change Dir** option.
2. Choose the directory you wish to sort and select **OK**.
3. In the Sort Order box, toggle on the key(s) by which you want to sort the directory.
4. Optionally toggle on the **Sort Subdirs** option.
5. Select **Re-Sort**. The new sort order will appear in the file list.
6. Select **Write** to write the new file arrangement to disk.

When DOS adds a file to a directory, it puts it at the bottom of the list of files already present. If, over time, you add many files to a directory, they will be in no particular order. DS allows you to organize your files.

Omit steps 1 and 2 above if you want to sort the current directory.

In version 7, you can select a directory by typing it at the path prompt or by selecting it from the Drive drop down list and the Subdirectories list. In version 6, you can choose a directory from the Drives and Subdirectories lists.

In step 3, the keys may be selected alone or in combination. When used in combination, the order in which you select the keys is significant. For example, if you select Extension and then Name, files will be sorted by extension, and all files with the same extension will be sorted by file name. Selecting these sort keys in the opposite order sorts files by name, and any files with the same name will also be sorted by extension. By default, files are sorted in ascending order (A–Z, 1–9). The plus sign next to a selected key indicates this. To sort in descending order (Z–A, 9–1), press the minus sign after selecting the key or click the mouse on the plus sign.

In step 4, the Sort Subdirs option will sort all subdirectories under the selected directory. When this option is off, only the current directory is sorted.

The sort is not made permanent until it is written to disk in step 6.

● **SYNTAX**

DS *keys*[–] *directory* [/S]

keys can be any of five sort keys: N (name), E (extension), D (date), T (time), or S (size). The keys may be used in any combination. Append the optional minus to a key to sort in descending order.

directory is the directory to sort.

/S sorts all subdirectories under *directory*.

DUPDISK
The Disk Duplicator

DUPDISK makes an exact copy of a floppy disk on another floppy disk of the same size and capacity. You can use it to make either a single copy or multiple copies of any given floppy disk

- **UPGRADE INFORMATION** DUPDISK is new to the Norton Utilities and is found only in version 7.

To Duplicate a Diskette

1. From the From: drop down list on the DUPDISK dialog box, select the source drive (the drive to copy from).

2. From the To: drop down list, select the target drive (drive to copy to), and select **OK**.

3. Insert the source diskette in the drive you have selected as the source drive, and select **OK**.

4. When DUPDISK has finished reading the source diskette, insert the target diskette in the drive you have selected as the target drive, and select **OK**.

5. If prompted, select **Yes** to overwrite existing data on the target diskette.

6. When the copy is complete, select **Yes** to make another copy, and go back to step 4. If you are finished, select **No**.

DUPDISK is much faster than DOS's DISKCOPY command because you have to swap disks only once when using a single floppy drive. For multiple copies of the same disk, DUPDISK saves you even more time because it holds the disk contents in memory rather than rereading the disk for each copy made. Unlike the DOS DISKCOPY command, DUPDISK copies the DOS system files and other hidden files, if present, as well as the volume label.

In step 4, if the target diskette you insert is not formatted, DUPDISK will ask you whether you wish to format it before copying. Select

Yes if you wish to format the target disk, or No if you do not wish to format the disk. If you select No, DUPDISK will prompt you to insert another target disk in the drive you have selected.

In step 5, if DUPDISK finds any files or subdirectories on the target diskette, it will ask you whether you wish to overwrite them. Once the contents of a diskette have been overwritten, it is impossible to recover them. **Do not use a target diskette that contains any data you want to keep**.

DUPDISK cannot copy a floppy disk to a disk of a different size or capacity. For example, DUPDISK cannot copy a 5¼" disk to a 3 ½" disk or a 1.2 MB disk to a 360K disk. To copy a floppy disk to a disk of a different capacity, use the DOS COPY command or the DOS XCOPY command with the /S switch if the source disk contains subdirectories. Make sure that the target disk has sufficient capacity to hold the data from the source disk. Remember that the DOS COPY and XCOPY commands will not copy hidden or system files.

• SYNTAX

DUPDISK [*sourcedrive*] [*targetdrive*]

sourcedrive is the drive indicator of the drive to copy from.

targetdrive is the drive indicator of the drive to copy to.

EP
Erase Protect-Version 6 Only

EP protects the data of specified files *after* deletion. Data from deleted files is held in a special subdirectory, virtually guaranteeing the successful unerasure of these files. Deleted files stored by EP are purged automatically after a specified number of days; you can purge them manually at any time.

- **UPGRADE INFORMATION** EP has been renamed SMARTCAN in version 7. The two programs are functionally identical, but each has a different organization. SMARTCAN, therefore, can be found in its own section.

To Activate File Protection

1. In the Erase Protect dialog box, select **Choose Drives**.
2. In the Choose Drives dialog box, select the drives to be protected and then select **ON**.
3. Select **File Protection** in the Erase Protect dialog box.
4. In the File Protection dialog box, specify the files you wish to protect.
5. At the **Purge Files Held Over** prompt, specify the number of days to protect erased files before they are automatically purged.
6. At the **Hold at Most** prompt, specify in kilobytes how much erased data to protect.
7. Select **OK**.
8. Select **Quit** in the Erase Protect dialog box to return to the DOS prompt and save the settings.

Under DOS, when a file is erased, its entry is removed from its directory and the FAT, but its data remains on the disk. This makes unerasure possible. However, because the space used by the erased file is made available by DOS to new files, unerasure is not always successful; the erased file's data will eventually be overwritten. EP virtually guarantees successful unerasure of files by storing "erased" data in a special subdirectory called TRASHCAN. TRASHCAN and its contents are not overwritten by DOS unless TRASHCAN is the only place left on the disk to put new files.

In step 4, select All Files to protect all files on the drive(s) selected in step 2. Select Only the Files Listed if you wish to protect only certain files. If you select this option, go to the Files list and type the extensions of the files you wish to protect (i.e., *.EXE or *.COM, to protect program files). Select All Files Except Those Listed if there are certain kinds of files you do not wish to protect. Type their extensions in the Files list (*.TMP to leave unprotected the temporary files created by certain programs during normal operations). Toggle on the Include Archived (Backed up) Files option if you wish to protect those files already backed up by the DOS BACKUP program (i.e., those files with the Archive attribute turned off).

In step 5, by default, erased files are protected for five days. Set this option to 0 to protect files indefinitely. Note, though, that this will fill the space you set aside for TRASHCAN fairly quickly, and when TRASHCAN is full, EP will empty it entirely as soon as you erase another file it needs to protect. Holding purged files indefinitely therefore really means holding purged files until TRASHCAN is full.

In step 6, you specify the size of TRASHCAN—how much data EP will protect. The minimum TRASHCAN size is 16K. Enter 0 to instruct EP to use as much space as is available.

EP is a Terminate-and-Stay-Resident (TSR) program that is loaded into memory when activated.

To Deactivate File Protection

1. In the Erase Protect dialog box, select **Choose Drives**.

2. Select **OFF** in the Choose Drives dialog box.

3. Select **Quit** in the Erase Protect dialog box to return to the DOS prompt.

EP is removed from memory when deactivated.

To Purge Files (Manually)

1. In the Erase Protect dialog box, select **Purge Files**.
2. Optionally select a drive containing files to be purged: In the Purge Deleted Files dialog box, select **Drive**, then select the drive letter and **OK**.
3. Mark the file or files you want to purge: Select **Tag** and enter the name of the file you want to mark in the Tag dialog box, or just double-click on the file(s) in the list.
4. Select **Purge**.
5. Select **Quit** in the Erase Protect dialog box to return to the DOS prompt.

Note that purged files are deleted permanently, and cannot be unerased.

- **SYNTAX**

    EP [/*options*]

    The options are the following:

    /**ON** activates EP and loads it into memory.

    /**OFF** deactivates EP and removes it from memory.

    /**STATUS** displays current status and settings.

    /**UNINSTALL** functions the same as /OFF.

    /**SKIPHIGH** loads EP into the main 640K of memory instead of High Memory. Use with the /ON option.

See Also SMARTCAN

FA
File Attributes

FA sets or clears file attributes.

Under DOS a file can have any of four attributes. These attributes give files different properties or allow it to be used in certain ways. The attributes are as follows:

- System: The DOS system files (IO.SYS and MSDOS.SYS in MS-DOS or IBMBIO.COM and IBMDOS.COM in PC-DOS) are frequently the only files that can have this attribute. System files make a disk bootable.

- Hidden: A file with the hidden attribute set on does not appear in a normal directory listing. Hiding files can give you an added measure of security. Also, some copy protection schemes write hidden files to your hard disk, and these files can remain behind even after the program has been removed. It is possible, in addition, to hide directories.

- Read-only: Files with this attribute set on cannot be edited or deleted.

- Archive: This attribute is primarily relevant to backup programs. This attribute is turned off when a file is backed up, and it is turned on when a file is created or modified. This allows backup programs to back up only those files that have been added or changed since your last backup.

- **UPGRADE INFORMATION**   FA 7 is identical to FA 6.

- **SYNTAX**

    FA *filespec* [*/options*]

    filespec is the file(s) or directory whose attributes will be changed.

The options are as follows:

/A[+ | −] sets (+) or clears (−) the Archive attribute.

/CLEAR clears all set attributes.

/DIR[+ | −] sets (+) or clears (−) the Hidden attribute for directories.

/HID[+ | −] sets (+) or clears (−) the Hidden attribute.

/P pauses the display after each full screen.

/R[+ | −] sets (+) or clears (-) the Read-Only attribute.

/S causes FA to work on all files or directories matching *filespec* in directories below the current directory.

/SYS[+ | −] sets (+) or clears (−) the System attribute.

/T causes FA to display only totals. Individual changes are not listed.

/U causes FA to work only on files with some attribute set.

- **NOTES** Running FA without any options displays the current settings for all files matching *filespec*.

See Also DISKEDIT, FILEFIND

FD

File Date and Time

FD changes the date and time stamp on files.

- **UPGRADE INFORMATION** FD 7 is identical to FD 6.

- **SYNTAX**

    FD *filespec* [*/options*]

    filespec is the file or files to stamp.

    The options are as follows:

    /D[*mm-dd-yy***]** sets the date to *mm-dd-yy*.

    /P pauses the display after each full screen.

    /S causes FD to work on all files matching *filespec* in all directories below the current directory.

    /T[*hh:mm:ss***]** sets the time to *hh:mm:ss*.

- **NOTES** Omit both the /D and /T options to stamp *filespec* with the current date and time.

    See Also DISKEDIT, FILEFIND

FILEFIND

FILEFIND is a multifaceted program. Its primary purpose is to find lost or misplaced files. It is also able to find directories and ASCII text; view files; change file attributes, dates, and times; and perform other related, miscellaneous tasks.

- **UPGRADE INFORMATION** FILEFIND 7 is functionally equivalent to FILEFIND 6. While there are quite a few cosmetic differences between the two versions, the only substantially new feature of FILEFIND 7 is the replace text option, which you can use to replace text strings you have searched for.

To Change File Attributes

1. Run a search for a file or files (see "To Find a File or Files").
2. In the list of found files that appears, highlight the file whose attributes you wish to change.
3. Pull down the Commands menu, and select the **Set Attributes** option. The Change Attributes dialog box appears.
4. In the Set Attributes box, select whether you want to change attributes of the highlighted file or of every file on the list.
5. Select the attributes you want to set or clear.
6. Select **OK**.
7. Select **OK** again to confirm the changes made.

The functions of the FA (File Attributes) program are also contained within FILEFIND.

In step 5, setting and clearing attributes differs between versions 6 and 7. In version 7, each attribute is set or cleared with one toggle box that has three settings instead of the usual two. When the Change Attributes dialog box appears, all toggles are in a "neutral" state—neither set nor cleared—regardless of whether any individual attribute is on or off. This "neutral" state of the toggle appears as a box within a box. To clear an attribute, toggle the box once by clicking on it once with the mouse or moving the cursor to the toggle box and pressing the spacebar once. A cleared attribute has an empty toggle box. To set an attribute, toggle the box twice. A set attribute has a checked toggle box.

In version 6, each attribute has two toggle boxes, one marked "Set" and one marked "Clear." Toggle on the "Set" toggle box to set an attribute; toggle on the "Clear" toggle box to clear an attribute.

It is also possible to change file attributes by using the DISKEDIT program (see "To Set File Attributes" in DISKEDIT), but using FA or FILEFIND is preferable, as it is more precise—you are more likely to make a serious error while editing a directory.

To Change File Dates and Times

1. Run a search for a file or files (see "To Find a File or Files").
2. On the list of found files that appears, highlight the file whose date and time you wish to set.
3. Pull down the Commands menu, and select the **Set Date/Time** option. The Set Date/Time dialog box appears.
4. In the Set Date/Time box, select whether you want to change only the highlighted file or every file on the file list.
5. To change the time, toggle the **Set Time To:** option on, and enter a new time.
6. To change the date, toggle the **Set Date To:** option on, and enter a new date.
7. Select **OK**.
8. Select **OK** again to confirm the changes made.

The functions of the FD (File Date and Time) program are also contained within FILEFIND.

It is also possible to change file dates and times by using the DISKEDIT program (see "To Change File Dates and Times" in DISKEDIT), but using FD or FILEFIND is preferable, as it is more precise—you are more likely to make a serious error while editing a directory.

To Configure the File List

1. Pull down the List menu and select the **Set List Display** option, or press **Ctrl-F**. The List Display dialog box appears.
2. In the List Format box, select how much file information you want to display.
3. In the Sort Criterion box, choose how you want to sort found files.
4. In the Sort Order box, choose whether you want sorted files to be listed in ascending or descending order.
5. Select **OK**.

In step 2, there are five options: You can display only the names of found files; file names and attributes; file names and sizes; file names, dates, and times; or file names, sizes, dates, and attributes (the default).

In step 3, found files can be sorted by file name, extension, date and time, size, or can be left unsorted. If you choose the Unsorted option, omit step 4. The Ascending and Descending options will have no effect.

To Create a Batch File

1. Pull down the List menu and select the **Create Batch** option, or press **Ctrl-B**.
2. In the Create Batch File dialog box and at the **Save the List To:** prompt, enter the name of the batch file you want to create.
3. Optionally toggle the **Save Full Path** and **Directory Title Line** options on.
4. At the **Text To Put before File Names:** prompt, optionally enter the text you want to put before file names in the batch file.

5. At the **Text To Put after File Names:** prompt, optionally enter the text you want to put after file names in the batch file.

6. At the **Text To Put before Directory Lines:** prompt, optionally enter the text you want to put before directory names in the batch file.

7. Select **OK**.

The Create Batch command is unavailable until there is a file list in the FileFind dialog box (i.e., until you run a find or search).

This command allows you to create a batch file from the file list that results from running a find or search. It is particularly useful for copying, deleting, or even running a particular group of files. Be certain, therefore, to define carefully the scope and condition of your search, as every file on the file list will be included in the batch file created.

In step 3, the Save Full Path option causes every file in the batch file to have its complete path attached (C:\NORTON\FILEFIND.EXE, as opposed to FILEFIND.EXE). Files are grouped by directory both in the file list and in resulting batch files. The Directory Title Line option causes the directory name for each of these groupings to be included in the created batch file.

Text entered in step 4 appears before each file name in the created batch file. Enter DOS commands here. For example, entering **del** produces

del *filename.ext*

for each file name that appears in the batch file.

Text entered in step 5 appears after each file name in the batch file. Enter DOS command arguments or parameters here. For example, if you entered **copy** in step 4, enter the target directory here:

c:\newdir

This produces

copy *filename.ext* **c:***newdir*

for each file name that appears in the batch file.

Text entered in step 6 appears before directory names in the batch file. Enter DOS directory commands here. For example, entering **cd** produces

cd c:*directory*

for every directory listed in the batch file. If the Directory Title Line option in step 3 is toggled off, omit step 6.

To Find a File or Files

1. In the FileFind dialog box, enter a file name and path (the path is optional; wildcards are OK) at the **File Name:** prompt.
2. Specify the search scope (the default drive only, the default directory, or on more than one drive), and optionally specify the search conditions (narrow the scope). See below for explanations.
3. Select **Find** to start the search (or **Start** in version 6), and select **OK** when it is finished.

To Search the Default Drive Only

1. In the FileFind dialog box, select the **Entire Disk** option.
2. Pull down the File menu and select the **Drive** option, or press **Ctrl-D**.
3. In the Change Drive dialog box, select the new default drive.
4. Pull down the Search menu and select the **Search Drives** option, or press **F2**.
5. In the Drives to Search dialog box, select the **Default Drive** option and select **OK**.

Default Drive is the default setting in the Drives to Search box in every new FILEFIND session. Therefore, omit steps 4 and 5 if you have not changed this setting in the current session.

To Search the Default Directory (and Its Subordinates)

1. In the FileFind dialog box, select the **Current Directory Only** option, or select the **Current Directory and Below** option to search the default directory and those directories below it.

2. Pull down the File menu and select the **Directory** option, or press **Ctrl-R**.

3. In the Change Directory dialog box, enter the new directory and path at the **Path** prompt (the **Current Directory** prompt in version 6) or select it from the Drives and Sub-Directories lists.

If the default directory is already properly set, omit steps 2 and 3.

To Search on More Than One Drive

1. In the FileFind dialog box, select the **Entire Disk** option.

2. Pull down the Search menu and select the **Search Drives** option, or press **F2** (**Alt-D** in version 6).

3. In the Drives to Search dialog box, select **All Drives** to search all drives installed on your system, or select **The Following Drives:** and then select specific drives to search.

To Narrow the Search

1. Pull down the Search menu and select the **Advanced Search** option, or press **F4**.

2. In the Advanced Search dialog box, optionally specify a range of dates at the **Date Is After:** and **Date Is Before:** prompts.

3. Optionally specify a range of file sizes at the **Size Is Greater Than:** and **Size Is Less Than:** prompts.

4. Optionally specify a file owner at the **Owner Is:** prompt.

5. In version 7 only, optionally specify a match criterion from the Find As: drop down list.

6. Optionally select one of five toggle options: **File Is Hidden**, **File Is System File**, **File Is Read-Only**, **Archive Bit Is Set**, and **Include Directories**.

These options narrow the search in that only files meeting *all conditions specified* in the Advanced Search dialog box are found (i.e., only files with dates, sizes, etc., in the specified range).

The Owner Is option in step 4 is for use on a network. It narrows the search to files belonging to one specific account or user.

The Find As option (Version 7 only) is an oddball function among those available on the Advanced Search dialog box. While all other functions narrow a search with reference to file characteristics (restricting matches to files with certain attributes), the Find As function narrows a search with reference to a text string contained within a file (restricting the strings FF considers a match). Therefore, you should use this function only when you are searching for files that contain a specific text string, which you specified at the Containing: prompt on the File Find dialog box. (See "To Search for Text.") There are four options on the Find As drop down list. Select Any Match if you do not wish to restrict your search in this way (or if you aren't searching for text within files). Select Full Word to restrict matches to exact matches of complete words. For example, if you are searching for the string "in," this option will match only files containing the word "in" and not the letters "i-n" that are part of a word such as "filefind." Select Prefix to restrict matches to words beginning with the text you specify. This option will match "*in*form," but not "in" or "filef*in*d." Select Suffix to restrict matches to words ending with the text you specify. This option will match "f*in*," but not "in," "filef*in*d," or "*in*form." The Find As option is especially useful if you intend to search a number of files for a common, nondistinctive word that could be part of another word.

The Hidden, System, Read-Only, and Archive toggles in step 5 narrow the search to those files with the indicated attributes set. The Include Directories option may seem misplaced, as it actually expands the search. When set, FILEFIND finds directories, as well as files that match the file name to search for.

To Go to a Specific File

1. Run a search for a file or files (see "To Find a File or Files").
2. On the list of found files that appears, highlight the file to which you wish to go in the files currently displayed.
3. Highlight a file on the file list.
4. In the FileFind dialog box, select **Go To**.

Quitting FILEFIND in the ordinary way leaves you in the current default directory. The Go To option also quits the program but leaves you in the directory that contains the highlighted file (i.e., a new default directory).

To Print the File List

1. Pull down the List menu and select the **Print List** option, or press **Ctrl-P**. The Print List dialog box appears.
2. In the Save the list to box, choose a destination for printing: the printer or a file. If you choose a file, specify a file name at the **File:** prompt.
3. In the Print List Format box, select how much file information you want to print.
4. Optionally select any of the three toggle options available: **Print Text Search Occurrences Per File**, **Print Directory Totals**, and **Print Totals for Entire List**.
5. Select **OK**.

This command is unavailable until there is a file list in the FileFind dialog box (i.e., until you run a find or search).

In step 2, if you print to a file, the default file name is FILELIST.BAT. Though it is quite possible to create a batch file with this option, the Create Batch option is preferable, as it is more powerful. (See "To Create a Batch File.")

In step 3, there are five options. You can print only file names; file names and attributes; file names and sizes; file names, dates, and times; or file names, sizes, dates, and attributes (the default).

If you run a text search, toggle the Print Text Search Occurences Per File option on to print the number of matches found in each file, along with the selected file information.

Toggle the Print Directory Totals option on to print the number of files found in each listed directory and the amount of space they use.

Toggle the Print Totals for Entire List option on to print a grand total summing all directory totals.

To Run a Target Fit

1. Run a search for a file or files (see "To Find a File or Files").
2. On the list of found files that appears, highlight the files for which you wish to run a target fit.
3. Pull down the Commands menu and select the **Target Fit** option.
4. Select the target drive and then select **OK**.
5. Select **OK** to acknowledge the results of the check.

Target Fit checks to see whether all the files on the current file list will fit on the target drive.

To Search for Text

1. In the FileFind dialog box, enter the name of the file(s) in which to search for desired text at the **File Name:** prompt (wildcards and a path are OK).
2. At the **Containing:** prompt, type the text string for which you want to search.
3. Optionally toggle on the **Replace With:** option and type your replacement text at the **Replace With:** prompt.
4. Optionally choose a case-sensitive search by turning off the **Ignore Case** toggle.

5. Specify the scope and the conditions of the search. (See "To Find a File or Files.")
6. In the FileFind dialog box, select **Find** (**Start** in version 6).
7. Select **OK** to acknowledge completion of the search.
8. If you have toggled on the **Replace With:** option in step 3, select **Replace**.
9. If you are doing a search and replace, make sure that the **Make Backup Files** option on the Search menu is toggled on.

In the resulting file list, the number of matches found in each file is displayed along with selected file information (see "To Configure the File List").

In step 1, specify the files in which FILEFIND is to search for text. To search all files in the designated scope, enter *.* after the prompt.

In steps 2 and 3, if you have toggled on the Replace With: option, you may search for and replace a string in either ASCII or hexidecimal form. To search for and replace a hexidecimal string, pull down the Search menu and select the Hex Strings option. Enter the hex codes for which you want to search at the Hex: prompt. Optionally toggle on the Replace With: option and enter the hex codes with which you would like to replace the ones you have searched for at the Hex: prompt. Select OK to proceed.

In step 4, the Ignore Case switch toggles case-sensitive searches on or off. If the switch is turned on (the default), the search is not case sensitive. Searching for *Linda* will find every consecutive occurrence of the letters *l-i-n-d-a* without regard to case: *Linda, LINDA, LiNdA*, etc. If the switch is turned off, the search will find only exact matches of the search string. Searching for *Linda* will find only *Linda*, not *LINDA, linda, lInDa*, etc.

In step 8, when you select Replace, the viewer displays the first found file containing searched for text. The first occurrence of this text is highlighted. Select Replace to replace this text with the replacement text you specified. Select No Change if you wish to leave this occurrence of the text unchanged. Repeat either of these selections for every subsequent occurrence of the searched for text. If you change your mind about a particular replacement, select Undo to change it back. Selecting Undo multiple times will undo your replacements one at a time in reverse order. Select Next File to leave the currently displayed file and make replacements in the next found file. Select This File to replace all occurrences of the searched for text in the file currently displayed. Select All Files to replace all occurrences of the searched-for text in all found files. Note you will not have the opportunity to undo this global change. When you are finished replacing, select Close and then select Yes to save your changes.

In step 9, when you select Make Backup Files, FILEFIND will make backup copies of all the files you have changed during a search and replace operation. This is a good idea in case you later regret the changes you have made to files. The backup copies retain the original filenames, but the file extensions are preceded by a curly bracket. For example,the backup file for SHARON.DOC would be named SHARON.{DO.

To View a File or Files

1. Run a find or search. (See "To Find a File or Files.")

2. In the FileFind dialog box, highlight a file on the file list and select **View**.

3. To scroll the file, use the arrow keys or, if you have a mouse, use the scroll bar on the right side of the screen.

4. To view the next file in the list, pull down the Viewer menu and choose the **Next File** option, or press **F8**. Or, in version 7 only, select the **Next File** option at the bottom of the screen.

5. To view the previous file in the list, pull down the Viewer menu and choose the **Previous File** option, or press **F7**. Or, in version 7 only, select the **Previous File** option at the bottom of the screen.

6. To see the next occurrence of the search string (if any) in the current file, pull down the Viewer menu and choose the **Next Match** option, or press **F6**. Or, in version 7 only, select the **Next Match** option at the bottom of the screen.

7. To see the previous occurrence of the search string (if any) in the current file, pull down the Viewer menu and choose

the **Previous Match** option, or press **F5**. Or, in version 7 only, select the **Previous Match** option at the bottom of the screen.

8. When you are finished reading, click on the Close option at the bottom of the screen in version 7, or, in version 6, click on the Main! menu to return to the FileFind dialog box.

Omit steps 6 and 7 if you did not run a text search, as the Next Match and Previous Match commands will be unavailable.

In version 7, you can view found files in ASCII or hexidecimal form. To select a viewer mode, pull down the Mode menu and select View ASCII or View Hex. Version 6 does not have a hexidecimal viewer.

• **SYNTAX**

FILEFIND [*filespec*] [*search string*] [*replace string*] [*/options*]

filespec is the file(s) to find. In addition to standard DOS file-naming conventions (including wildcard use), FILEFIND also observes the following: .*.* searches for every file in the current directory, and *:*.* searches for every file on every drive.

search string is the text to search for in a Text Search.

replace text (version 7 only) is the text with which you wish to replace the text string you are searching for. The options are the following:

/A[+|-] sets (+) or clears (-) the archive attribute for *filespec*.

/BATCH causes FILEFIND to exit to DOS when the search specified on the command line is finished. Use only with the /O:*filename* option.

/C searches for *filespec* in the current directory only. Equivalent to the Current Directory Only option.

/CLEAR clears all file attributes from *filespec*.

/CS performs a case-sensitive search. Equivalent to toggling the Ignore Case option off.

/D[*mm-dd-yy*] sets the file date for *filespec* to a specific month (*mm*), date (*dd*), and year (*yy*).

/HID[+ | –] sets (+) or clears (–) the hidden attribute for *filespec*.

/NOW sets the file date and time for *filespec* to the current system time.

/O:*filename* prints the file list resulting from the search for the specified file.

/R[+ | –] sets (+) or clears (–) the read-only attribute for *filespec*.

/S searches for *filespec* in the current directory and all its subdirectories. Equivalent to the Current Directory and Below option in the FileFind dialog box.

/SYS[+ | –] sets (+) or clears (–) the system attribute for *filespec*.

/T[*hh*:*mm*:*ss*] sets the file time for *filespec* to a specific hour (*hh*), minute (*mm*), and second (*ss*).

/TARGET:*drive* performs a target fit—checks to see whether *filespec* will fit on the specified drive.

FILEFIX

FILEFIX reconstructs new, error-free copies of damaged files. It repairs damaged spreadsheet files—those created with Lotus 1-2-3, Symphony, QuattroPro, and Excel—database files—those created with dBASE and Clipper—and word processing files created with WordPerfect.

- **UPGRADE INFORMATION** FILEFIX 7 is functionally equivalent to FILEFIX 6, although there are quite a few cosmetic differences between the two versions. FILEFIX 7 performs the same operations that FILEFIX 6 does; it just does so on two additional types of spreadsheet files (QuattroPro and Excel) and word processing files created by WordPerfect.

To Fix a Database File Automatically

1. In the File Fix dialog box, highlight **dBASE & Clipper** and then select **Proceed**. In version 6, select **dBASE**.
2. In the Choose File to Repair dialog box, specify the name of the file you want to repair.
3. In the Repair dBASE File dialog box, specify the name of the new, reconstructed file, select **Fully Automatic** as the Repair Mode, specify the repair options, and then select **Begin**.
4. Select **Skip Review**.
5. Select the destination of the repair report—**Printer** or **File**—or select **No Report**.
6. In the File Fix dialog box, select another kind of file to fix or **Quit** to exit DOS. In version 6, select **Yes** to fix another file or select **No** to exit to DOS.

In step 2, in version 7, you can select a file by typing a complete filename and path (if necessary) at the File: prompt and selecting OK. Or, you may select a file by double-clicking in the Directories and

Files list boxes (you may select a file on a drive other than the current one by first selecting a drive from the Drive: drop down list). In version 6, specify the file you want to fix by typing its name at the File name: prompt or by selecting its name from the Drives, Dirs, and Files lists.

In step 3, you have three repair options: Use Clipper Field Limits, Fix Shifted Data Automatically, and Strict Character Checking. If you are repairing a Clipper file, turn on the first option. If you are repairing a dBASE file, turn it off.

In damaged database files, data may shift some number of spaces to the left or right across field boundaries. Turn on the second option to have FILEFIX fix this. In general, this option should be turned on.

The third option should almost always be turned on. Turn it off only if you have special graphics characters embedded in your fields. Such graphics are not produced with dBASE or Clipper but with a few third-party applications.

The damaged file is repaired automatically unless its header is corrupted. The file header contains information about the structure of the database (i.e., the number, name, size, type, etc., of component fields). If this is the case, the header must be manually repaired. This will occur after step 3. You may first be prompted to specify the version under which the damaged file was created; select Review Fields, then follow the steps in the section "To Fix a Database File's Structure."

If you want to review or change header information, even though the header itself is undamaged, select Review Fields in step 4 instead of Skip Review.

To Fix a Database File Manually

1. In the File Fix dialog box, highlight **dBASE & Clipper** and then select **Proceed**. In version 6, select **dBASE**.
2. In the Choose File to Repair dialog box, specify the name of the file you want to repair.

3. In the Repair dBASE File dialog box, specify the name of the new, reconstructed file, select **Review Damaged Records** or **Review All Records** as the Repair Mode, specify the repair options, and select **Begin**.

4. Select **Skip Review.**

5. For each record at which FILEFIX stops, select an action: **Accept, Reject, Shift, or Mode.**

6. Select the destination of the repair report—**Printer** or **File**—or select **No Report**.

7. In the File Fix dialog box, select another kind of file to fix or **Quit** to exit to DOS. In version 6, select **Yes** to fix another file or select **No** to exit to DOS.

In step 2, in version 7, you can select a file by typing a complete filename and path (if necessary) at the File: prompt and selecting OK. Or, you may select a file by double-clicking in the Directories and Files list boxes (you may select a file on a drive other than the current one by first selecting a drive from the Drive: drop down list). In version 6, specify the file you want to fix by typing its name at the File Name: prompt or by selecting its name from the Drives, Dirs, and Files lists.

In step 3, database files can be repaired in two ways: You can choose to review every record or only those that are damaged.

Also in step 3, you have three repair options: Use Clipper Field Limits, Fix Shifted Data Automatically, and Strict Character Checking. For an explanation of these options, see "To Fix a Database File Automatically."

If the file header (which contains information about the structure of the database) is damaged, you will be prompted to repair this after step 3. You may first be prompted to specify the version under which the damaged file was created; select Review Fields, then follow the steps in the section "To Fix a Database File's Structure." When you are finished, you will return to step 5.

If you want to review or change header information, even though the header itself is undamaged, select Review Fields in step 4 instead of Skip Review.

110 FILEFIX

In step 5, there are a number of options. For each record, select Accept to keep the record in its current state, and select Reject to discard the record. Select Shift and then press ← and → to properly align data within fields. When data is properly aligned, select Done and then Accept. Select Mode to change the Repair Mode.

To Fix a Database File's Structure

1. Select **Revise**.
2. Select **Import**.
3. In the Choose Import File dialog box, specify the database containing the structure you want to import.
4. In the Repair dBASE File dialog box, select **Accept**.

OR

1. Select **Revise**.
2. Select **Edit**.
3. Press ← or → until the data in the first field of the first record in the file sits next to the left edge of the on-screen box, and then select **OK**. This marks the beginning of file data.
4. Press ← or → until data is aligned in proper columns and then select **OK**. This establishes record size.
5. For each field displayed, press ← and → until data is correctly displayed within the field, select **Edit**, and specify the correct field name and type.
6. Once each field is finished, select **OK**.
7. Select **Accept**.

The structure of a database file can be fixed in one of three ways:

- Import the structure from another, healthy database file. To do this, use the first sequence of steps.
- Edit the structure manually. To do this, use the second sequence of steps.

- Import a similar but nonidentical structure from a healthy database and tailor it to a proper fit. To do this, use both sequences of steps, omitting step 4 from the first sequence.

To Fix a Spreadsheet File

1. In the File Fix dialog box, select the kind of spreadsheet file you want to fix and, in version 7 only, select **Proceed.**
2. In the Choose File to Repair dialog box, specify the name of the file you want to fix.
3. In the Repair File dialog box, specify the name of the new, reconstructed file, specify the repair mode, and select **Begin**.
4. Select the destination of the repair report—**Printer** or **File**—or select **No Report.**
5. In the File Fix dialog box, select another kind of file to fix or **Quit** to exit to DOS. In version 6, select **Yes** to fix another file or select **No** to exit to DOS.

In step 2, in version 7, you can select a file by typing a complete filename and path (if necessary) at the File: prompt and selecting OK. Or, you may select a file by double-clicking in the Directories and Files list boxes (you may select a file on a drive other than the current one by first selecting a drive from the Drive: drop down list). In version 6, specify the file you want to fix by typing its name at the File Name: prompt or by selecting its name from the Drives, Dirs, and Files lists.

In step 3, you can select one of two repair modes: Attempt Recovery of All Data and Recover Cell Data Only. In almost all cases, it is possible to reconstruct an entire spreadsheet, so you should routinely choose the first option. If, however, damage to the file is particularly severe and complete recovery is not possible, choose the second option.

To Fix a WordPerfect File (Version 7 Only)

1. In the File Fix dialog box, highlight **WordPerfect** and select **Proceed**.

112 FILEFIX

2. In the Choose File to Repair dialog box, specify the name of the file you want to fix.
3. In the Repair WordPerfect File dialog box, specify the name of the new, reconstructed file.
4. Specify the repair mode to use and select **Begin**.
5. Select **OK** to acknowledge the completion of repairs.
6. Select another file to fix or quit to return to DOS.

In step 2, you can select a file by typing a complete filename and path (if necessary) at the File: prompt and selecting OK. Or, you may select a file by double-clicking in the Directories and Files list boxes (you may select a file on a drive other than the current one by first selecting a drive from the Drive: drop down list).

In step 4, choose Recover Document since this will auto-repair the file if possible. If Recover Document does not work, you will be prompted to repair the file's prefix, etc. (See "To Repair a WordPerfect File's Prefix.")

To Repair a WordPerfect File's Prefix

1. In the Repair WordPerfect Prefix dialog box, select **Build Simple File Prefix**.
2. Select **Begin** to build a simple file prefix.
3. Select **OK** to acknowledge that the simple file prefix has been built.
4. Return to step 6 under "To Fix a WordPerfect File."

OR

1. In the Repair WordPerfect Prefix dialog box, select **Import File Prefix**.
2. Select **Begin** to import a file prefix.
3. In the Choose Import File dialog box, specify the file from which to import the file prefix by typing a complete filename and path (if necessary) at the **File**: prompt and selecting **OK**. Or, you may select a file by double-clicking in the Directories and Files list boxes (you may select a file

on a drive other than the current one by first selecting a drive from the Drive: drop down list).

4. Select **OK** to import the file prefix.
5. Select **OK** to acknowledge the completion of the importation.
6. Return to step 6 under "To Fix a WordPerfect File."

OR

1. In the **Locate Start Of Document** viewer in the **Repair WordPerfect Prefix** dialog box, place the cursor block at the beginning of the file's text.
2. Select **Repair Document Offset**.
3. Select **Begin**.
4. Select **OK** to acknowledge the fix.
5. Return to step 6 under "To Fix a WordPerfect File."

● SYNTAX

FILEFIX [*filename.ext*]

When you indicate the file name and extension on the command line, FILEFIX senses the type of file with which you are working. Accordingly, it skips those steps where you enter the file type and name. Thus, in "To Fix a Spreadsheet File" and in "To Fix a Database File" (both automatically and manually), you begin at step 3.

● **NOTES** FILEFIX 6 works on files created by Lotus 1-2-3 versions 1, 1A, and 2, Symphony versions 1.0 and 1.1, and dBASE versions III, III+, and IV. One-hundred-percent-compatible files are also supported.

FILEFIX 7 works on files created by Lotus 1-2-3 versions through (and including) 3.1, Symphony versions 1.0 and 1.1, dBASE III, III+ and IV, Excel versions through (and including) 4.0, and WordPerfect through (and including) 5.1.

FL

File Locate

FL is a small and efficient file find program. FL is not as powerful as FILEFIND, as FL can only search for files by name and not by any other criteria. However, since FL lacks an interactive mode and can only be used from the command line, it is faster to use.

- **UPGRADE INFORMATION** FL 7 contains all of the functions of FL 6 and adds the ability to search in a path you specify.

- **SYNTAX**

    FL *filespec* **[/options]**

filespec is the file or files to find. Drive letter, path, and wild cards all may be used.

The options are the following:

/**A** searches on all drives.

/**E:***envar* searches only the the path specified in the *envar* environment variable.

/**F***#* finds only the first # files that match *filespec*. By default, # equals 1.

/**P** pauses the display after each full screen.

/**T** searches only in those directories listed in the PATH.

/**W** lists files in the landscape or "wide" format.

See Also FILEFIND

FS
File Size

FS totals the size of a group of specified files. This is most useful when you are copying files and you need to determine if there is sufficient space on your target drive. As such, FS is akin to FILEFIND's Target Fit function, though it is more efficient as it lacks an interactive mode and runs only from the command line.

- **UPGRADE INFORMATION**   FS 7 is identical to FS 6.

- **SYNTAX**

    FS *filespec* [*drive*:] [*/options*]

    filespec is the file or files to size. Drive letters, path, and wild cards all may be used.

    drive: is the target drive. FS measures free space on this drive to see if *filespec* will fit.

    The options are the following:

    /P pauses the display after each full screen.

    /S sizes files matching *filespec* in all subdirectories under the specified directory.

    /T suppresses the file list and displays totals only.

    See Also   FILEFIND

IMAGE

The IMAGE program protects your disks against accidental formatting. It saves essential disk information—the boot record, FAT, and root directory—to the file IMAGE.DAT. This file can then be used by UNFORMAT to restore data to a formatted disk and by UNERASE to unerase files (See UNERASE, UNFORMAT).

IMAGE does not have an interactive mode and can be used only from the command line.

- **UPGRADE INFORMATION** IMAGE 7 contains all of the functions of IMAGE 6 and adds the ability to save essential disk information without displaying the output.

- **SYNTAX**

    IMAGE [*drive*:] [/NOBACKUP] [OUT]

    drive: specifies the drive for which IMAGE saves essential information. If *drive*: is omitted, the default drive is used.

    /NOBACKUP causes IMAGE not to create the backup file IMAGE.BAK when it saves essential disk information.

    /OUT causes IMAGE to run without displaying any messages or information on the screen.

- **NOTES** IMAGE can protect both floppy disks and hard disks from accidental formats. However, only floppies formatted with Norton's Safe Format can be recovered. Floppies formatted with a DOS format cannot be recovered, as they are completely overwritten in the process (i.e., the IMAGE.DAT file, used to reconstruct the disk, is itself overwritten). Hard disks, by contrast, can almost always be unformatted, regardless of the formatting method. Hard-disk data is not overwritten during a format.

The file IMAGE.DAT *must* reside in the root directory in order for a disk to be properly unformatted. IMAGE automatically places IMAGE.DAT properly. Do not move this file.

INSTDOS

Version 7 Only

INSTDOS installs selected Norton Utilities programs in their own group under Microsoft Windows 3.0 or 3.1.

To Run INSTDOS

1. Start Microsoft Windows 3.0 or 3.1.
2. Pull down the File menu and select **Run**.
3. At the **Command Line:** prompt in the Run window, type **instdos** (including a path if necessary).
4. Select **OK** to acknowledge completion of the installation.

INSTDOS installs DISKREET, FILEFIND, FILEFIX, NCD, NDOS, NORTON, SAFE FORMAT, and SYSINFO in a group called "Norton Utilities for DOS" under Windows 3.0 or 3.1.

LP
Line Print

LP formats and prints text files to your printer or to another file on disk.

- **UPGRADE INFORMATION** LP 7 contains all of the functions of LP 6 and adds a few additional options. It allows you to print a file using a printer configuration file you create with NUCONFIG and to append output generated by LP to an existing file. Note that because some of the options have been renamed, there are two separate lists of options below, one for version 7 and the other for version 6.

- **SYNTAX**

    LP *filespec destination* [*/options*]

    filespec is the name of the text file or files to print. Wild cards are acceptable. Include a path if necessary.

    destination is the name of the printer port or file to which you want *filespec* sent. The default is PRN:.

The options for version 7 are as follows:

/80 | 132 prints the file in 80 or 132 columns.

/A appends the output generated by LP to *destination* file.

/B# sets the bottom margin to # lines. The default is 5.

/CONFIG:*filename* prints a file using a printer configuration file you created with NUCONFIG. If you regularly print to different printers or with different printing formats or setup files, using printer configuration files to switch printers or formats is a good idea; it eliminates unnecessary repetition of command-line switches. If you use LP with printer configuration files, you may still use the LP command-line switches. However, since some switches may duplicate settings already established in a configuration file, there is no need to repeat them. See "To Create or Modify Printer Files" in NORTON.

/EBCDIC prints files in the EBCDIC format, a format often used on IBM mainframes.

/HEADER[0 | 1 | 2] sets one of three headers. /HEADER0 sets no header. /HEADER1 sets a header containing the current date and time. /HEADER2 sets a two-line header containing the current date and time on one line, and file name, and creation or modification date and time on the other.

/HI# sets the height of the paper in lines. The default is 66.

/L# sets the left margin to # columns. The default is 5.

/N turns on line numbering.

/PA# sets the starting page number to #. The default is 1.

/PR:*printertype* specifies what type of printer you are using. Printer type may be TT(y), GE(neric), EP(son), PR(oprinter), QU(ietwriter), TO(shiba), LA(serjet), or PO(stscript).

/R# sets the right margin to # columns. The default is 5.

/SET:*setupfile* sends the printer control codes stored in the setup file "setupfile" to the printer before printing begins. Printer control codes differ for every printer. See your printer manual for more information.

/SP# sets the line spacing to # lines. The default is 1.

/T# sets the top margin to # lines. The default is 3.

/TAB# sets the tab value for # spaces. The default is 8.

/W# sets the width of the paper to # columns. The default is 85.

/WS prints files in WordStar format.

The options for version 6 are as follows:

/80 | 132 prints the file in 80 or 132 columns.

/B# sets the bottom margin to # lines. The default is 3.

/EBCDIC prints files in EBCDIC format, a format often used on IBM mainframes.

/H# sets the height of the paper in lines. The default is 66.

/HEADER[0 | 1 | 2] sets one of three headers. /HEADER0 sets no header. /HEADER1 sets a header with current date and time. /HEADER2 sets a two-line header containing current date and time on one line, and file date and time on the other. The default is /HEADER1.

/L# sets the left margin to # columns. The default is 5.

/N turns on line numbering.

/P# sets the starting page number to #. The default is 1.

/PS prints the file in PostScript format.

/R# sets the right margin to # columns. The default is 5.

/S# sets the line spacing to # lines. The default is 1.

/SET:*setupfile* prints using printer control codes stored in *setupfile*. Printer control codes differ for every printer. See your printer manual.

/T# sets the top margin to # lines. The default is 3.

/TAB# sets the tab value to # spaces. The default is 8.

/W# sets the width of the paper to # columns. The default is 85.

/WS prints files in WordStar format.

NCACHE2/NCACHE

Disk caches speed up the operation of a computer by placing data recently read from disk in a memory buffer. When this data is needed again, it is read from memory, which is considerably faster than reading it from disk. Caches can also place data to be written to disk in a buffer, speeding up operation by controlling exactly when disk writes occur.

- **UPGRADE INFORMATION** NCACHE2 (version 7) contains all of the functions of NCACHE (version 6) and adds several new ones, which give you increased control over when cached data is written to disk. Note the file name change: NCACHE2.EXE in version 7, NCACHE.EXE in version 6.

- **SYNTAX**

    [DEVICE=*path*]NCACHE2.EXE /*sizeoption* [/*options*]

NCACHE2 can be loaded from the command line or from your CONFIG.SYS file as a device driver. Cache size and options can be specified when loading the NCACHE2 from either source.

path is the directory in which NCACHE2.EXE is located.

/sizeoption specifies the cache size when loading NCACHE2. You can specify *sizeoption* by using one of four options: /INSTALL, /EXT, /EXP, or /DOS. See below for explanations.

The options are as follows:

/[+ | -]A activates (+) or deactivates (−) the cache but does not remove the cache from memory. (The default is +.)

/BLOCK=bytes specifies cache-block size. *Bytes* can equal 512, 1K, 2K, 4K, or 8K.

/[+ | -]C activates (+) or deactivates (−) caching of additional data—that is, freezes cache contents when turned off. (The default is +.)

/DELAY=*secs.hths* delays disk writes by the specified amount of time. *Secs* must be an integer from 0 to 59, *hths* an integer from 0 to 99. Use when IntelliWrites is enabled. See the /I option, below.

/DISKRESET = on | off (version 7 only) specifies that NCACHE2 should write all cached data to disk after an application makes a disk reset request. The requesting program suspends operation until NCACHE2 finishes writing. If this switch is off, NCACHE2 ignores disk reset calls. (The default is on.)

/DOS=[[-*bytes*] sizes the cache to *bytes* of conventional memory. If *bytes* is preceeded by a minus sign, the cache is sized to all available conventional memory, minus *bytes*. If *bytes* is omitted, NCACHE2 will use 128K.

/DUMP (version 7 only) writes to disk any data that has not yet been written to disk because the write has been deferred.

/EXP=[[-*bytes*[,*winbytes*]] sizes the cache to *bytes* of expanded memory. If *bytes* is preceeded by a minus sign, the cache is sized to all available expanded memory, minus *bytes*. *Winbytes* specifies the amount of expanded memory to use as a cache when running Windows 3.0 or higher in 386 Enhanced mode. If *bytes* is omitted, the NCACHE2 will use all available expanded memory. If *winbytes* is omitted, *winbytes* is set equal to *bytes*.

/EXT=[[-*bytes*[,*winbytes*]] sizes the cache to bytes of extended memory. If *bytes* is preceeded by a minus sign, the cache is sized to all available extended memory, minus *bytes*. *Winbytes* specifies the amount of extended memory to use as a cache when running Windows 3.0 or higher in 386 Enhanced mode. If *bytes* is omitted, the NCACHE2 will use all available extended memory. If *winbytes* is omitted, *winbytes* is set equal to *bytes*.

/F empties the cache. NCACHE2 will write all deferred disk writes to disk before flushing the cache.

/G=*bytes* sets the group sector size to *bytes*. This sets the maximum amount of buffer space that any one read can occupy. (The default is 128K.)

/I[+ | -] activates (+) or deactivates (-) intelligent disk writes (IntelliWrites). Speeds up operation by writing data to disk more efficiently—maximizing the amount of data written in any given revolution of the disk and writing data to disk while control has returned to the current application (i.e., in the background).

/INI=*path* specifies the location of the NCACHE2 configuration file NCACHE.INI. This file is created with the /SAVE option.

/INSTALL installs and configures NCACHE2 according to the defaults in the NCACHE.INI file. You can override these defaults by specifying other switches when you install the program. NCACHE2 remains resident until you uninstall the cache or turn off your computer.

/MULTI = on ¦ off (version 7 only) enables the multitasking write ability of NCACHE2. With /MULTI on, NCACHE2 writes in the background while DOS executes applications in the foreground. With /MULTI off, NCACHE2 suspends the foreground application while writing data in the background. (The default is off.)

/OPTIMIZE=S ¦ E ¦ M automatically sets the /BLOCK, /DELAY, /READ, and /WRITE options, optimizing them for system speed (S), efficiency of reads and writes (E), or memory usage (M). Individual settings of these options, however, take precedence.

/[+ ¦ –]P activates (+) or deactivates (–) write protection for cached drives.

/QUICK=ON ¦ OFF activates (ON) or deactivates (OFF) quick prompts. Use when IntelliWrites is enabled (see the /I option, above). Speeds up operation by returning to the DOS prompt before all disk writes are complete.

/QUIET reduces NCACHE2 feedback such that no messages are displayed on the screen unless there is an error.

/R=[D]*sectors* causes NCACHE2 to read ahead *sectors* sectors. Speeds up operation by reading the next most likely group of sectors into the cache, before they are actually requested by the application. Adding the D prefix ("dynamic") enables reading ahead only when probable sectors are sitting sequentially on the disk.

/READ=*bytes* specifies the size of the buffer into which sectors "read-ahead" are placed. *Bytes* must be an integer value greater than or equal to 8K and less than or equal to 64K. Setting *bytes* to 0 disables the read-ahead feature. See the /R option, above.

/REPORT[=ON | OFF] Displays a detailed NCACHE2 status screen. If ON is specified, the detailed status screen will appear after any NCACHE2 operation.

/RESET resets the cache for all drives to its newly loaded state. Similar to /F.

/SAVE saves the current configuration to the file NCACHE.INI.

/STATUS[=ON | OFF] displays a summary NCACHE2 status screen. If ON is specified, the summary screen will appear after any NCACHE2 operation.

/UNINSTALL removes NCACHE2 from memory. NCACHE2 cannot be removed if it was loaded as a device through CONFIG.SYS. NCACHE2 cannot be removed if another Terminate-and-Stay-Resident (TSR) program was loaded after it and remains in memory.

/USEHIGH=ON | OFF when set ON, loads NCACHE2 itself (i.e., the memory management apparatus, rather than the cache) into Upper Memory Blocks.

/USEHMA=ON | OFF when set ON, loads NCACHE2 itself (i.e. the memory management apparatus, rather than the cache) into the DOS High Memory Area.

/[+ | -]W activates (+) or deactivates (−) Write-through. Caches disk writes as well as disk reads. It has no effect when Intelli-Writes is enabled.

/WRITE=*bytes* specifies the size of the IntelliWrites buffer. *Bytes* must be an integer value greater than or equal to 8K and less than or equal to 64K. Setting *bytes* to 0 disables the Intelli-Writes feature. See the /I option, above.

- **NOTES** Do not use NCACHE2 with the DOS FASTOPEN program, as NCACHE2 takes over its functions.

Do not use NCACHE to cache a compressed drive. Cache the host drive instead.

NCC
Norton Control Center

NCC gives you control over a number of system options and settings: cursor size; text, background, border, and palette colors; video mode; keyboard repeat rate; mouse sensitivity; serial port configuration; and system date and time. It also provides four stopwatches.

- **UPGRADE INFORMATION** NCC 7 is nearly identical to NCC 6. The only differences between the two programs are that NCC 7 no longer allows you to change the background to bright or blinking in the DOS colors option, there are a few new command-line switches, and the procedure to exit NCC has been changed slightly.

To Change Cursor Size

1. In the Select Item box, select **Cursor Size**.
2. In the Cursor Size box, adjust the size of the cursor by repositioning the Start and End arrows.
3. Select **OK**.

The Start and End arrows can be adjusted with ↑ and ↓ or by dragging with the mouse. (You can select the arrows with ← and → if you don't have a mouse.).

The results of adjusting cursor size are at all times previewed in the Actual Size box.

In step 2, you may return the cursor to its default size by selecting Default in the Cursor Size box.

To Change DOS Colors
(Text, Background, and Border)

1. In the Select Item box, select **DOS Colors**.

2. In the DOS Colors box and in the Text Color box, select the DOS text color and background color.
3. In the Border Color box, select a border color.
4. Version 6 only. In the Background box, select whether background colors should be **Bright** or **Blinking.**
5. Select **OK.**

If you are going to use the DOS Colors function, you should load the ANSI.SYS driver in your CONFIG.SYS file. Although this is not necessary, the color changes you make are less likely to be undone by programs that themselves set text, border, and background colors.

In step 2, the text color and background color are set in combination; that is, all possible combinations of text and background colors are available in the Text Color box.

The default colors can be reset by selecting the Default option in the DOS Colors box.

To Change Palette Colors

1. In the Select Item box, select **Palette Colors.**
2. In the Palette Colors box, use the pointer arrows to indicate the color you want to change.
3. Select the **Change** option.
4. In the Change Color dialog box, select a new color and then select **OK.**
5. Repeat steps 2 through 4 for each color you want to change.
6. In the Palette Colors box, select **OK** when finished.

This function is available only if you have a monitor with EGA or VGA graphics.

To return an individual color to its default setting, choose the Default option in the Change Color dialog box in step 4.

To return all colors to their default settings, choose the Default option in the Palette Colors box.

To Change Selected Country Information

1. To change the selected country and country information, choose **Country Info** in the Select Item box.
2. In the Country Info box, highlight the country whose formats you want to use and select **OK**.

This function is only available if the COUNTRY parameter has been set in your CONFIG.SYS file or the NLSFUNC program has been run. See your DOS manual for details.

In step 2, when you select a new country, the Time, Date, Currency, List, and Numbers formats change accordingly.

To Change System Date and Time

1. In the Select Item box, select **Time and Date**. The Time and Date box appears.
2. In the Date box, highlight the month, date, and year; use the plus (+) key to change the values upward, and the minus (–) key to change them downward.
3. In the Time box, highlight the hour, minutes, and seconds; use the plus key to change the values upward, and the minus key to change them downward.
4. Select **OK**.

On computers where the system configuration is stored in CMOS, this function changes the CMOS date and time, thereby making the changes permanent. On computers that have only a clock/calendar or nothing at all, the date and time are changed for the current session only. After rebooting or powering up, the date and time have to be reset.

To Change the Video Mode

1. In the Select Item box, select **Video Mode.**
2. In the Video Mode box and in the Display Lines box, select the number of lines of text to display on the screen.
3. In the Display Mode box, select either the **Black and White** option or the **Color** option.
4. Select **OK**.

The options available to you with the Video Mode function depend entirely on the kind of video card installed in your system. In step 2, the option to change the number of display lines is only available if you have an EGA- or VGA-equipped system. Neither the Display Lines option nor the Display Mode options are available on a system with monochrome graphics (Hercules and compatible graphics).

To Configure Serial Ports

1. In the Select Item box, select **Serial Ports.**
2. At the top of the Serial Ports box, highlight the port to be configured.
3. In the Baud box, select the rate at which the serial port communicates.
4. In the Parity box, select the parity setting at which the serial port communicates.
5. In the Data Bits box, select the number of data bits in each byte transmitted.
6. In the Stop Bits box, select the number of stop bits to be sent after each byte of data sent.
7. Repeat steps 2 through 6 for each port.
8. Select **OK**.

In order for your computer to communicate via a serial port with any external device (mouse, laser printer, modem, etc.), the serial port must be properly configured. The port and the external device must use the same protocols and settings (whatever those may be; it is entirely dependent on the device in question).

To Restore Saved Settings

1. Pull down the File menu and select the **Load Settings** option, or press **F3**.

2. In the Load Settings dialog box, enter the name of the file that contains the settings you want to load and then select **OK**.

To Save NCC Settings to a File

1. Pull down the File menu and select the **Save Settings** option, or press **F2**. The Save Settings dialog box appears.

2. In the Settings box, toggle on the settings to be saved.

3. In the File Name box, type the name of the file that will contain the saved settings.

4. Select **OK**.

Settings that are saved in a file can be implemented simultaneously. You do not have to reset everything each time you use your computer. (See "To Restore Saved Settings.")

To Set the Keyboard Repeat Rate

1. In the Select Item box, select **Keyboard Speed.**

2. In the Keyboard Speed box, set the keyboard repeat rate by moving the top "belt buckle" left or right.

3. Set the repeat delay by moving the second "belt buckle" left or right.

4. Optionally hold down a key to test the new settings. Results are visible at the Keyboard Test Pad prompt.

5. Select **OK**.

The *keyboard repeat rate* is the rate at which a character is repeated on the screen when a key is depressed and held down. It can be set as slow as 2 characters per second and as fast as 30 characters per second. The keyboard repeat rate can be set on all 286, 386, and 486 computers and on some 8088 and 8086 computers.

The *repeat delay* is the length of time a key must be held down before a character is repeated. It can be set as slow as 1 second and as fast as 0.25 seconds and works on 286, 386, and 486 computers.

In steps 2 and 3, "belt buckles" can be moved with the ←, →, Home, and End keys or by dragging with the mouse.

Repeat rate and delay can be set automatically to their fastest settings by selecting Fast in the Keyboard Speed box.

To Set Mouse Sensitivity

1. In the Select Item box, select **Mouse Speed**.

2. In the Mouse Speed box, move the "belt buckle" to adjust mouse sensitivity.

3. Optionally move your mouse to test the new settings.

4. Select **OK**.

In step 2, the "belt buckle" can be moved with the ←, →, Home, and End keys or by dragging with the mouse.

Mouse sensitivity can be returned to its default setting by selecting the Default option in the Mouse Speed box.

To Use Stopwatches/Timers

1. In the Select Item box, select **Watches**.

2. In the Watches box, select any of four watches you want to use.

3. Select **Start** to start the watch, **Pause** to stop it, or **Reset** to reset it to zero.

When you first start a watch, the current system time is displayed.

• SYNTAX

NCC [*filename*] [**/SET**]

OR

NCC [*/options*]

filename specifies the file containing saved NCC settings. If *filename* is specified, the /SET option must be used to load the settings.

The options are the following:

/25 sets number of display lines to 25.

/35 sets number of display lines to 35 (EGA only).

/40 sets number of display lines to 40 (VGA only).

/43 sets number of display lines to 43 (EGA only).

/50 sets number of display lines to 50 (VGA only).

/BW80 sets display to black and white, 80 columns, 25 rows.

/C:*comment* displays *comment*. Comments that include spaces must be enclosed in quotation marks.

/CO80 sets display to color, 80 columns, 25 rows.

/CURSOR (version 7 only) should be used when loading options from *filename*. It sets only the cursor size and ignores all other options saved in *filename*.

/DOSCOLOR (version 7 only) should be used when loading options from *filename*. It sets only the DOS text and border colors and ignores all other options saved in *filename*.

/FAST sets keyboard repeat rate and delay to the fastest settings.

/L displays current time and date on the left side of the screen.

/N suppresses display of current time and date.

/PALETTE (version 7 only) should be used when loading options from *filename*. It sets only the palette colors and ignores all other options saved in *filename*.

/START:# starts the stopwatch with the specified number. If # is omitted, watch number 1 is started.

/STOP:# stops the stopwatch with the specified number. If # is omitted, watch number 1 is stopped.

NCD
Norton Change Directory

NCD is a subdirectory manager. It lets you create, delete, and rename subdirectories, as well as navigate easily among them.

- **UPGRADE INFORMATION** NCD 7 contains all of the functions of NCD 6 and adds the ability to view the contents of a directory and to see how much free space remains on a drive. In addition, a few more of NCD's functions are available through command-line options.

To Change Directories

1. Highlight the directory that you want to change to.
2. Press ↵.

In step 1, highlight the target directory by using ↑ and ↓ or the built-in Speed Search function. To use Speed Search, simply type the first letter or letters of the directory you want to highlight. Each time you type a letter, the highlight bar jumps to the next directory name beginning with the letter typed. Pressing Ctrl-↵ cycles the highlight bar through all directories that match the letters you typed.

To Change Drives

1. Pull down the Disk menu and select the **Change Disk** option, or press **F3**.
2. In the dialog box that appears, select a new drive.

To Change the Number of Display Lines

1. Pull down the View menu.
2. Select the number of lines to display on screen.

This function is available only if you have EGA or VGA graphics.

134 NCD

The choices available in step 2 are determined by the kind of graphics card you have.

This function changes the display for the NCD program only. If you want to change the display lines systemwide, use the NCC program (see NCC, "To Change the Video Mode").

To Change or Delete a Volume Label

1. Pull down the Disk menu and select the **Volume Label** option, or press **Ctrl-V**.
2. In the Volume Label dialog box, type the new volume label and select **OK**.

To delete a drive's volume label, select the Delete option in the Volume Label dialog box in step 2.

To Configure NCD

1. Pull down the Directory menu and select the **Configure** option.
2. Select any of three available options.
3. Select **OK**.

In step 2, there are three options. Enable Copy Tree enables or disables the Copy Tree function (see "To Copy a Directory"). Enable Remove Tree enables or disables the Remove Tree function (see the second sequence of steps under "To Delete a Directory"). Enable Prune & Graft enables or disables the Prune & Graft function (see "To Rearrange a Directory Tree").

To Copy a Directory

1. Highlight the directory you want to copy.
2. Pull down the Directory menu and select the **Copy Tree** function, or press **Alt-F5**.

3. In the Copy Directory to: dialog box (called the Select Directory dialog box in version 6), specify the directory to which you will copy the highlighted directory.

4. Optionally toggle the **Delete Original Files** option.

5. Select **OK**.

This function copies a directory, all of its subdirectories, and all of their files to the directory you specify (i.e., the copied directory becomes a subdirectory of the target directory).

In step 3 in version 7, you may specify the target directory by typing it at the Path: prompt or by selecting it from the Drives drop down list and the Subdirectories list. In version 6, type the target directory at the Copy the Tree to: prompt or select it from the Drives and Subdirectories lists.

In step 4, the Delete Original Files option deletes the directory and its files after they have been copied. This option, then, allows you to move rather than copy a directory.

For reasons of safety, the Copy Tree function is disabled by default. See "To Configure NCD" to enable this function.

To Delete a Directory

1. Highlight the directory you want to delete.

2. Pull down the Directory menu and select the **Delete** option, or press **F8**.

3. If the directory contains files, review the file list in the caution box and select **Yes** to proceed with the deletion.

OR

1. Highlight the directory you want to delete.

2. Pull down the Directory menu and select the **Remove Tree** option, or press **Alt-F8**.

3. Select **Remove** on the warning dialog box that appears.

4. Select **Yes** on the second warning dialog box.

The Delete option deletes only the highlighted directory and any files it contains. It is unable to delete any directory that contains subdirectories. The Remove Tree option, by contrast, deletes in one operation the highlighted directory, all of its subdirectories, and all of their files.

You cannot use either option on the root directory of any drive.

For reasons of safety, the Remove Tree option is disabled by default. See "To Configure NCD" to enable this function.

To Get Directory Size Information

1. Highlight the directory you wish to size.
2. Pull down the Directory menu and select the **Tree Size** option.
3. Select **OK** to acknowledge the Tree Size dialog box.

This option provides the total size of all files contained in the selected directory and the total disk space allocated to it. The latter measure includes the size of all of the directory's files, the size of their slack space, and the size of the directory itself.

To List Files (Version 7 Only)

1. Pull down the Directory menu and select the **File List** option or press **F4**.
2. Optionally reorder the file list by toggling on the keys by which you wish to sort and then selecting **Re-Sort**.
3. Select **Close** to return to NCD.

This option allows you to see the contents of a directory.

In step 2, the keys may be selected alone or in combination. When used in combination, the order in which you select the keys is significant. For example, if you select Extension and then Name, files will be sorted by extension, and all files with the same extension will be sorted by file name. Selecting these sort keys in the opposite order sorts files by name, and any files with the same name will also be sorted by extension. By default, files are sorted in ascending order (A-Z, 1-9). The plus sign next to a selected key indicates this. To sort in descending order (Z-A, 9-1), press the minus sign after selecting the key or click the mouse on the plus sign.

To Make a Directory

1. Highlight the directory that will contain the new directory (i.e., highlight the parent-to-be directory).

2. Pull down the Directory menu and select the **Make** option, or press **F7**.

3. In the dialog box that appears, enter the name of the directory you want to create and select **OK**.

In step 1, highlight the directory by using the arrow keys or Speed Search. (See "To Change Directories" for an explanation.)

To Print the Directory Tree

1. In version 7, pull down the Disk menu and select **Print Tree** or press **Alt-P**. In version 6, pull down the Directory menu and select the **Print Tree** option, or press **Alt-P**.

2. In the Print Tree dialog box and at the **Print the Directory Structure To:** prompt, specify where the tree is to be printed.

3. In the Tree Format box, specify the format with which the tree is to be printed.

4. Select **Print.**

Trees can be printed to a printer or a file, so in step 2, specify either a file name or the device to which a printer is attached (PRN, LPT1:, LPT2:, etc.). If you print a tree to a file, there is an added step: Select OK to acknowledge the creation of a new file.

In step 3, there are three possible tree formats:

- Select Tree, Graphic Chars to print the tree as it appears on screen: directory names connected by lines.

- Select Tree, Non-Graphic Chars if your printer is unable to print graphics. This prints a tree with hyphens, plus signs, etc.

- Select List to get a simple list of directories not in tree format.

To Rearrange a Directory Tree

1. Select the drive whose tree you wish to rearrange. See "To Change Drives" if necessary.
2. Pull down the Directory menu and select the **Prune & Graft** option, or press **Alt-G**.
3. On the Prune & Graft dialog box, highlight the directory you wish to relocate.
4. Select **Prune**.
5. Highlight the directory under which you wish to place the directory pruned in steps 3 through 4.
6. Select **Graft**.
7. Repeat steps 3 through 6 as necessary.
8. Select **Close**.

The Prune & Graft function allows you to rearrange the directory tree, making any directory a subdirectory of another, regardless of original hierarchy.

Unlike the Copy function (see "To Copy a Directory"), this function only works on the current drive. If you wish to rearrange the tree of a drive other than the default, you must select that drive in step 1.

In step 3, all subdirectories of the directory you highlight will be moved along with it.

In steps 3 and 5, you may use the Speed Search function to highlight a directory. See "To Change Directories" for an explanation of Speed Search.

For reasons of safety, the Prune & Graft option is disabled by default. See "To Configure NCD" to enable this function.

To Rename a Directory

1. Highlight the directory you want to rename.
2. Pull down the Directory menu and select the **Rename** option, or press **F6**.
3. In the dialog box that appears, type the new directory name and select **OK.**

In step 1, highlight the directory by using the arrow keys or Speed Search. (See "To Change Directories" for an explanation.)

This function is unavailable if you are using a DOS version prior to 3.0.

To Rescan a Disk

1. Pull down the Disk menu and select the **Rescan Disk** option, or press **F2**.
2. In the Rescan Disk dialog box, select **Yes.**

When NCD is run on a drive for the first time, it stores directory information in a file named TREEINFO.NCD (though this file will not be used on drives with three or fewer directories.) In subsequent uses of the program, NCD reads directory information from this file rather than rescanning the drive, which saves you some time. Changes made to the directory tree (for example, renaming, adding, or deleting a directory) with NCD are reflected automatically in TREEINFO.NCD. Changes made with DOS or some other utility are not. If, then, you make a change to a directory and run NCD, the directory tree displayed is not accurate. You have to rescan the disk to put current information in TREEINFO.NCD.

To View Disk Space Information (Version 7 Only)

1. Pull down the Disk menu and select the **Free Space** option or press **Ctrl-F**.
2. Select **OK** to return to NCD when you have finished viewing the information.

This option tells you how much total space is available on the currently selected drive, how much of this space is in use, and how much is free.

- **SYNTAX**

    NCD [MD ¦ RD ¦ SIZE] [*drive:*] [*dir*] **/**options

    dir is the name of the directory you wish to make (NCD MD *dir*), remove (NCD RD *dir*), size (NCD SIZE *dir*), or change to. If you are changing to a directory, only the lowest-level directory in the target path has to be specified (for example, DOCS for \WP\WORD\DOCS).

    drive: is the drive on which **dir** resides. Specify only if **dir** is on a drive other than the current drive.

    The options are the following:

    /A displays the directory tree for all drives on your system, excluding floppies. Use with the /L option.

    /G displays the directory tree using lines instead of plus and minus signs. Use with the /L option.

    /L[:*filename*] displays the directory tree. If you specify :*filename*, the tree will be printed to this file instead.

    /N (version 7 only) causes NCD not to save changes in TREEINFO.NCD.

    /NG displays the directory tree using plus and minus signs instead of lines. Use with the /L option.

    /P pauses the display after each full screen.

    /R (version 7 only) rescans the directory structure of *drive*.

    /T displays directory size information. Use with the /L option.

    /V:*label* (version 7 only) places the volume label specified by *label* on *drive*. If you omit *label* you will be prompted to enter a disk label or to delete the current one.

OR

  NCD COPY *dir1 dir2* **[/DELETE]**

This copies *dir1* and makes it a subdirectory of *dir2*. This is the same as the Copy Tree command. Use the /DELETE function if you want to delete *dir1* after the copy is complete.

OR

NCD GRAFT *dir1 dir2*

This relocates *dir1* as a subdirectory of *dir2*. This is the same as the Prune & Graft command.

OR

NCD RMTREE *dir* [/BATCH]

This deletes *dir1*, all of its subdirectories, and all of their files. This is the same as the Remove Tree command. Use the /BATCH for automatic execution (i.e., no dialog boxes, and return to the DOS prompt when done).

- **NOTES** The TREEINFO.NCD file is placed in the root directory of a drive. If you move it, NCD will be unable to locate it and will rescan the disk and recreate the file.

NDD
Norton Disk Doctor

NDD checks for and repairs errors in the system area—specifically, the partition table, boot record, directory tree, and file allocation table (FAT)—and errors on the disk medium itself (i.e., physically damaged sectors).

- **UPGRADE INFORMATION** NDD 7 contains all of the functions of NDD 6 and adds the ability to run a surface test independently of system area tests. In addition, NDD 7 provides more flexible repair options, tests compressed drives and host drives, and makes more functions accessible through the command line.

To Configure NDD

1. In the Norton Disk Doctor dialog box, select **Options**.
2. Select one of the configuration sequences below.
3. In the Disk Doctor Options dialog box, select **OK** to set these options for the current NDD session only, or select **Save** (**Save Settings** in version 6) to set options for both current and future sessions. Select **Cancel** to cancel the changes you made.

To Enable/Disable Surface Testing (Version 7 Only)

1. In the Norton Disk Doctor Options dialog box, select **General**.
2. Select the radio button for the surface test mode you want.
3. Select **OK**.

In NDD 7, the surface test can be run in combination with NDD's system area tests, independently, or not at all. Select Always Perform Surface Test to run the surface test automatically when NDD tests a disk. If you select this option, skip steps 6 through 10 in "To Test (and Repair) a Disk." Select Never Perform Surface Test to disable surface testing. If you select this option, skip steps 6 through 10 in "To Test (and Repair) a Disk." Select Prompt Before Surface Test to run a surface test when NDD tests a disk and to set surface test options before it does so. If you select this option, you will follow steps 6 through 10 in "To Test (and Repair) a Disk."

To Set Auto-Repair Options (Version 7 Only)

1. In the Norton Disk Doctor Options dialog box, select **Auto-Repair**.
2. In the Automatic Repair Options dialog box, select how NDD should repair various problems of your disk.
3. Select **OK**.

In step 2, you determine whether NDD will repair problems with partition tables, FATs, directory structures, compression structures, and surface errors of or on your disk. If you select Prompt, NDD will prompt you for confirmation before making repairs. If you select Auto, NDD corrects any problems automatically; no prompts appear. If you select Never, NDD identifies, but does not correct, problems it finds.

To Set a Custom Error Message

1. In the Norton Disk Doctor Options dialog box, select **Custom Message**.
2. In the Set Custom Message dialog box, toggle the **Prompt with Custom Message** option on.
3. Press **F2** to select a text attribute for the message.
4. Type the message in the message square.
5. Select **OK**.

Using a custom message prevents NDD from correcting system area errors (i.e., errors in the FAT, directory structure, boot record, etc.) and makes steps 4 and 5 in "To Test (and Repair) a Disk" unnecessary.

In step 3, there are four text attributes from which to choose: normal, bold, underline, and reverse. The text you type appears in whatever attribute is selected. You can, therefore, produce messages with multiple attributes by repeating steps 3 and 4 for different parts of the message.

To Set Surface Test Options

1. In the Norton Disk Doctor Options dialog box, select **Surface Test**.
2. Set surface test options exactly as in steps 6 through 9 in "To Test (and Repair) a Disk."

To Skip Certain Tests (Version 7 Only)

1. In the Norton Disk Doctor Option dialog box, select **General**.
2. Toggle on any of six Skip options.
3. Select **OK**.

In step 2, there are four tests that you can have NDD skip:

- Select Skip Partition Tests to omit testing of the integrity of the partition table on your hard disk. Some proprietary partitioning software may cause NDD difficulty.

- Select Skip CMOS Tests to omit testing of your machine's CMOS (where date, time, and configuration information is stored).

- Select Skip Compression Tests to omit testing of the host drive on which a compressed structure resides

- Select Skip Host Drive Tests to omit testing of drives that contain other logical or compressed drives.

There are two further Skip options:

- Select Only 1 Hard Disk if your computer has only one physical hard drive installed but NDD reports more than one.

- Select Drives To Exclude if you do not want NDD to test certain entire drives. Type the drive letters of the drives you wish to skip at the Drives To Exclude: prompt.

To Skip Certain Tests (Version 6 Only)

1. In the Disk Doctor Options dialog box, select **Tests To Skip**.
2. In the Tests to Skip dialog box, select the test or tests you want to skip.
3. Select **OK**.

In step 2, there are four tests you can have NDD skip:

- Select Skip Partition Tests to omit testing of the integrity of the partition table on your hard disk. Some proprietary partitioning software may cause NDD difficulty.

- Select Skip CMOS Tests to omit testing of your machine's CMOS (where date, time, and configuration information is stored).

- Select Skip Surface Tests to omit testing of your disk for physical errors. Selecting this option automatically skips steps 6 through 10 in "To Test (and Repair) a Disk."

- Select Only 1 Hard Disk if your computer has only one physical hard-disk drive installed but NDD reports more than one.

To Run a Surface Test Alone (Version 7 Only)

1. In the Norton disk Doctor dialog box, select **Surface Test**.
2. On the Surface Test Notice dialog box, if it appears, select **OK** when you are finished reading
3. In the Select Drives to Surface Test dialog box, select the disk(s) you want to test and then select **OK**.
4. Set surface test options exactly as in steps 6 through 8 in "To Test (and Repair) a Disk."
5. Select **Begin Test**. The test may take a while.

6. On the summary screen, optionally print a surface test report by selecting **Report**.

7. On the Report for Drive screen, select **Print** to print the report, or select **Save As** to save it in a file. If you choose **Save As**, enter the name of the report file in the Save Report dialog box.

8. If you do not wish to print or save the report, select **Done**.

In version 7, the surface test can be run by itself, as here, or in combination with NDD's system area tests (see "To Test (and Repair) a Disk.") Note that if you have disabled surface testing, the Surface Test option is unavailable (see "To Enable/Disable Surface Testing"). You must enable surface testing to run a surface test.

To Test (and Repair) a Disk

1. In the Norton Disk Doctor dialog box, select **Diagnose Disk**.

2. In the Select Drives to Diagnose dialog box, select the disk or disks you want to test, and then select **Diagnose**.

3. If errors are found, read the explanation box(es) and select **Continue**.

4. When prompted to correct errors, select **Yes** to correct them or **No** to let them alone.

5. Follow any prompts NDD presents to correct errors.

6. In the Surface Test dialog box and in the What To Test box (which is called the Test box in version 6), select whether you want NDD to test the entire surface of the disk for damage or just the space occupied by files.

7. In the Type of Test box (which is called the Test Type box in version 6), select the surface test depth (how thoroughly NDD tests the disk surface).

8. In the Passes box, select how many times you want NDD to perform the surface test.

9. Version 6 only. In the Repair Setting box, select a repair option.

10. Select **Begin Test**.

11. On the summary screen, optionally print a report of NDD findings and actions by selecting **Report**.

12. On the Report for Drive screen, select **Print** to print the NDD report, or select **Save As** to save it in a file. If you choose **Save As**, enter the name of the report file in the Save Report dialog box.

13. If you do not wish to print or save the report, select **Done**.

In step 2, select the drives you want to diagnose by highlighting them and pressing the spacebar or by clicking on them once with the mouse.

If you select No in step 4, NDD does not correct the errors it has found, and you skip to step 6.

In step 5, the actual dialog boxes you see depend on the errors found. However, make sure, when prompted, to select the Create UNDO File option and then select the drive on which this file is stored. Doing so allows you to undo any changes NDD makes. See "To Undo NDD Corrections."

Steps 6 through 10 constitute the surface test, which checks for physical errors on a disk. If you want to skip these steps, select **Cancel** in step 6 and go to step 11. Otherwise, in step 6, select **Entire Disk Area** (called Disk Test in version 6) to have NDD test the entire disk surface for physical errors, or select **Area Used by Files** (called **Files Test** in version 6) to have it test only the areas of the disk with data on them (i.e., files).

In step 7, if you are using version 7, there are three types of tests:

- Select Normal Test to have NDD perform a "light" test.

- Select Thorough Test to have NDD perform a more thorough (and longer) test.

- Select Thorough Test Only on Fridays (the default) if you are going to use NDD every day for preventive maintenance.

In version 6,

- Select Daily to have NDD perform a "light" test.

- Select Weekly to have NDD perform a more thorough (and longer) test.
- Select Auto Weekly (the default) if you are going to use NDD every day for preventive maintenance.

In step 8, select Repetitions to specify exactly how many times the surface test is to be done. Select Continuous to run the surface test until you interrupt it.

In step 9, version 6 only, you set the repair options for the surface test, not the system area test that occurs in steps 2 through 5.

- Select Don't Repair if you want to leave any surface errors NDD finds.
- Select Prompt before Repairing to have NDD prompt you before it fixes a surface error.
- Select Repair Automatically to have NDD fix any errors it finds without prompting you first.

To Undo NDD Corrections

1. In the Norton Disk Doctor dialog box, select **Undo Changes**.
2. In the Undo Changes dialog box, select **Yes**.
3. Select the drive containing the Undo file.
4. Select **Yes** in the confirmation box.
5. Select **OK** to acknowledge completion of the operation.

This function allows you to undo the changes or corrections made with NDD. To undo NDD corrections, however, you must have saved an Undo file in step 5 of "To Test (and Repair) a Disk."

The Undo file is always called NDDUNDO.DAT and is stored in the root directory.

● **SYNTAX**

NDD [*drive:*] [*drive:*] [*/options*]

drive: specifies the drive(s) to test and repair.

NDD 149

The options are the following:

/C tests the system area and performs a surface test on the indicated drive(s).

/DT performs a surface test only.

/FIXSPACES repairs file names with spaces in them.

/NOCOMP omits testing any compressed structure.

/NOHOST omits testing the host drive of any compressed volume.

/Q tests the system area but does not perform a surface test.

/R:*filename* sends a report to the specified file. Use this option with /Q or /C.

/RA:*filename* appends a report to the specified file. Use this option with /Q or /C.

/REBUILD has NDD attempt to reconstruct a critically damaged disk.

/SKIPHIGH causes NDD to use conventional memory.

/UNDELETE undeletes a partition.

/UNDO undoes repairs made in an earlier NDD session.

/X:*drive* excludes the specified drive from testing. Excluded drives do not appear for selection in the Select Drives to Diagnose dialog box.

See Also DISKTOOL

● **Notes** NDD tests for and repairs errors on compressed drives such as those created by DOS 6's DoubleSpace.

NDIAGS
The Norton Diagnostics

NDIAGS provides 34 diagnostic tests for most, if not all, aspects of your computer's hardware. The tests tell you whether each component or part is functioning properly.

- **UPGRADE INFORMATION** NDIAGS is new to the Norton Utilities and is found only in version 7.

To Configure NDIAGS

1. Pull down the File menu and select the **Options** option.
2. Toggle on the **Use Optional Loopback Plugs** option if you have loopback plugs with which to test your serial and parallel ports.
3. Toggle on the **Display Introductory Screens** option if you wish to have NDIAGS display an explanatory screen before each test.
4. Toggle on the **Use Alternate Speaker Test** option to test the speaker with a series of notes instead of a spoken phrase.
5. Select **OK**.

In step 2, toggle this option on if you have loopback plugs for parallel and serial ports tests. A loopback plug facilitates port tests by allowing a port to send and receive data to and from itself.

In step 3, it is worth toggling this option off after you become familiar with all NDIAGS tests because the introductory screens will become annoying. These screens can also be disabled by toggling on the Disable Intro. Messages option at the bottom of any introductory screen.

To Display Ports and the Keyboard Configuration

1. Pull down the File menu and select the **Hardware Configuration** option.
2. In the Hardware Configuration dialog box, optionally specify the memory address, interrupt, and type for each serial port you have.
3. Optionally specify the memory address and interrupt for each parallel port.
4. Optionally pull down the **Keyboard Type** drop down list and select the kind of keyboard you have.
5. Select **OK** to change settings for the current session, **Save** to save settings for current and future sessions, or **Reset** to change settings back to their defaults.

This function is more useful for displaying, rather than changing, port and keyboard configuration since these settings rarely, if ever, need to be changed. In fact, if you do make changes to these settings, it is likely that you will disable or impair your ports and keyboard.

To Print a Complete System Summary Report

1. Pull down the File menu and select the **Report** option.
2. In the Topics list, select the tests whose results you wish to include in the report.
3. If you wish to run the same report again in the future, select **Save** and enter a file name in the Save Report Options dialog box that appears.
4. Select a destination for the report from the **Destination** drop down list.
5. Select **OK**.

This function allows you to print the results of multiple tests in one report. The Topics list has an entry for every diagnostic test, (and two others that allow you to place a header and notes on your report). Note that all tests on the Topics list marked with an asterisk require user input.

In step 2, every test you select from the Topics list will run before the report is generated. This is a way, therefore, to run a batch of diagnostic tests. If you have previously saved a set of tests for a report, you may load it here instead of selecting the tests all over again. To do so, select the Load option and then select the name of the set from the Load Report Options dialog box that appears.

In step 3, you can save the set of tests you selected in step 2, thereby simplifying future runs of the same report.

In step 4, you may send the report to one of three destinations: the screen, your printer, or a file. If you select File here, enter a file name after you select OK in step 5.

To Print the Results of One Test

1. Select the **Print** option at the bottom of the test screen.
2. In the Print Current Information dialog box, select **Printer** to send the results to your printer. Select **File** to save the results to a file.
3. If you are saving to a file, type its filename (and path, if necessary) and select **OK**.
4. Select **OK** to acknowledge completion.

Omit step 3 if you are sending the results to your printer.

To Run a Particular Diagnostic Test

Each diagnostic test is run by selecting one option from one menu. In the following list, the tests are given by their option name, which is indicative of the nature of the test. The name of the menu on which the option appears is given in parentheses. The tests are the following:

16550A (Comprehensive): a serial port's ability to send and receive data, its interrupt, and its buffer. For use primarily on IBM PS/2's and other IBM computers.

Base Memory (Memory): the first 640K of RAM.

CMOS (System): CMOS contents and status

Color (Video): all colors in all video modes.

Expanded Memory (Memory): all installed EMS expanded memory.

Extended Memory (Memory): all installed XMS extended memory.

Floppy Disks (Disks): head positioning, data reading, drive RPM, detection of swapped and write-protected disks. Requires a formatted floppy.

Floppy Disks, Comprehensive (Comprehensive): sequential and random reads and writes. Requires a formatted floppy.

Hard Disks (Disks): drive RPM, head positioning, data reading.

Keyboard Lights (Other): Num Lock, Caps Lock, Scroll Lock lights.

Keyboard Press (Other): scan codes for all keys.

Memory Test, Comprehensive (Comprehensive): Rigorous bit-by-bit test of all installed memory. Can take from 2 to 24 hours. This test requires that you first boot your system "clean" with no TSR's or drivers loaded.

Mouse (Other): mouse buttons and movement.

Parallel Ports (System): data transfer, registers.

Run Calibrate (Comprehensive): runs the CALIBRAT program.

Serial Ports (System): data transfer, registers.

Speaker (Other): speaker sound, function.

System Board (System): CPU functions, registers, and modes (real and protected), math coprocessor functions and registers, DMA controller, interrupt controller, timers, and real-time clock.

System Information (System): identifies type of main processor, math coprocessor, BIOS, video standard, mouse, keyboard, and bus.

Video Grid (Video): all supported graphics modes.

Video Memory (Video): all video RAM.

Video Mode (Video): all supported video modes.

To Run Diagnostic Tests Consecutively

- At the bottom of any test screen, select Next Test to run the next test in sequence.

The order in which NDIAGS runs its diagnostic tests corresponds to the order of options on the pull down menus. The first test (System Information) is the first option on the first test menu (System), the second test is the second option, etc. Note that when you first start NDIAGS, the System Information test is run automatically. From this test screen you will always select Start Tests instead of Next Test.

- **SYNTAX**

    NDIAGS [/options]

The options are the following:

/AUTO:# cycles continuously through all noninteractive tests at intervals of # seconds. Press **Esc** to stop and return to DOS.

/BURNIN:# cycles continuously through all noninteractive tests # times.

/COMP runs the comprehensive memory test. This test requires that you first boot your system "clean," with no TSR's or drivers loaded.

/REP:*filename* prints a report of tests run to *filename*. Use with the /AUTO and /SPEC options.

/RESET resets NDIAGS's record of your computer's configuration. Use this option only when you have changed any hardware on your system.

/SPEC:*setname* runs the set of tests saved as *setname*.

NDOS

The NDOS program is a substitute for COMMAND.COM. NDOS allows the user to access a set of new and improved DOS and batch file commands. Following is a reference of NDOS commands.

- **UPGRADE INFORMATION** NDOS 7 contains all of the functions found in NDOS 6 and adds seven new NDOS commands. Although a few of the NDOS 7 commands that were present in NDOS 6 have been modified slightly, most of these modifications involve no more than the addition of a few new command line switches.

In Common with DOS

APPEND
ASSIGN
BACKUP
CHKDSK
CHOICE
(DOS 6 only)
COMMAND
COMP
DEBUG
DEFRAG
(DOS 6 only)
DELTREE
(DOS 6 only)
DISKCOMP
DISKCOPY
DOSKEY
DOSSHELL
EDIT
EDLIN
EMM386
EXE2BIN
EXPAND
FASTOPEN
FC
FDISK
FIND
FORMAT
GRAFTABL
GRAPHICS
JOIN
KEYB
LABEL
LOADFIX
MEM
MODE
MORE
MSBACKUP
(DOS 6 only)
NLSFUNC
POWER
(DOS 6 only)
PRINT
QBASIC
RECOVER
REPLACE
RESTORE
SETVER
SHARE
SORT
SUBST
SYS
TREE
XCOPY

ALIAS

ALIAS allows you to abbreviate frequently used or complex commands by assigning them to any name you choose. You can then run the command by entering the name you chose, i.e., an alias, instead.

- **SYNTAX**

    ### ALIAS [/options] [alias][=command]

    alias is the short or mnemonic name you choose to which you are assigning a command.

    command is the command you are abbreviating with *alias*. You can assign multiple commands, in effect making a batch file, by separating them with a caret (^) and enclosing the alias arguments in reverse quotes (')

    The options are as follows:

    /P pauses the display after each full screen.

    /R *filename* allows you to read in a file of previously defined aliases. *Filename* should be an ASCII file with each alias on its own line in the form *alias=command*.

- **EXAMPLE** If you often reformat a 360K disk to erase it, you might make an alias such as

    ### alias fmt360=sformat /a /q /f:360

    Norton Safe Format automatically reformats a 360K disk and returns you to the DOS prompt.

- **NOTES** Omitting *alias* and *command* displays a list of current aliases. Omitting *command* displays the command assigned to alias.

ATTRIB

ATTRIB sets or clears file attributes or directory attributes.

● SYNTAX

ATTRIB [/options] [+ | -attributes] filespec

filespec is the file(s) or directory whose attributes you wish to change.

The options are as follows:

/D sets or clears the attributes of the directory specified in *filespec*.

/S sets or clears the attributes of the files specified in *filespec* in all subdirectories below the current directory or below the directory specified in *filespec*.

/Q (version 7 only) causes ATTRIB to run in quiet mode; no filenames are displayed.

attributes may be any of the following:

A sets (+) or clears (–) the Archive attribute.

H sets (+) or clears (–) the Hidden attribute.

R sets (+) or clears (–) the Read-Only attribute.

S sets (+) or clears (–) the System attribute.

● **EXAMPLE** To set all of your .DOC files to read-only and hidden for an added measure of security, enter

attrib +rh *.doc

● **NOTES** Omitting all options and attributes displays any attributes currently set for *filespec*.

BEEP

BEEP sounds a tone or tones of specified frequency or duration. BEEP is similar to the BE BEEP command.

● SYNTAX

BEEP [*pitch length*]

pitch is the frequency in Hertz. The default is 440.

length is the duration of the tone in 18ths of a second. The default is 2.

● **EXAMPLE**   To sound an "A" tone over middle C for one second, enter

beep 440 18

To sound it twice, enter

beep 440 18 440 18

CANCEL

CANCEL stops the execution of any and all batch files currently running and returns you to the NDOS prompt.

● SYNTAX

CANCEL (value)

value (version 7 only) sets the ERRORLEVEL to the specified value.

See Also   QUIT command.

CD

CD (Change Directory) is a slightly enhanced version of the DOS CD command. Flexibility has been added in the use of periods to represent directory levels (see "Example" below).

● SYNTAX

CD *path*

path is the directory you wish to make current. Path may be prefaced with a drive letter if you wish to change the current directory on a drive other than the current drive.

● **EXAMPLE** To change to a directory one level above the current directory (i.e., to the parent directory), enter

cd ..

This can be done in DOS as well. However, in NDOS, to change to a directory two levels above the current directory, enter

cd ...

The use of more than two periods is not allowed in DOS; NDOS allows the use of as many as necessary.

CHDIR

CHDIR is the same as CD above.

CDD

CDD (Change Drive and Directory) allows you to change either the default drive or the default directory, or both together. In DOS, changing both the default drive and default directory requires you to enter two commands.

● SYNTAX

CDD [*drive:*][*dir*]

drive: is the drive to which you wish to change.

dir is the directory to which you wish to change.

- **EXAMPLE** To change from the root directory of drive C to the \NORTON directory on drive D, enter

    cdd d:\norton

CLS

The NDOS CLS command is an enhanced version of the DOS CLS command. NDOS's CLS allows you to change text and background colors as well as clear the screen.

- **SYNTAX**

    CLS [[BRIGHT][BLINK] *textcolor* **ON** *background* **[BORDER** *bdrcolor*]]

    BRIGHT (version 7 only) causes the text to appear brighter than normal.

    BLINK causes the text to blink.

    textcolor sets the color of text. Valid colors are black, blue, green, cyan, red, magenta, yellow, white, bright blue, bright green, bright cyan, bright red, bright magenta, bright yellow, and bright white.

    background sets the background color. Valid colors in version 7 are black, blue, green, cyan, red, magenta, yellow, and white. In version 6, valid colors are all of the above plus gray.

    bdrcolor (version 7 only) sets the color of the screen border. Valid colors are black, blue, green, cyan, red, magenta, yellow, and white.

- **EXAMPLE** To clear the screen and set the screen colors to green on black, enter

    cls green on black

COLOR

COLOR allows you to change text and background colors.

- **SYNTAX**

    COLOR [[BRIGHT] [BLINK] *textcolor* **ON** *background* **[BORDER** *bdrcolor*]]

    BRIGHT (version 7 only) causes the text to appear brighter than normal.

    BLINK causes the text to blink.

    textcolor sets the color of text. Valid colors are the same as for the CLS command above.

    background sets the background color. Valid colors are listed under the CLS command.

    bdrcolor (version 7 only) sets the color of the screen border. Valid colors are listed under the CLS command above.

- **EXAMPLE** To set the screen colors to green on black, enter

    color green on black

COPY

The NDOS COPY command is an enhanced version of the DOS COPY command, allowing you to to specify more than one source file to copy. NDOS COPY also provides a set of useful options.

- **SYNTAX**

    COPY [*options*] *file1*[+...+*filen*][/A/B] *target*

    file1 and *filen* are the files to be copied. You may specify any number of files to copy. File names may be prefaced with a path.

    + concatenates source files into one file named *target*. If *target* is omitted, files are appended to the first source file listed.

    target specifies the destination of the file(s) being copied or the name of the file created by the copy operation.

The options are as follows:

/A treats the files copied or created as ASCII files (i.e., copies the contents of a source file only up to the first ^Z (end of file) character, or adds a ^Z character to the end of the target file).

/B treats the files copied or created as binary files (i.e., ignores all ^Z characters).

/C (version 7 only) copies changed files only.

/H (version 7 only) copies hidden files.

/M copies only files that have the Archive attribute set.

/N (version 7 only) tests the results of the copy.

/P asks for confirmation for every file to be copied.

/Q turns off the display of name of files copied.

/R (version 7 only) displays a prompt before overwriting an existing file.

/S (version 7 only) copies files from the current directory and its subdirectories.

/U (version 7 only) copies only those source files that are newer than a matching target file or those for which there is no existing target file.

/V verifies each copy.

- **EXAMPLE** To copy two files that cannot be described together with wild cards, such as testtest.dat and budget.wks, to the root directory of drive D:, enter

copy testtest.dat budget.wks d:

To concatenate the two files ONE.TXT and TWO.TXT into a file called THREE.TXT, enter

copy one.txt+two.txt three.txt

DEL

The NDOS DEL function is an expanded version of the DOS DEL function. It allows you to put more than one *filespec* on the command line and it adds options.

SYNTAX

DEL [/options] filespec

filespec is the file or files to be deleted. You may specify any number of files to delete.

The options are as follows:

/**N** (version 7 only) tests the results of the deletion.

/**P** asks you to confirm the deletion of each file.

/**Q** turns off the display of name and number of files deleted.

/**S** (version 7 only) deletes files from the current directory and its subdirectories.

/**X** (version 7 only) removes empty subdirectories.

/**Y** turns off all confirmation by assuming an affirmative reponse (to **del** *.*, for example).

/**Z** deletes hidden, read-only, and system files.

- **EXAMPLE** To delete two read-only files, enter

del /z file.one file.two

To delete an entire directory with confirmation, enter

del /p *.*

DELAY

DELAY pauses execution for a specified number of seconds.

SYNTAX

DELAY *secs*

- **EXAMPLE** To pause a batch file for 5 seconds, one line should read

delay 5

DESCRIBE

DESCRIBE allows you add 40 character descriptions of files and directories to your directory listings.

● SYNTAX

DESCRIBE *filespec* ["*text*"]

filespec is the file or directory to which you are adding a description.

text is the description you are adding. If you omit text from the command line, you are prompted for it.

● **EXAMPLE** To add a description to an alternate AUTOEXEC file containing Windows drivers, enter

describe autoexec.win "Boot machine configured for Windows."

● **NOTES** Descriptions are only visible using the NDOS DIR command and a one-column file display. Descriptions can be edited by opening the hidden file in which they are contained. The file is named DESCRIPT.ION and is located in the same directory as the files whose description it contains.

DIR

The DIR command is an expanded version of the DOS DIR command.

● SYNTAX

DIR [/A:[*attributes*]] [/O:[*sortkeys*]] [/*options*] [*filespec*]

/A: Lists only files with certain file attributes set. You specify which files are to be listed with *attributes*. The *attributes* can be any combination of the following:

(-)A lists files with the Archive attribute set. Append the optional minus sign to list all files without the Archive attribute set.

(-)D lists directories. Append the optional minus sign to list files and not directories.

(-)H lists hidden files. Append the optional minus sign to list all files that are not hidden.

(-)R lists read-only files. Append the optional minus sign to list all files that are not read-only.

(-)S lists system files. Append the optional minus sign to list all files that are not system files.

/O: sorts the directory listing according to sortkeys. The sortkeys can be any combination of the following:

(-)D sorts numerically by file date and time. Append the optional minus sign to sort in descending order.

(-)E sorts alphabetically by file extension. Append the optional minus sign to sort in descending order.

(-)G puts directories at the top of the listing (assumed by default). Append the optional minus sign to list directories at the bottom.

(-)I sorts alphabetically by file description created by the DESCRIBE command. Append the optional minus sign to sort in descending order.

(-)N sorts alphabetically by file name. Append the optional minus sign to sort in descending order.

(-)S sorts numerically by file size. Append the optional minus sign to sort in descending order.

(-)U displays files in the order they were placed in the directory (COMMAND.COM's default). Append the optional minus sign to display this in reverse.

The options are as follows:

/1 lists files in one column (the default).

/2 lists files in two columns.

/4 lists files in four columns. Displays only file name and size.

/B turns off volume and directory ID's at the top of the file listing, and file size and free space totals at the bottom.

/C (version 6 only) displays directory listing in uppercase letters.

/C (version 7 only) gives the compressed ratio of files.

/D (version 7 only) disables colors.

/E (version 7 only) displays directory listings in uppercase letters.

/F (version 7 only) gives the full path of each filename.

/J lists file extensions in their own column rather than right next to the file names.

/K turns off volume and directory ID's at the top of the listing.

/L displays file names in lowercase letters (the default).

/M turns off file size and free space totals at the bottom of the directory listing.

/N lists the directory using all default values.

/P pauses the display after each full screen.

/S lists the contents of the specified directory and all subdirectories below it.

/T displays file attributes set.

/U displays only file size and free space totals.

/V sorts multicolumn displays (/2, /4, /W) down the column instead of left to right.

/W displays the directory in "wide," or landscape format.

filespec is the directory or files to be listed.

- **EXAMPLE** To list the files in the current directory in two columns, sorted by file extension, enter

    dir /o:e /2

To list all spreadsheet files on the C drive with the Archive attribute set (i.e., files that have not been backed up), enter

    dir /A:a /s c:*.wk?

DIRS

Displays the directory stack. The directory stack is created and used by the PUSHD and POPD commands.

• SYNTAX

DIRS

See Also   PUSHD and POPD commands

DRAWBOX

DRAWBOX draws a box at specified screen coordinates. It is similar to the BE BOX command.

• SYNTAX

DRAWBOX *TLCrow TLCcol BRCrow BRCcol borders* **[BRIGHT | BLINK]** *boxcolor* **ON** *background* **[FILL** *color*] **[SHADOW]**

TLCrow TLCcol are the screen coordinates for the top-left corner of the box. *TLCrow* is the row in which this corner sits, and *TLCcol* is the column.

BRCrow BRCcol are the screen coordinates for the bottom-right corner of the box. *BRCrow* is the row in which this corner sits, and *BRCcol* is the column.

borders specifies the border style of the box. Borders can be the following:

  0 draws no border

  1 draws a single-line border

  2 draws a double-line border

  3 draws a single-line border on the top and bottom of the box, and a double-line border on the sides.

  4 draws a double-line border on the top and bottom of the box, and single-line borders on the sides.

BRIGHT (version 7 only) causes the box to appear brighter than normal.

BLINK causes the box to blink.

boxcolor specifies the color of the box. Valid colors in version 7 are black, blue, green, cyan, red, magenta, yellow, white, bright blue, bright green, bright cyan, bright red, bright magenta, bright yellow, and bright white. In version 6, valid colors are all of the above plus gray.

background specifies the background color. Valid colors are black, blue, green, cyan, red, magenta, yellow, and white. In version 6, valid colors are all of the above plus gray.

FILL fills the box with color. Valid colors are the same as for the background option.

SHADOW (version 7 only) draws the box with a transparent drop shadow.

- **SYNTAX** To draw a small, green box with double borders in the upper-left corner of your screen, enter

    drawbox 1 1 10 10 2 green on black

DRAWHLINE

DRAWHLINE draws a horizontal line at specified screen coordinates.

- **SYNTAX**

    DRAWHLINE *startrow startcol length style* **[BRIGHT | BLINK]** *linecolor* **ON** *background*

    startrow and ***startcol*** are the screen coordinates of the left endpoint of the line. *Startrow* is the row in which this point sits, and *startcol* is the column.

    length is the length of the line.

    style specifies whether the line is drawn as a single line or a double line. Style may be set to 1 or 2.

    BLINK causes the line to blink.

    BRIGHT (version 7 only) causes the text to appear brighter than normal.

    linecolor specifies the color of the line. Valid colors are the same as for the boxcolor option under DRAWBOX above.

background specifies the background color. Valid colors are the same as for the background option under DRAWBOX above.

- **EXAMPLE** To draw a green double line across the center of your screen, enter

    drawhline 12 0 79 2 green on black

DRAWVLINE

DRAWVLINE draws a vertical line at specified screen coordinates.

- **SYNTAX**

    DRAWVLINE *startrow startcol length style* **[BRIGHT | BLINK]** *linecolor* **ON** *background*

startrow and *startcol* are the screen coordinates of the top endpoint of the line. *Startrow* is the row in which this point sits, and *startcol* is the column.

length is the length of the line.

style specifies whether the line is drawn as a single line or a double line. *Style* may be set to 1 or 2.

BRIGHT (version 7 only) causes the line to appear brighter than normal.

BLINK causes the line to blink.

linecolor specifies the color of the line. Valid colors are the same as for the boxcolor option under DRAWBOX above.

background specifies the background color. Valid colors are the same as for the background option under DRAWBOX above.

- **EXAMPLE** To draw a green double line down the center of your screen, enter

    drawvline 0 39 25 2 green on black

ECHOS

ECHOS displays text without a trailing carriage return and line feed.

- **SYNTAX**

    ECHOS ON | OFF | *message*

    /ON turns **ECHO** default on.
    /OFF turns **ECHO** default off.

    message is the text of the message you wish to display.

- **EXAMPLE** echo this is a test message will print "this is a test message" on your screen without putting a carriage return at the end of the line.

ENDLOCAL

ENDLOCAL restores the disk drive, directory, environment variables, and aliases saved in memory with SETLOCAL.

- **SYNTAX**

    ENDLOCAL

    Use SETLOCAL and ENDLOCAL in batch files, not aliases.

- **EXAMPLE** The following batch file fragment saves the aliases, environment, drive, and current working directory, changes the drive and directory, modifies some environment variables, runs the program TEST1, and then restores the original values.

    ```
    setlocal
    cdd d:\test
    set path = c:\; c:\dos; c:\util
    set lib = d:\lib
    test1
    endlocal
    ```

ERASE

The ERASE command is identical to DEL above.

ESET

ESET allows you to edit an alias or an environment variable "on the fly." This means the change takes effect immediately and there is no need to reboot your machine.

- **SYNTAX**

    ESET [*/options*] *name*

    name is the alias or environment variable to edit.

    /A (version 7 only) assumes the argument is an alias so you can edit an alias with the same name as an environment variable.

    /M (version 7 only) edits an environment variable in the master environment rather than the local environment.

- **EXAMPLE** To edit your path, enter

    eset path

    and make your changes.

EXCEPT

EXCEPT allows you to execute a command on all but the file or files specified.

- **SYNTAX**

    EXCEPT (*filespec*) *command*

    filespec is the file or files you wish to exempt from command.

    command is the command you are executing or program you are running.

- **EXAMPLE** To delete all .BAK files in your root directory, except for AUTOEXEC.BAK, enter

    except (autoexec.bak) del *.bak

EXIT

EXIT is the same as the DOS EXIT command, and it exits you from NDOS as well.

- **SYNTAX**

    EXIT

FOR

FOR allows you to repeat a command several times using different parameters each time. The NDOS FOR command is similar to the DOS FOR command.

- **SYNTAX**

    FOR [/A *options*] **%***var* **IN (***parameters***) [DO]** *command*

    The **/A** switch (version 7 only) allows the selection of files for processing based on attributes. It may be used with any combination of the following:

    r selects files with the read-only attribute set. Append the optional minus sign to select all files without the read-only attribute set

    h selects hidden files. Append the optional minus sign to select all files that are hidden.

    s selects system files. Append the optional minus sign to select all non-system files.

    d selects subdirectories.

    a selects files with the archive attribute set. Append. the optional minus sign to select all files without the archive attribute set.

%var is the variable by means of which parameters are passed to *command*.

parameters is the list of different parameters *command* will use. *Command* executes once for each parameter listed.

command is the command to execute. It can be any NDOS command, DOS command, batch file, or alias.

- **EXAMPLE** To copy all .DOC files in two different directories to a backup disk using only one operation, enter

    for %doc in (c:\memos*.doc c:\word*.doc) do copy %doc b:

The copy command then executes twice. First it copies all .DOC files in the directory c:\memos to drive B. Then it copies all .DOC files in c:\word to drive B.

FREE

FREE displays the amount of free space, occupied space, and total space on specified drives.

- **SYNTAX**

    FREE *drive1*: [*driven*:]

    drive1: is the drive to examine. Multiple drives can be specified on the command line.

- **EXAMPLE** To examine free space on drives C and D, enter

    free c: d:

GLOBAL

GLOBAL executes a command in the current directory and all subdirectories below it.

SYNTAX

GLOBAL [/options] command

command is the command to execute. It can be any NDOS command, DOS command, batch file, or alias.

The options are as follows:

/H (version 7 only) processes hidden subdirectories.

/I ignores errors that will terminate execution before completion.

/P (version 7 only) issues a prompt confirming whether the command should be executed in each directory.

/Q turns off display of directory names during command execution.

- **EXAMPLE** To delete all .BAK files on the current drive, enter

    global del *.bak

GOSUB

GOSUB provides the ability to use subroutines in a batch file. Execution switches to the label specified, and returns upon encountering the RETURN command.

SYNTAX

GOSUB *label*

label is the label to jump to.

- **EXAMPLE** The following batch file fragment illustrates the concepts of jumping to a label and returning:

    echo Jump to a label, check free space...
    gosub space
    echo ... and return
    goto quit
    :space

```
free c:
return
:quit
```

See Also   RETURN command

HELP

HELP provides help for NDOS and DOS.

For Help in version 7, press F1.

● SYNTAX (Version 6)

HELP [*subject*] [*/options*]

subject is one of the predefined help topics. You can specify one if you know it.

The options are as follows:

/BW sets display to black and white.

/HERC sets display for use with Hercules graphics.

/LCD sets display for use on LCD screens.

/G0 displays Help with no graphical elements.

/G1 displays Help with graphical controls (radio buttons, toggle options, and check marks).

/G2 displays Help with graphical controls and a graphical mouse pointer.

HISTORY

HISTORY displays the command stack and allows you to manipulate it to some extent. The command stack is a list of commands you have entered on the command line in the current session. Rather than retyping a command, you may access it from the stack by pressing the ↑ and ↓ keys.

176 NDOS

● **SYNTAX**

HISTORY [/*options*]

The options are as follows:

/A *command* (version 7 only) adds the specified command to the command stack.

/F clears the command stack.

/P pauses the display after each full screen when listing the command stack.

/R *filename* allows you to create your own stack of frequently used commands by reading them in from the file *filename*. *Filename* must be an ASCII file and each command should appear on its own line.

● **EXAMPLE** To create your own command stack from the file named *commands*, enter

history /r commands

IF

IF gives you the ability to put If—Then statements in batch files. It does so by executing the specified command if the given condition is true. The NDOS IF command is an expanded version of the DOS IF command.

● **SYNTAX**

IF [NOT] *condition* [AND | OR | XOR] [NOT] *condition... command*

command is the command to execute if condition is true. *Command* can be any NDOS command, DOS command, batch file, or alias.

NOT causes *command* to execute if *condition* is false.

condition can take the form of two values separated by a logical operator. The values are often a variable (%1, %a, etc.) and a text string ("some text", "1"). The logical operators you can use are as follows:

AND (version 7 only) requires both condit.ions to be true before a command is executed

OR (version 7 only) requires either one condition or both conditions to be true before a command is executed.

XOR (version 7 only) requires that *only* one condition be true before a command is executed.

Operator	Meaning	Example
==	Equals	%a == "text"
EQ	Equals	%a EQ "text"
GE	Greater than or equal to	%a GE "1"
GT	Greater than	%a GT "1"
LE	Less than or equal to	%a LE "5"
LT	Less than	%a LT "5"
NE	Not equals	%a NE "text"

Condition can also take one of the following other forms:

ERRORLEVEL *operator #* where *operator* is one of the operators from the list above and # is an integer. This condition allows you to test the current ERRORLEVEL.

EXIST *filename* where *filename* is the name of a file. This condition allows you to test whether a file exists.

ISALIAS *name* where *name* is any name. This condition allows you to test whether an alias exists.

ISDIR *dir* where *dir* is the name of a directory. This condition allows you to test whether a directory exists.

ISINTERNAL *command* (version 7 only) is true if *command* is an internal command.

ISLABEL *command* (version 7 only) is true if the specified label exists.

string1 *locicaloperator* **string2** (version 7 only) compares two strings. This command is not case-sensitive.

Note that you can use multiple conditions.

● **EXAMPLE** To remove the AUTOEXEC.BAT file from your root directory, if the file exists, enter

if exist c:\autoexec.bak del c:\autoexec.bak

This example checks to see if the alias "fmt360" exists, and, if it does not, creates it.

if NOT isalias fmt360 alias fmt360 = sformat a: /f:360 /a /q

See Also INKEY and INPUT for more examples using other conditions

IFF

IFF gives you the ability to put If—Then—Else statements into your batch files. It is a further elaboration of the IF command. It executes the specified command(s) if the given condition is true, and it executes a different command(s) if the condition is false.

● **SYNTAX**

IFF [NOT] *condition* **[AND | OR | XOR] [NOT]** *condition*... **THEN**
commands1

  .
  .
  .

ELSE
commands2

  .
  .
  .

ENDIFF

commands1 is the command or commands to execute if *condition* is true. *Commands1* can be any NDOS command, DOS command, batch file, or alias.

commands2 is the command or commands to execute if *condition* is false. *Commands2* can be any NDOS command, DOS command, batch file, or alias.

NOT causes *commands1* to execute if *condition* is false and *commands2* to execute if *condition* is true.

condition may be any of the conditions specified under the IF command. You can use multiple conditions.

- **EXAMPLE** The following example checks to see if the alias "fmt360" exists. If it does, the alias is deleted and recreated. If it does not, the alias is simply created.

```
iff isalias fmt360 then
  unalias fmt360
  alias fmt360 = format a: /4
else
  alias fmt360 = format a: /4
endiff
```

INKEY

INKEY allows you to input one character from the keyboard and assign that character to a variable. This can be most useful when used with the IF and IFF commands.

- **SYNTAX**

    INKEY [/K "keystrokes"] [/W#] [*prompt*] %%*variable*

/K (version 7 only) defines the allowable *keystrokes*. *Keystrokes* must be enclosed in double quotation marks. If you wish to read a control or function key as part of *keystrokes*, enclose them in square brackets.

/W# causes execution to pause and wait # seconds for a response. If # seconds pass and no key is pressed, the command falls through and %%*variable* is not assigned.

prompt is text to be displayed while waiting for a response.

%%variable is the variable to which you will assign the key pressed.

- **EXAMPLE** The following example is the skeleton of a menu:

   ```
   @echo off
   cls
   echo 1. Word Processing
   echo 2. Database
   echo 3. Spreadsheet
   inkey Your selection? %%select
   if "%select" == "1" call wp.bat
   if "%select" == "2" call dbase.bat
   if "%select" == "3" call 123.bat
   ```

INPUT

INPUT allows you to input multiple characters from the keyboard and assign them to a variable. This can be most useful with the IF and IFF commands.

- **SYNTAX**

   INPUT [/W#] [*prompt*] %%*variable*

   /W# causes execution to pause and wait # seconds for a response. If # seconds pass and nothing has been typed, the command falls through and %%*variable* is not assigned.

   prompt is text to be displayed while waiting for a response.

   %%*variable* is the variable to which you will assign the keys pressed. Every key pressed, up to but not including ↵, is assigned to %%*variable*.

- **EXAMPLE** The following is the skeleton of a menu.

   ```
   @echo off
   cls
   echo Enter "wp" for Word Processing
   echo Enter "db" for Database
   echo Enter "ss" for Spreadsheet
   input Your selection? %%choice
   call %choice.bat
   ```

KEYSTACK

KEYSTACK automatically feeds keystrokes to a program from a batch file or alias.

- **SYNTAX**

    KEYSTACK ["keystrokes"] [#] [@#] [!] [/W#]

    keystrokes are the characters you wish to store in the keyboard buffer. Enclose *keystrokes* in double quotation marks.

    # allows inclusion of ASCII decimal codes.

    @# allows inclusion of extended keyboard codes (keystrokes generated by the Alt key, the cursor pad keys, and the function keys).

    ! clears all pending keystrokes, both in the KEYSTACK buffer and the keyboard buffer.

    /W# tells KEYSTACK to wait *#* seconds for a keystroke.

- **EXAMPLE** The following batch file will change to drive b: and delete all of the files on b: without requiring the user to confirm the deletion by typing "Y."

    b:\
    keystack "Y"
    del *.*

- **NOTES** The KSTACK.COM TSR must be loaded to use KEYSTACK.

LH

LH loads Terminate-and-Stay-Resident programs (TSRs) into Upper Memory (i.e., the memory between 640K and 1024K).

- **SYNTAX**

    LH *filespec*

    filespec is the TSR to be loaded into Upper Memory.

- **NOTES** To use LH, you must be running DOS 5 or 6. The command DOS=UMB must appear in your CONFIG.SYS file.

LIST

LIST is a rudimentary ASCII file viewer.

- **SYNTAX**

    LIST [/options] filespec

    filespec is the file(s) you wish to view.

The options are as follows:

/H views WordStar files.

/S allows you to view output piped from commands you execute.

/W wraps text at the right side of your screen.

You can scroll through the displayed file with the direction keys. You may also use the following:

Home brings you to the top of the file.

End brings you to the bottom of the file.

Esc exits the current file.

F finds text you specify.

N repeats the find specified with "F."

P prints the file to LPT1:.

Ctrl-c quits LIST.

- **EXAMPLE** To view your AUTOEXEC.BAT file, enter

    list autoexec.bat

To view the current command stack, enter

   history | list /s

LOADBTM

When turned on, LOADBTM runs your batch files by loading them into memory first. While the speed difference for small batch files is negligible, it can be significant for large batch files.

- **SYNTAX**

    LOADBTM ON | OFF

- **NOTES** LOADBTM must be executed from within a batch file.

LOADHIGH

LOADHIGH is the same as LH, above.

LOG

LOG creates a file that records every command you enter from the command line and when the command was issued. If you work at home, this can be useful for tax purposes.

- **SYNTAX**

    LOG [options]

The options are as follows:

comment is the text you want to add to your log file.

ON | OFF turns logging on or off.

/W filename allows you to specify the name of your log file. If omitted, the default name is C:\NDOS.LOG.

- **EXAMPLE** To turn on logging and add a comment about the day's work, enter

    log /w c:\mylog
    log Wrote the section on NDOS.

MEMORY

MEMORY details the disposition of memory on your system. MEMORY shows how much conventional, expanded, and extended memory is installed and how much is available for use. It also shows the size of the DOS environment (i.e., how much memory is set aside for environment variables, the path, etc.), how much for aliases, and how much for the command stack or history.

- SYNTAX

    MEMORY

MOVE

MOVE moves files from one directory to another. In effect, MOVE works by copying a file and then deleting the original.

- SYNTAX

    MOVE *sourcefile target* [*/options*]

    sourcefile is the file or files to be moved. You may specify more than one file here.

    target is the directory to which *sourcefile* is to be moved. If you also specify a file name, *sourcefile* will be both moved and renamed.

The options are as follows:

/C (version 7 only) moves changed files only.

/D (version 7 only) specifies that the destination must be a directory.

/H (version 7 only) moves hidden files.

/N (version 7 only) tests the results of the move.

/P prompts you for confirmation for each file moved.

/Q turns on the display of name and number of files moved.

/R prompts you for confirmation before overwriting a file.

/S (version 7 only) directs MOVE to move files from the current directory and its subdirectories.

/U (version 7 only) moves the file(s) to the destination only if the destination file exists and is older.

- **EXAMPLE** If you have two different AUTOEXEC files, you can use MOVE to switch them efficiently.

    move autoexec.bat temp
    move autoexec.win autoexec.bat
    move temp autoexec.win

To move all files in the directory \OLDFILES off of your hard disk and on to a floppy, enter

    move \oldfiles*.* a:

POPD

Changes the current directory to the most recent directory added to the directory stack. A directory is added to the directory stack when you change directories using the PUSHD command. If, then, you change a series of directories using PUSHD, you can change back in the reverse order using POPD.

- **SYNTAX**

    POPD [*]

    * clears the directory stack

- **EXAMPLE**

    C:\> pushd c:\wp   --> C:\WP>
    C:\WP> pushd c:\word --> C:\WORD>
    C:\WORD> popd --> C:\WP>
    C:\WP> popd --> C:\>

See Also DIRS and PUSHD commands

PROMPT

PROMPT modifies the command prompt. The NDOS PROMPT command is an enhanced version of the DOS PROMPT command.

- **SYNTAX**

    PROMPT [*prompt*]

    prompt is text you wish to appear in your prompt. You may embed in *prompt* command strings in the form $*i* to achieve certain effects. $*i* can be repeated any number of times and *i* can be any of the following:

    b displays the | character.

    c displays the (character.

    d displays the current date as day mmm dd, yyyy.

    e returns ASCII 27, the Escape character. This allows you to send ANSI codes to change screen colors, redefine keys, etc.

    f displays the) character.

    g displays the > character.

    h backspaces over the previous character.

    l displays the < character.

    n displays the letter of the current drive.

    P displays the current drive and directory in uppercase letters.

    p displays the current drive and directory in lowercase letters.

    q displays the = character.

    s displays a space.

    t displays the current time as hh:mm:ss.

    v displays the current DOS version.

    X*j*: displays the current directory in uppercase letters on drive *j*. *j* may be any drive on your system.

    x*j*: displays the current directory in lowercase letters on drive *j*. *j* may be any drive on your system.

    z displays the current NDOS shell level. That is, if you are running multiple copies of NDOS, say because you shelled out of a program, this option shows you which is current. **0** represents the main or primary copy.

$ displays the $ character.

_ returns a CR/LF (carriage return/line feed).

If you omit $i, the default for floppy drives is ng and the default for all other drives is pg.

- **EXAMPLE** Entering

    prompt This is lp$g

displays this prompt:

This is <c:\wp>

or whatever the current drive and directory may be.

PUSHD

PUSHD changes directories and adds the previous directory (i.e., the directory you just left) to the directory stack. This allows you to change directories "backwards" (i.e., in the reverse order) using the POPD command.

- **SYNTAX**

    PUSHD *path*

    path is the directory that you wish to make current. You may preface *path* with a drive letter so you can change to a directory on another drive.

- **EXAMPLE**

    C:\> pushd d:\wp --> D:\WP>
    D:\WP> pushd c:\word --> C:\WORD>
    C:\WORD> popd --> D:\WP>
    D:\WP> popd --> C:\>

See Also DIRS and POPD commands

QUIT

QUIT terminates the current batch file. If the batch file you QUIT is a nested batch file, control returns to the batch file that called it. This is in contrast to the CANCEL command, which terminates all running batch files.

- **SYNTAX**

    QUIT value

    value (version 7 only) sets the ERRORLEVEL to the specified value.

    See Also   CANCEL command

RD

RD (Remove Directory) is nearly identical to the DOS RD command. The only difference is that NDOS RD supports the use of wildcards so you can remove multiple directories simultaneously.

- **SYNTAX**

    RD *path*

    path is the full path name of the directory to be deleted. It may be prefaced with a drive letter. A directory must be empty before it can be removed.

- **EXAMPLE**   To remove all subdirectories on drive C, enter

    rd c:*.*

REBOOT

REBOOT reboots your computer system.

● SYNTAX

REBOOT (/options)

The options are as follows:

/N prompts the user to confirm the reboot.

/C performs a "cold" reboot, which has nearly the same effect as turning the computer off and then on again.

● **EXAMPLE** To "warm" boot your computer, simply type REBOOT.

REN

REN renames files or directories. REN is a slightly expanded version of the DOS REN command because it can rename directories and more files.

● SYNTAX

REN [/options] original new

original is the name of the file or directory to be renamed. You may use wild cards in *original*, thereby renaming multiple files or directories in one operation.

new is the new name of *original*. If you are renaming files, *new* may be prefaced with a path, allowing you to move a file by renaming it. Such movement, however, is restricted to the current drive only.

The options are as follows:

/N (version 7 only) tests the results of the renaming.

/P prompts you for confirmation for each file renamed.

/Q turns off the display of files renamed.

/S (version 7 only) allows you to rename subdirectories with a wildcard file specification.

- **EXAMPLE** To rename a directory you might enter

    ren \WP \WORD

To rename and move a file you might enter

   ren c:\test.txt c:\temp\hold.txt

This moves the file TEST.TXT to the \TEMP directory and renames it HOLD.TXT.

RENAME

RENAME is the same as REN, above.

RETURN

RETURN completes the execution of a batch file subroutine, started with the GOSUB command.

- **SYNTAX**

    RETURN

- **EXAMPLE** Jumping to a label with GOSUB and returning is illustrated below:

    echo Jump to a label, check free space...
    gosub space
    echo ... and return
    goto quit
    :space
    free c:
    return
    :quit

See Also GOSUB command

RMDIR

RMDIR is the same as RD, above.

SCREEN

SCREEN moves the cursor to the specified screen coordinates and optionally writes text there.

● **SYNTAX**

SCREEN *row col* [*text*]

row is the row where you want to move the cursor.

col is the column where you want to move the cursor.

text is any text you want written at the new cursor position.

● **EXAMPLE** This example places the message "a box" inside a green box drawn with the DRAWBOX command.

    drawbox 10 30 14 50 1 green on black
    screen 12 38 a box

SCRPUT

SCRPUT moves the cursor to specified screen coordinates and writes text there in color.

● **SYNTAX**

SCRPUT *row col* [BRIGHT | BLINK] *textcolor* ON *background text*

row is the row where you want to move the cursor.

col is the column where you want to move the cursor.

BRIGHT (version 7 only) causes the text to appear brighter than normal.

BLINK causes text to blink.

textcolor is the color of text. Valid colors in version 7 are black, blue, green, cyan, red, magenta, yellow, white, bright blue, bright green, bright cyan, bright red, bright magenta, bright yellow, and bright white. In version 6, valid colors are all of the above plus gray.

background is the background color of text. Valid colors are black, blue, green, cyan, red, magenta, yellow, and white. In version 6, valid colors are all of the above plus gray.

text is any text you want written at the new cursor position.

- **EXAMPLE** This example places the message "a box" in inverse video (black on white) inside a green box drawn with the DRAWBOX command.

    drawbox 10 30 14 50 1 green on black
    scrput 12 38 black on white a box

See Also SCREEN command

SELECT

SELECT executes the specified command on a group of files you choose from a file list.

- **SYNTAX**

    SELECT [/A:*attributes*] [/C][/D][/O:*sortkeys*] *command* [*filespec*]

    command is the command to execute. *Command* may be an NDOS command, DOS command, batch file, or alias.

    filespec specifies the group of files you wish to display in the file list. You may specify multiple file groups (*.com *.bat). This causes multiple file lists to appear, one after another.

    /A: limits the file list by causing only files with certain attributes set to appear. You can specify the files to appear by specifying attributes, which can be any combination of the following:

    (-)A displays files with the Archive attribute set. Append the optional minus sign to display all files without the Archive attribute set.

    (-)D displays directories. Append the optional minus sign to display files and not directories.

(-)H displays hidden files. Append the optional minus sign to display all files that are not hidden.

(-)R displays read-only files. Append the optional minus sign to display all files that are not read-only.

(-)S displays system files. Append the optional minus sign to display all files that are not system files.

/C (version 7 only) displays the file list in uppercase letters.

/D (version 7 only) disables directory colorization.

/O: sorts the file list according to *sortkeys*. The sortkeys can be any combination of the following:

(–)D sorts files numerically by file date and time. Append the optional minus sign to sort in descending order.

(–)E sorts files alphabetically by file extension. Append the optional minus to sort in descending order.

(–)G puts directories at the top of the listing (assumed by default). Append the optional minus sign to list directories at the bottom.

(–)I sorts files alphabetically by file description created by the DESCRIBE command. Append the optional minus sign to sort in descending order.

(–)N sorts files alphabetically by file name. Append the optional minus sign to sort in descending order.

(–)S sorts files numerically by file size. Append the optional minus sign to sort in descending order.

(–)U displays files in the order they were placed in the directory (COMMAND.COM's default). Append the optional minus sign to display this in reverse.

When the file list appears, you may scroll through it using the ↑, ↓, PgUp, and PgDn keys. You select files with the following keys:

+ selects the highlighted file.

– deselects the highlighted file.

spacebar selects or deselects the highlighted file.

* selects the entire file list.

When all the files you want are selected, press ↵ to execute the command.

- **EXAMPLE**   To make a backup copy on floppy disk of some of your word processing files, you could enter

    select /o:n copy (*.doc) a:

Note here that *a:* is part of the copy command and must be included.

SET

SET gives you control over environment variables. It is a slightly expanded version of the DOS SET command.

- **SYNTAX**

    SET [*/options*] [*var* [=*value*]]

    var is the variable you wish to create or delete. Omitting *var* (and *value*) displays all environment settings.

    value is the value you wish to assign to *var*. If *var* does not exist, it is created. If *var* already exists, it is given a new value. If you omit *value*, *var* is deleted.

    The options are as follows:

    /M displays or modifies the master environment rather than the local copy of the environment.

    /P pauses the display after each full screen.

    /R *filename* allows you to read in a file of previously defined variables. *Filename* should be an ASCII file with each variable in the form *var=value* on its own line or separated by the compound character (^).

- **EXAMPLE**   To reset the path, enter

    set path=c:\;c:\wp;c:\norton

SETDOS

SETDOS configures NDOS.

● **SYNTAX**

SETDOS [/options]

The options are as follows:

/**A**# determines the method NDOS uses to clear the screen (using ANSI codes or not). # may have one of three values:

0 lets NDOS determine whether an ANSI driver is loaded and clear the screen accordingly. This is the default. Unless you are using a nonstandard ANSI driver, the default is sufficient.

1 forces NDOS to clear the screen using ANSI codes.

2 forces NDOS to clear the screen without using ANSI codes.

/**C**# specifies the character used to separate multiple commands listed on the same line. The default is the caret (^). You cannot use the pipe [|] or redirection characters (<>) or the white-space character.

/**E**# specifies the Escape character. This character allows you to display characters on screen that would otherwise have a different function or not be displayable (e.g., control characters, such as carriage return or backspace). The default is set to Ctrl-X. You cannot use the pipe [|] or redirection characters (>) or the white-space character.

/**F**# enables (# = 0) or disables (# = 1) abbreviation of long path and file names that otherwise wouldn't fit on screen. The default is 0. Use 1 for full filenames.

/**H**# (version 6 only) specifies the minimum length for a command to be added to the command stack when executed. The default is 0.

/**I** [+| -] command (version 6 only) enables (+) or disables (−) command (a specified internal NDOS command).

/**L** is a command-line input switch between the NDOS editor and other editors that also provides an aliasing ability.

/M# sets NDOS command line editing to insert mode (# = 1) or overstrike mode (# = 0). The default is 0.

/N# enables (# = 1) or disables (# = 0) NOCLOBBER. That is, when NOCLOBBER is on, files may not be overwritten by redirection (i.e., dir > *filename*). The default is 0.

/R# sets the number of rows displayed on your screen. This is usually determined automatically.

/Ss:e (version 6 only) sets the cursor size by specifying the starting (s) and ending (e) scan lines. The defaults are 6 and 7 respectively.

/So:i (version 7 only) sets the cursor size by specifying the percentage of the character cell used in (o) overstrike mode and (i) insert mode.

/U# displays file names in uppercase (# = 1) or lowercase (# = 0) for NDOS internal commands. The default is 0.

/V# enables (# = 1) or disables (# = 0) echoing of commands in batch files. The default is 1. You can override this setting with the ECHO command.

If all options are omitted, the current settings are displayed.

SETLOCAL

SETLOCAL saves a copy of the current disk drive, directory, environment variables, and aliases to a reserved block of memory. You can then change their values and later restore their original values with ENDLOCAL.

• SYNTAX

SETLOCAL

Use SETLOCAL and ENDLOCAL in batch files, not aliases.

• **EXAMPLE** See ENDLOCAL for an example of how to use SETLOCAL and ENDLOCAL.

SWAPPING

SWAPPING, when enabled, allows NDOS to relocate a portion of itself (about 80K) from conventional memory to expanded or extended memory, if available, or to disk if they are not. There usually is no need to turn this option off, though it can, on occasion, slow down batch-file execution if you are swapping to disk.

- **SYNTAX**

    SWAPPING [ON | OFF]

    ON | OFF enables or disables NDOS relocation. If you enter SWAPPING without ON or OFF, the current SWAPPING status is displayed.

TEE

TEE provides a more flexible kind of output redirection. That is, you can both view output on screen and redirect it to a file in one operation. Standard redirection (>) allows one but not the other.

- **SYNTAX**

    TEE [/A] *filename*

    /A appends output to *filename*.

    filename is the name of the file to which output is copied.

- **EXAMPLE** To view a directory listing and, at the same time, copy it to a file called DIR.DAT, enter

    dir | tee dir.dat

TEXT/ENDTEXT

TEXT allows you to display multiple lines of text in a batch file.

NDOS

- **SYNTAX**

    TEXT
    text to display
    text to display
    .
    .
    ENDTEXT

TIMER

TIMER provides you with a stopwatch, or, in version 7, three stopwatches.

- **SYNTAX**

    TIMER [/#] [/S] [ON]

    /# turns on timer #. Valid values of # are 1, 2, and 3. Thus, TIMER /1 turns on the first timer, TIMER /2 the second, and TIMER /3 the third.

    /S shows you a split time without stopping the watch.

    ON forces the specified timer to restart.

Entering TIMER/# once starts the specified watch. Entering it again stops the watch and shows you the elapsed time. Entering TIMER /S shows a split time. Entering TIMER ON forces the timer to restart.

TRUENAME

TRUENAME finds and displays the full, true path and filename for a specified file.

- **SYNTAX**   **TRUENAME** *filespec*

filespec is the file or files whose true name and path you wish to find.

TYPE

- **NOTES** TRUENAME will see through JOIN and SUBST commands. It requires DOS 3.0 or later.

TYPE

TYPE displays ASCII files on screen. The NDOS TYPE command is a more flexible version of the DOS TYPE command.

- **SYNTAX**

    TYPE [/options] *filespec*

    filespec is the file or files to display. If you specify more than one file, they are viewed in series.

    The options are as follows:

    /L turns on line numbering.

    /P pauses the display after each full screen.

- **EXAMPLE** To view both your AUTOEXEC.BAT file and your CONFIG.SYS file, enter

    type /p autoexec.bat config.sys

UNALIAS

UNALIAS deletes an alias.

- **SYNTAX**

    UNALIAS *alias*

    alias is the alias you wish to delete. You may specify more than one alias.

- **EXAMPLE** To delete the alias "fmt360," enter

    unalias fmt360

See Also ALIAS command

UNSET

UNSET deletes an environment variable.

● **SYNTAX**

> **UNSET** *var*

OR

> **UNSET (/M)***

var is the variable you wish to delete. You may specify more than one variable.

/M removes the environment variable from the master environment rather than the local environment.

* deletes all environment variables.

● **EXAMPLE** To delete the environment variables *VAR1* and *VAR2*, enter

> **unset** *var1 var2*

See Also SET and ESET commands

VOL

VOL displays the volume labels of the specified drive or drives. The NDOS VOL command is more flexible than the DOS VOL command, as it can display the volume labels of multiple drives in one operation.

● **SYNTAX**

> **VOL** *drive:*

drive: is the drive whose volume label you wish to display. You may specify more than one drive.

- **EXAMPLE** To display the volume labels of your two hard disks, C and D, enter

    vol c: d:

VSCRPUT

VSCRPUT allows you to display text in a vertical column in a specified color.

- **SYNTAX**

    VSCRPUT *row column* **[BRIGHT | BLINK]** *textcolor* **ON** *background text*

    row is the row on the screen where you wish the text to start being displayed.

    column is the column on the screen where you wish the text to start being displayed.

    BRIGHT causes the text to appear brighter than normal.

    BLINK causes the text to blink.

    textcolor sets the color of the text. Valid colors are the same as for the CLS command above.

    background sets the background color. Valid colors are listed under the CLS command above.

- **EXAMPLE**

    vscrput 5 5 blink red on green This is a test!

    will cause "This is a test!" to be displayed in blinking red letters on a green background beginning at row 5 and column 5 on your screen.

Y

Y provides flexible output redirection by allowing you to append the contents of a file or files to standard output.

● SYNTAX

Y *filespec*

filespec is the file that you will append to any output. You may specify multiple files here.

● **EXAMPLE** To append the contents of the file DIR.DAT to the listing of your root directory, enter

dir | ydir.dat

NORTON
Norton Utilities Shell

The NORTON program is a shell from which you can run any of the programs that make up the Norton Utilities or any other frequently used program. NORTON also provides the ability to configure the Norton Utilities.

- **UPGRADE INFORMATION** NORTON 7 contains all of the functions of NORTON 6 and expands your ability to configure the Norton Utilities. There are, in addition, a few cosmetic changes in the interface, which are noted below.

To Add a Program (or Command) to the Program List

1. Pull down the Menu menu and select the **Add Menu Item** option.
2. In the Add Menu Item box, select **Command**.
3. At the **Name in Menu:** prompt, type the program (or command) name as you want it to appear in the program list.
4. At the **DOS Command:** prompt, type the DOS command that runs the program (or that is the command in question). Include a path if necessary.
5. In the Topic box, select the topic under which the program (or command) should be listed when the program list is sorted by topic.
6. Select **Description**.
7. Press **F2** to select a text attribute for the description.
8. In the Description box, type a description of the program (or command).
9. Select **OK** twice.

This function allows you to run any program (or execute any command) from NORTON.

When the program list is sorted by name, step 2 is omitted.

In step 7 in version 7, there are four text attributes from which to choose: normal, bold, bold reverse, and reverse. In step 7 in version 6, there are also four text attributes from which to choose: normal, bold, underline, and reverse. The text you type appears in whatever attribute is selected. You can, therefore, produce descriptions with multiple attributes by repeating steps 7 and 8 for different parts of the description.

To Add a Topic to the Program List

1. Sort the program list by topic. (See "To Sort the Program List.")
2. Pull down the Menu menu and select the **Add Menu Item** option.
3. In the Add Menu Item dialog box, select **Topic**.
4. Type the name of the new topic.
5. Select **Description**.
6. Press **F2** to select a text attribute for the description.
7. In the Description box, type a description of the topic.
8. Select **OK** twice.

This function is only possible when the program list is sorted by topic. (You can have as many as ten topics.)

In step 6 in version 7, there are four text attributes from which to choose: normal, bold, bold reverse, and reverse. In step 6 in version 6, there are also four text attributes from which to choose: normal, bold, underline, and reverse. The text you type appears in whatever attribute is selected. You can, therefore, produce descriptions with multiple attributes by repeating steps 6 and 7 for different parts of the description.

To Change Program Colors

1. Pull down the Configuration menu, and select the **Video and Mouse** option.
2. On the Configure Video/Mouse dialog box (which is called the Video and Mouse Options dialog box in version 6), select **Customize Colors**.
3. On the Customize Colors dialog box (which is called the Custom Color Setup dialog box in version 6), and on the display components list on the left-hand side, highlight the component whose colors you wish to change.
4. Select **Color** in version 7, or **Change** in version 6.
5. In the Colors: dialog box (which is called the Select New Color dialog box in version 6), select the text and background color combination you wish to use.
6. Select **OK**.
7. Repeat steps 3 through 6 as necessary.
8. Select **OK** in version 7, or **Save** twice in version 6.

This option allows you to change the color of any part of the Norton Utilities display, from the color of dialog boxes, to the color of option hot keys, to the color of scroll bars. Note that any color change you make will be uniform across all of the Norton Utilities (i.e., all scroll bars on all programs will be bright cyan on magenta, and so on).

In step 3, all of the display parts whose colors you can change are listed and are grouped by category—all button elements are grouped together under the heading "Buttons," etc. The part you select, in its current colors, appears in the display on the right-hand side of the screen.

In step 4, you can select the Default option to change all parts back to their default colors.

In step 5, all combinations of text and background colors are available for you to choose. You can select the Default option to return the selected part back to its default colors.

To Configure the Screen and Mouse

1. Pull down the Configuration menu and select the **Video and Mouse** option.

2. In the Configure Video/Mouse dialog box (which is called the Video and Mouse options dialog box in version 6), and from the Screen Colors drop down list in version 7 or in the Screen Colors box in version 6, select a color mode.

3. Version 7 only. From the Display Lines drop down list, select the number of lines you would like on your display.

4. From the Display Mode drop down list in version 7 or in the Graphics Options box in version 6, select a graphics mode.

5. From the four toggle boxes in the lower left of the Screen Options box in version 7 or in the Screen Options box in version 6, specify box and background options.

6. In the Mouse Options box, select the desired mouse options.

7. Select **OK** in version 7 or **Save** in version 6.

In step 2, there are seven available color modes:

- Select **Greyscale (Laptop)** in version 7 (which is called **Laptop** in version 6) if you are using a laptop computer.

- Select **Black and White** if you are using a composite monitor.

- Select **Monochrome** if you are using a monochrome monitor.

- Select **CGA Colors** if you are using a CGA monitor or want a display with fewer available colors.

- Select one of two **EGA/VGA Color** options if you have an EGA or VGA display.

- Select **Custom Colors** if you want to make your own color set without disturbing any of the other color sets.

In step 3, select the number of lines you would like your screen to display. The numbers available depend on the type of video card you have. Some video cards may not support this feature.

In step 4, the graphics options control the appearance of the scroll and title bars, mouse pointer, buttons, toggle boxes, and check marks. In version 7, there are three options:

- Select All Graphical Controls if you wish to provide graphical scroll bars and title bars, complete circles for radio buttons, complete squares for toggle boxes, and check marks to indicate that an option is toggled on.

- Select Some Graphical Controls if you wish to provide round option buttons and square check boxes, but no special graphical icons in the Norton Utilities.

- Select Standard if you wish to display parentheses for nongraphics characters and square brackets for option buttons and check boxes.

In version 6, there are four options:

- Select Graphical Dialogs to provide graphical scroll bars and dialog box title bars, an arrow for the mouse pointer, complete circles for radio buttons, complete squares for toggle boxes, and check marks to indicate that an option is toggled on.

- Select Graphical Mouse to provide all of the above except graphical scroll and title bars.

- Select Graphical Controls to provide all of the above except graphical scroll and title bars and the arrow mouse pointer (which becomes a block).

- Select Standard to draw all of these options as ASCII characters instead of graphics. The mouse pointer is a block, buttons are parentheses, toggle boxes are square brackets, and check marks are X's.

In step 5, toggle Zooming Boxes on to have dialog boxes "explode," or expand, from their centers when drawn. Toggle Solid Background on or off to switch between a solid background and a tessellated background. In version 6, toggle the Ctrl-↵ Accepts option on to use Ctrl-↵ instead of f to OK a dialog box.

Toggle the Button Arrows option on to have arrows appear on the default dialog box buttons. In version 7 only, toggle the Block Cursor option on to make the cursor appear as a blinking block instead of a blinking underline.

In step 6, toggle on Left-Handed Mouse to reverse the functions of the mouse buttons. Toggle on Fast Mouse Reset for automatic, proper positioning of the mouse pointer and the most efficient use of the Norton Utilities. In step 6 in version 7 only, you can adjust your mouse's double-clicking speed, sensitivity, and acceleration from the appropriately named drop down lists. Toggle on Graphical Mouse to have your mouse pointer appear as an arrow and not as a rectangle. Toggle on Enter Moves Focus to move between dialog box choices with ↵ instead of the tab key. Note that this requires you to OK dialog boxes with Ctrl-↵ instead of ↵.

To Create or Modify Printer Configuration Files (Version 7 Only)

1. Pull down the Configuration menu and select **Printer Setup**.
2. In the Configure Printer dialog box, select **Add**.
3. In the Configuration Name dialog box, type the name of the Configuration file and select **OK**.
4. In the Printer Settings dialog box, and in the Options box, toggle options for compressed print, wrapped lines, or numbered lines.
5. Pull down the Printer Type drop down list and select your printer, or the one that most closely resembles it.
6. In the Margins box, set the width of top and bottom margins in lines and the width of the left and right margins in columns.
7. In the Page Size box, set the width of the page in columns and the height of the page in lines.

8. In the Line Spacing box, set the line spacing and the width of tabs in spaces.

9. In the Header box, select the type of header you want from the Kind of Header drop down list. Toggle on the **Bold Headers** option if you wish headers to be boldfaced.

10. From the Output Destination drop down list, select the port to which your printer is attached, or select **Disk File** if you are printing to a file.

11. From the Data Format drop down list, select ASCII, unless you are printing to a file and wish to create a file in WordStar or EBCDIC format.

12. From the Orientation drop down list, select whether you wish to print in Portrait or Landscape orientation.

13. Select **OK**.

14. Highlight the printer configuration file you wish to use and select **Select**.

15. Select **Close**.

This function allows you to create a simple printer definition for use with the LP program. Rather than throw a complex set of switches every time you use LP, you set the options only once here.

In step 2, if you wish to modify a configuration file rather than create one anew, highlight it on the Configuration Files list and select Edit. Skip step 3 if you are editing, rather than adding a configuration file.

In step 4, the Wrap Lines option should be toggled on.

In step 7, a standard 8½ x 11 page is 80 columns wide and 66 (or 60) lines high.

In step 9, you may select single-line or double-line headers, or None, to have no header at all.

In step 12, the list will not be available if the printer you selected in step 5 does not support landscape printing.

To Delete a Program or Topic from the Program List

1. In the Norton Utilities dialog box and in the Commands box (program list), highlight the program or topic you want to delete.
2. Pull down the Menu menu. Select the **Delete Menu Item** option.
3. In the Delete Menu Item dialog box, select **Yes** to confirm the deletion.

To delete a topic, the program list must be sorted by topic. Programs (or commands) can be deleted regardless of sort order.

A topic cannot be deleted if it has programs (or commands) listed beneath it.

To Edit a Program Entry on the Program List

1. Highlight the program (or command) you want to edit.
2. Pull down the Menu menu. Select the **Edit Menu Item** option.
3. Follow steps 3 through 9 in "To Add a Program (or Command) to the Program List," changing the current information as you go.

To Edit a Topic Entry on the Program List

1. Highlight the topic you want to edit.
2. Pull down the Menu menu. Select **Edit Menu Item**.
3. Follow steps 4 through 8 in "To Add a Topic to the Program List," changing the current information as you go.

To Enable or Disable Menu Editing

1. Pull down the Configuration menu, and select the **Menu Editing** option.

2. On the Norton Menu Editing dialog box, select the **Enable Editing** or **Disable Editing** option.

3. Select **OK**.

This option enables or disables your ability to edit the Program List. See "To Add a Program (or Command) to the Program List," "To Add a Topic to the Program List," etc.

To Expand Norton Program Files (Version 6 Only)

1. Pull down the Configuration menu, and select the **Expand Programs** option.

2. Select **OK** to acknowledge the information dialog box.

3. In the Expand Program Files dialog box, toggle the programs you wish to expand by highlighting them and pressing the spacebar.

4. Select **Expand**.

The Norton Utilities may be installed in compressed format, such that they occupy approximately 40% less disk space than they would if expanded. The trade-off, however, is that compressed programs must decompress before they execute. While the delay caused by decompressing programs is minimal or unnoticeable on faster machines, it can be significant on slower machines. Use this function to expand the programs, thus speeding their execution (at the expense of disk space). Note that, once expanded, programs cannot be recompressed.

To Lengthen or Shorten Norton Program File Names

1. Pull down the Configuration menu, and select the **Alternate Names** option.

2. Choose long or short names for each of the programs displayed.

3. Select **OK**.

This option allows you to rename programs with long names with two-letter mnemonics (e.g., DISKEDIT.EXE to DE.EXE). This cuts down on typing.

In step 2, you may select the All Short option to shorten the names of all listed programs, or the All Long option to restore the long names of all of the programs.

To Load and Configure Startup Programs

In version 7, follow these steps:

1. Pull down the Configuration menu and select **Startup Programs**.
2. Select the programs you wish to use at startup from the Startup Programs list and configure as necessary. See below for explanations.
3. Select **Save** to make the relevant changes to your AUTOEXEC.BAT and CONFIG.SYS files.
4. Select **OK** to acknowledge.
5. Quit the NORTON program.
6. Reboot your computer so that the changes you have made will take effect.

In version 6, all relevant options are found on the Configuration menu. For specific instructions, see the sequences of steps marked version 6 below. When you are finished loading and configuring, quit NORTON and reboot your machine.

To Load and Configure DISKMON

1. Highlight Start Disk Monitor on the Startup Programs list and select **Configure**.
2. On the Configure Disk Monitor dialog box, optionally toggle on the **Monitor Disk Accesses** option to write-protect certain areas of your disk.
3. Optionally toggle on the **Display Disk Light** option to turn on the drive activity indicator.

4. Select **OK**.

In step 2, the areas of your disk to be protected must be specified by running DISKMON. See DISKMON, "To Use Disk Protect."

To Load and Configure DISKMON (Version 6)

1. Pull down the Configuration menu and select **AUTOEXEC.BAT**.
2. In the AUTOEXEC.BAT Setup dialog box, toggle on the **Load the DISKMON Utility** option.
3. Select **OK**.
4. Select **Save**.

To Load the DISKREET Driver

- Select **Start DISKREET Encryption Driver**.

To Load the DISKREET Driver (Version 6)

1. Pull down the Configuration menu and select **CONFIG.SYS**.
2. In the CONFIG.SYS Setup dialog box, toggle on the **Load the DISKREET.SYS Driver** option.
3. Select **OK**.
4. Select **Save**.

To Load IMAGE

1. Highlight Save Disk Format Data and select **Configure**.
2. On the Protect Disk Format Data dialog box, set the drive(s) you wish to IMAGE.
3. Select **OK**.

To Load and Configure IMAGE (Version 6)

1. Pull down the Configuration menu and select **AUTOEXEC.BAT**.
2. On the AUTOEXEC.BAT Setup dialog box, toggle on the **Run the IMAGE Utility** option.
3. Select **OK**.
4. Select **Save**.

To Load and Configure NCACHE2

1. In version 7, highlight Start Norton Cache on the Startup Program list and select **Configure**. In version 6, pull down the Configuration menu and select **Norton Cache.**
2. In the Norton Cache dialog box and in the Loading box, select the source from which you wish to load the cache.
3. In the High Memory box, select where in memory the cache program will load itself.
4. In the Cache Options box, select whether you wish to cache floppy drives and enable IntelliWrites.
5. In the Memory Usage box, select how much memory will be allocated to the cache.
6. Optionally select the **Advanced** option.
7. In the Norton Cache-Advanced Option dialog box and in the buffering box, select buffering and delay options.
8. In the Optimize box, optionally optimize the cache for speed, efficiency, or memory, and select **OK**.
9. Select **OK** again.

All of the options here are equivalent to command-line options explained under NCACHE/NCACHE2. Indeed, all options set here are saved in the file NCACHE.INI as if you had saved them with the NCACHE /SAVE command. See NCACHE /SAVE and NCACHE /INI.

In step 2, you may choose to load NCACHE from your AUTO-EXEC.BAT file or your CONFIG.SYS file, or you may choose not to load it at all.

In step 3, you may choose to load the NCACHE program itself (i.e., NCACHE's memory management apparatus, rather than the memory buffer) into High Memory or conventional memory.

In step 4, it is *not* recommended that you cache floppy drives. IntelliWrites allow data to be written to disk more efficiently and in the background. See NCACHE /I.

In step 5, select whether the memory cache will use Extended, Expanded, or Conventional memory, and how much. You cannot mix and match types. See NCACHE /DOS, NCACHE /EXT, and NCACHE /EXP.

In step 6, if you do not choose to set advanced options, skip to step 9.

In step 7, you can set various buffer and delay options, as follows:

- The Read-Ahead Buffer option specifies the size of the buffer into which sectors "read-ahead" are placed. You must set it to an integer value between 8 and 64, inclusive. Setting it to 0 disables the read-ahead feature. See the NCACHE /R and NCACHE /READ options.

- The Write-Back Buffer option specifies the size of the IntelliWrites buffer. You must set it to an integer value between 8 and 64, inclusive. Setting it to 0 disables the IntelliWrites feature. See step 4 above, and NCACHE /WRITE and NCACHE /I.

- The Cache Buffer Blocks option sets the size of cache data blocks. Valid sizes are 512, 1024, 2048, 4096, 8192. See NCACHE /BLOCK.

- The Delay Before Sectors option delays disk writes by the specified amount of time. The time value you select represents seconds and hundredths of seconds—an integer from 0 to 59 inclusive, and an integer from 0 to 99, inclusive. Use when IntelliWrites is enabled. See step 4 above, and the NCACHE /DELAY and NCACHE /I options.

- The Don't Wait for Write-Back... option speeds up operation by returning to the DOS prompt before all disk writes are complete. Use when IntelliWrites is enabled. See step 4 above, and the NCACHE /QUICK and NCACHE /I options.
- The Wait for Disk Writes option enables or disables multi-tasking disk writes.

To Load KEYSTACK:

- Select Start Keystack from the Startup Programs list.

If you wish to use KEYSTACK, you must use NDOS (See "To Load and Configure NDOS")

To Load KEYSTACK (Version 6):

1. Pull down the Configuration menu and select the **CONFIG.SYS File** option.
2. In the CONFIG.SYS Setup dialog box, toggle on the **Load the NDOS.COM Command Shell** option.
3. Select **OK**.
4. Select **Save**.

If you wish to use KEYSTACK, you must use NDOS (See "To Load and Configure NDOS (Version 6)".)

To Load and Configure NDD:

1. Highlight Diagnose Disk Problems on the Startup Programs list and select **Configure**.
2. In the Check Disks for Problems dialog box, select the drive(s) you wish NDD to check.
3. Select **OK**.

Running NDD from here causes NDD to check system areas on selected drives each time your machine is rebooted, but not to perform a surface test.

To Load and Configure NDD (Version 6)

1. Pull down the Configuration menu and select **AUTOEXEC.BAT**.
2. On the AUTOEXEC.BAT Setup dialog box, toggle on the **Run the NDD Utility...** option.
3. Select **OK**.
4. Select **Save**.

Running NDD from here causes NDD to check system areas on selected drives, but not to perform a surface test.

To Load and Configure NDOS

1. Highlight Use NDOS Command Processor on the Setup Programs list and select **Configure**.
2. In the General box in the NDOS Configuration dialog box, toggle on any of the four general NDOS options.
3. In the Sizes box, specify the amount of space (in bytes) to reserve for environment variables, aliases, and the command history.
4. In the Beeps box, specify the frequency (in Hertz) and the duration (in microseconds) of the beeps issued by NDOS. Select **Test** to hear the results of your beep specifications.
5. In the Other box, specify the minimum length necessary for a command to be put in the command history, and specify the maximum file description length.
6. Select **OK**.

In step 2, the two load options allow you to relocate NDOS and the DOS environment into your upper memory, thereby freeing up some conventional memory. The Insert Mode When Editing... option causes the NDOS command line to start in insert mode rather than typeover mode. You can change between insert and typeover modes at the command line by pressing the insert key. The Use Underscore for Insert Mode... causes the NDOS cursor to appear as an underscore. When this option is off, the cursor appears as a block in insert mode.

In step 5, commands issued that are shorter than the minimum history command length specified here are not saved in the command history. Set this option to 0 to have all commands put in the command history.

To Load and Configure NDOS (Version 6)

1. Pull down the Configuration menu and select **CONFIG.SYS File**.
2. In the CONFIG.SYS Setup dialog box, toggle on the **Load the NDOS.COM Command Shell** option.
3. Select **OK**.
4. Select **Save**.

To Load SMARTCAN

- Select **Start SMARTCAN** from the Startup Programs list.

To Load EP (Erase Protect) (Version 6)

1. Pull down the Configuration menu and select the **AUTOEXEC.BAT File** option.
2. On the AUTOEXEC.BAT Setup dialog box, toggle on the **Load the Erase Protect Utility** option.
3. Select **OK**.
4. Select **Save**.

To Password Protect the Norton Utilities (Version 7)

1. Pull down the Configuration menu and select the **Passwords** option.
2. In the Password Protection dialog box, toggle the programs you wish to password protect.
3. Select **OK**.
4. In the Password dialog box, type your password at the **New Password:** prompt.
5. Retype your password at the **Confirm New Password:** prompt.
6. Select **OK**.

This function makes it so that a password is required to use selected Norton programs. Note that the password selected in steps 4 and 5 will be used to protect all programs selected in step 2. Also in step 2, optionally select the Select All option to password protect all Norton programs listed.

In step 4, you may change a password already assigned by typing it at the Old Password: prompt and then typing the new password as in steps 4 and 5 above.

To Password Protect the Norton Utilities (Version 6)

1. Pull down the Configuration menu, and select the **Passwords** option.
2. In the Password Protection dialog box, toggle the programs you wish to password protect.
3. Select **Set Password**.
4. In the Set Password dialog box, type your password and select **OK**.
5. In the Verify Password dialog box, retype your password and select **OK**.

This function makes it so that a password is required to use selected Norton programs. Note that the password specified in steps 4 and 5 will be used to protect all programs selected in step 2.

To Run a Program (or Command) from NORTON

1. In the Norton Utilities dialog box and in the Commands box (program list), highlight the name of the program you want to run.
2. On the command line at the cursor, next to where the name of the program to run appears, type any required arguments or switches.
3. Press ↵.

To Sort the Program List

1. Pull down the Menu menu.
2. Choose the **Sort by Name** option or press **Alt-N** to sort the list by program name. Choose **Sort by Topic** or press **Alt-T** to sort by topic.

• SYNTAX

NORTON (/options)

The options are the following:

/BW specifies use of the Black and White mode and is for use with composite monitors.

/G0 specifies use of the Standard graphics option. (See "To Configure the Screen and Mouse," step 4.) EGA and VGA only.

/G1 (version 6 only) specifies use of the Graphical Controls graphics option. (See "To Configure the Screen and Mouse," step 4.) EGA and VGA only.

/G2 (version 6 only) specifies use of the Graphical Mouse graphics option. (See "To Configure the Screen and Mouse," step 4.) EGA and VGA only.

/LCD specifies use of the Laptop color mode and is for use with LCD displays.

/M0 disables the graphics (small arrow) mouse.

/NOZOOM tells Norton not to use exploding dialog boxes. (See "To Configure the Screen and Mouse," step 3.)

NUCONFIG

The NUCONFIG program lets you configure the Norton Utilities. All but one of the options in the program are available in the NORTON program, and, as such, instructions will refer you to the relevant NORTON section.

- **UPGRADE INFORMATION** NUCONFIG 7 contains a number of functions absent in NUCONFIG 6, such as specifying the locations of temporary files and creating printer setup files. In addition, there are more functions available for loading and configuring the Norton Utilities.

To Change Program Colors

In version 7, follow these steps:

1. In the Configure Norton Utilities dialog box, select the **Video and Mouse** option.

2. Follow steps 2 through 8 in the NORTON "To Change Program Colors" section.

In version 6, follow these steps:

1. In the Norton Utilities Configuration dialog box, select the **Video and Mouse** option.

2. Follow steps 2 through 8 in the NORTON "To Change Program Colors" section.

To Configure the Screen and Mouse

In version 7, follow these steps:

1. In the Configure Norton Utilities dialog box, select the **Video and Mouse** option.

2. Follow steps 2 through 7 in the NORTON "To Configure the Screen and Mouse" section.

In version 6, follow these steps:

   1. In the Norton Utilities Configuration dialog box, select the **Video and Mouse** option.

   2. Follow steps 2 through 7 in the NORTON "To Configure the Screen and Mouse" section.

To Create or Modify Printer Configuration Files (Version 7 Only)

   1. In the Configure Norton Utilities dialog box, select the **Printer Setup** option.

   2. Follow steps 2 through 15 in the NORTON "To Create or Modify Printer Configuration Files" section.

To Enable or Disable Menu Editing

In version 7, follow these steps:

   1. In the Configure Norton Utilities dialog box, select the **Menu Editing** option.

   2. Follow steps 2 through 3 in the NORTON "To Enable or Disable Menu Editing" section.

In version 6, follow these steps:

   1. In the Norton Utilities Configuration dialog box, select the **Menu Editing** option.

   2. Follow steps 2 through 3 in the NORTON "To Enable or Disable Menu Editing" section.

To Expand NORTON Program Files (Version 6 Only)

   1. In the Norton Utilities Configuration dialog box, select the **Expand Programs** option.

2. Follow steps 2 through 4 in the NORTON "To Expand Norton Program Files" section.

To Lengthen or Shorten Norton Program File Names

In version 7, follow these steps:

1. In the Configure Norton Utilities dialog box, select the **Alternate Names** option.

2. Follow steps 2 through 3 in the NORTON "To Lengthen or Shorten NORTON Program File Names" section.

In version 6, follow these steps:

1. In the Norton Utilities Configuration dialog box, select the **Alternate Names** option.

2. Follow steps 2 through 3 in the NORTON "To Lengthen or Shorten NORTON Program File Names" section.

To Load and Configure Startup Programs (NDOS, KEYSTACK, NDD, IMAGE, SMARTCAN (EP), NCACHE, DISKMON, DISKREET.SYS)

In version 7, follow these steps:

1. In the Configure Norton Utilities dialog box, select the **Startup Programs** option.

2. See the relevant subsection for each program under the NORTON "To Load and Configure Startup Programs" section.

In version 6, follow these steps:

- See the relevant subsection for each program under the NORTON "To Load and Configure Startup Programs" section. Note, though, that in NUCONFIG, the options in step 1 above are all selected from the Norton Utilities Configuration dialog box and not the Configuration menu.

To Password Protect the Norton Utilities

In version 7, follow these steps:

1. In the Configure Norton Utilities dialog box, select the **Passwords** option.
2. Follow steps 2 through 6 in the NORTON "To Password Protect the Norton Utilities" section.

In version 6, follow these steps:

1. In the Norton Utilities Configuration dialog box, select the **Passwords** option.
2. Follow steps 2 through 5 in the NORTON "To Password Protect the Norton Utilities" section.

To Set the Location of Temporary Files (Version 7 Only)

1. In the Configure Norton Utilities dialog box, select the **Temporary Files** option.
2. In the Temporary Files dialog box, and at the **Swap Files Directory**: prompt, type the name of the directory to which you would like the Norton Utilities to write its swap files.
3. At the **Temporary Files Directory**: prompt, type the name of the directory to which you would like the Norton Utilities to write its temporary files.
4. Select **OK**.

In step 2, the Norton Utilities will sometimes swap data out of memory and write it to disk, so as to use the newly-freed memory for something else, or write temporary files to disk. Both are part of normal operation. This function allows you to specify where the Norton Utilities will do such writing and is particularly useful if you specify a RAM drive, since reading and writing from RAM drives is much faster than reading and writing to your hard disk.

RESCUE

RESCUE stores a copy of vital hard disk information on a floppy disk. Specifically, it stores a copy of your boot record, partition table, CMOS information, and AUTOEXEC.BAT and CONFIG.SYS files. In the event that any of this information is lost, you can retrieve it from the RESCUE disk. In addition, you may store a copy of some NORTON data recovery programs such as NDD, UNERASE, UNFORMAT, etc.

- **UPGRADE INFORMATION** In version 6, RESCUE existed as the Create a Rescue Disk function in the DISKTOOL program and copied only the boot record, CMOS, and partition table data to the rescue disk. In version 7, it is broken out as a separate program, and copies in addition the AUTOEXEC.BAT and CONFIG.SYS files and optionally, data recovery programs.

To Create a Rescue Disk

1. In the Rescue Disk dialog box, select **Create**.

2. From the Save Rescue Information To: drop down list in the Create Rescue Disk dialog box, select the drive to which you wish to copy rescue information.

3. From the Rescue Diskette Type: drop down list, select the size of the diskette onto which you will copy the rescue information.

4. Toggle on the **Format Rescue Diskette** option if your diskette is not formatted.

5. Toggle on the **Update Changed Files Only** option if you have already created a rescue disk and wish to update its contents.

6. From the Rescue Disk Contents list, select the recovery programs you wish to include on your rescue disk.

7. Select **Create**.

8. Place the floppy disk in the drive specified in step 2 and select **OK**.
9. Select **OK** to acknowledge the overwrite warning (if any).
10. Select **OK** to acknowledge completion.

In step 2, although it is possible to select a hard disk as a rescue disk, it is not wise to do so. If your hard disk is inaccessible (because you have lost CMOS information or because of a corrupted partition table, for example), you will not be able to access the rescue data to fix the problem.

To Restore Rescue Information

1. Put the rescue disk in a floppy drive and start the RESCUE program from that disk.
2. In the Rescue Disk dialog box, select **Restore**.
3. At the **Restore Rescue Information From:** prompt in the Restore Rescue Information dialog box, type the name of the drive containing your rescue disk.
4. In the Items to Restore box, toggle the rescue data you wish to restore.
5. Select **Restore**.
6. Select **Yes** to confirm.
7. Remove the rescue disk from your floppy and select **Reset** to reboot your machine.

In step 3, the program will not let you proceed until you type the name of a drive containing rescue information. Make sure to indicate floppy drives with a colon following the drive letter (A:, for example).

In step 4, you may select CMOS information, boot record information, or partition table information in any combination for restoration.

• SYNTAX

RESCUE /options

The options are as follows:

/CREATE:*drive* creates a rescue disk on drive *drive*.

/RESTORE:*drive* restores a rescue disk from drive *drive*.

/SKIPHIGH causes RESCUE to use conventional rather than high memory.

SFORMAT
Safe Format

SFORMAT is better than the FORMAT program in DOS, as it is able to format disks more quickly and in such a way that they can be unformatted without data loss.

- **UPGRADE INFORMATION** SFORMAT 7 is functionally identical to SFORMAT 6, though there are some differences in their interfaces.

To Allow or Disallow Formatting of Hard Disks

In version 7,

1. In the Safe Format dialog box, select **Configure**.
2. Toggle the **Allow Hard Disk Formatting** option at the bottom of the box.
3. Select **OK**.

In version 6,

1. Pull down the Configure menu and select the **Hard Disks** option, or press **Alt-H**.
2. In the Hard Disk Formatting box, toggle the **Allow Hard Disk Formatting** option on or off, and select **OK**.

To prevent accidental formatting of hard disks, this option is turned off by default.

To Format a Disk

1. In the Safe Format dialog box and on the Drive drop down list in version 7, (or in the Drive box in version 6), select the drive you want to format.

2. If you are formatting a floppy, select the desired disk capacity from the Size drop down list in version 7 (or in the Size box in version 6).

3. From the Format Type drop down list in version 7 (or in the Format Mode box in version 6), choose what kind of format you want to execute.

4. From the System Files drop down list in version 7 (or in the System Files box in version 6), choose what you want to do with the DOS system files.

5. At the **Volume Label:** prompt, type the volume label you want to assign to the formatted disk, if any.

6. Optionally toggle the **Save Image Info** option on. (This option is called **Save UNFORMAT Info** in version 6.)

7. Select **Format** in version 7 or **Begin Format** in version 6.

8. Select **Yes** if a confirmation box appears.

9. Select **OK** to acknowledge format completion.

In step 2, the sizes you can choose from depend on the types of drives you have. Five-and-a-quarter-inch drives can be formatted to 1.2MB, 360K, 320K, 180K, and 160K. Three-and-a-half-inch drives can be formatted to 2.88MB (version 6 only), 1.44MB, and 720K. This option is not available if you are formatting a hard disk.

In step 3, you have three options:

- Select Safe to perform a safe format, which allows you to unformat the disk and recover any data on it, if necessary.

- Select Quick to perform the fastest format. This effectively blanks the disk by overwriting system information (directory structure, boot record, FAT).

- Select DOS to perform a normal DOS format.

In step 4, you have three options:

- Select None in version 7 (or Don't Put on Disk in version 6) if you do not want to create a bootable disk.

- Select Put on Disk if you want to create a bootable disk.

SFORMAT

- Select Leave Space if you are undecided. This option allows you to add the system files subsequently with the DOS SYS command.

In step 6, the Save Image Info option (version 7) or the Save Un-Format Info option (version 6) must be toggled on if you are doing a safe format. Image information allows a formatted disk to be recovered with the UNFORMAT program. (See UNFORMAT and IMAGE.)

To Save Current Settings

- In version 7, on the Safe Format dialog box, toggle on the **Save Settings on Exit** option. In version 6, pull down the Configure menu, and select the **Save Settings** option.

To Set Default Floppy Types

In version 7,

1. In the Safe Format dialog box, select **Configure**.
2. In the Floppy Drive box, select the floppy drive whose default type you wish to set.
3. In the Type for Drive box, select your default size and capacity.
4. Select **OK**.

In version 6,

1. Pull down the Configure menu and select the **Floppy Types** option. The Floppy Types dialog box appears.
2. In the Floppy Drives box, select the drive whose default type you want to set.
3. In the Type for Drive box, specify the default floppy type and size.
4. Select **OK**.
5. Save your settings. (See "To Save Current Settings.")

Use this function if, for example, you frequently format 360K disks in a 1.2MB drive.

The Prompt For Missing Diskettes option is on by default and should remain so. This option will provide a warning if you attempt to format a floppy disk when the drive door is open.

● SYNTAX

SFORMAT [drive:] [/options]

drive: is the drive you want to format or the target drive.

The options are the following:

/1 formats a single-sided disk.

/4 formats a double-density (360K) disk in a high-density (1.2MB) disk drive.

/8 formats the target disk with 8 sectors per track instead of the usual 9.

/A formats the target drive automatically, using current or default settings, and quits to DOS.

/B formats the target drive, leaving space for the DOS system files. Allows you to subsequently make the disk bootable with the SYS command in DOS.

/D performs a normal DOS format.

/F:*bytes* specifies the formatted size of the target disk.

/N:# specifies the number of sectors per track; # can equal 8, 9, 15, 18, or 36.

/Q performs a quick format.

/S makes the target drive bootable.

/T:# specifies the number of tracks to be written on the disk; # can equal 40 or 80.

/U formats without providing overwrite warnings.

/V:*label* attaches the specified volume label to the formatted drive.

- **NOTES** During installation of the Norton Utilities, you have the option to rename the DOS FORMAT program XXFORMAT and to rename the SFORMAT program FORMAT.

See Also IMAGE, UNFORMAT

SMARTCAN
Version 7 Only

SMARTCAN, known as EP (Erase Protect) in version 6, protects the data of specified files *after* deletion. Data from deleted files is held in a special subdirectory, virtually guaranteeing the successful unerasure of these files. Deleted files stored by SMARTCAN are purged automatically after a specified number of days; you can purge them manually at any time.

- **UPGRADE INFORMATION** SMARTCAN was known as EP in version 6. SMARTCAN contains the same features as EP, but the interfaces of the two programs are different.

To Activate File Protection

1. In the Configure SmartCan dialog box, toggle on the **Enable SmartCan** option.
2. Select **Drives**.
3. In the Drives dialog box, select the drives to be protected and then select **OK**.
4. In the Files to Protect box in the Configure SmartCan dialog box, select which files you wish to protect.
5. In the SmartCan Storage Limits box, toggle on the **Purge Files Held Over...** option and the **Hold at Most...** option.

Under DOS, when a file is erased, its entry is removed from its directory and the FAT, but its data remains on the disk. This makes unerasure possible. However, because the space used by the erased files is made available by DOS to new files, unerasure is not always successful; the erased file's data will eventually be overwritten. SMARTCAN virtually guarantees successful unerasure of files by storing "erased" data in a special subdirectory called SMARTCAN. SMARTCAN is a TSR that occupies about 10K of RAM when activated.

In step 3, you may select one or more of the installed drives from the list of drives on the left-hand side of the Drives dialog box. Or, you may select drives by group from the Drive Types box. Select All Floppy Drives to protect all floppy drives on your system, All Local Drives to protect all non-floppy, non-network drives, or All Network Drives to protect network volumes to which you are connected.

In step 4, select All files to protect all files on the drive(s) you selected in step 3. Select Only the Files Listed to protect only files of your choosing. Specify these files at the File Extensions prompt, listing them by extension (*.COM, *.EXE, etc). Select All Files Except Those Listed to protect all files but those of your choosing. Specify the files exempt from protection by extension at the File Extensions prompt. Files that have been backed up through use of a Backup program (i.e., those files with the Archive attribute turned off) will not be protected unless the Protect Archived (Backed Up) Files option is turned on.

In step 5, the default storage limits are five days or 20MB, whichever comes first.

To Deactivate File Protection

1. In the Configure SmartCan dialog box, toggle the **Enable SmartCan** option off.
2. Select **OK** in the Configure SmartCan dialog box to return to the DOS prompt.

SMARTCAN is removed from memory when disabled.

To Purge Files (Manually)

1. In the Configure SmartCan dialog box, select **Purge**.
2. Optionally select a drive containing files to be purged: In the Purge Deleted Files dialog box, select **Drive**, then select the drive letter and **OK**.
3. Mark the file or files you want to purge: Select **Tag** and enter a filespec for the file(s) you want to mark in the Tag dialog box, or just double-click on the file(s) in the list.

4. Select **Purge**.
5. Select **Cancel** in the Purge Deleted Files dialog box, then **OK** in the Configure SmartCan dialog box to return to the DOS prompt.

Note that purged files are deleted permanently, and cannot be unerased.

● SYNTAX

SMARTCAN (/options**)**

The options are the following:

/CONVERT searches for and converts EP (Erase Protect) TRASHCANS for use with SMARTCAN.

/ON activates SMARTCAN and loads it into memory.

/OFF deactivates SMARTCAN and removes it from memory.

/STATUS displays current status and settings.

/UNINSTALL functions the same as /OFF.

/SKIPHIGH loads SMARTCAN into the main 640K of memory instead of High Memory. Use with the /ON option.

SPEEDISK
The Disk Defragmentation Program

When DOS writes a file to disk, the first cluster in the file is placed in the first available cluster on disk, the next cluster in the file is placed in the next available cluster, and so on, filling the disk from front to back. As a result, when files are copied onto an empty hard disk, each file's clusters sit together in one area of the disk.

After much use, however, a file's clusters can be scattered over different areas of the disk. For example, if a 20K file is deleted and a 25K file is written to the disk, the first 20K of the new file fits into the vacated space, while the remaining 5K must be placed elsewhere. Although this is simply a result of normal DOS bookkeeping, a hard disk with files scattered all over will noticeably slow down your computer. The read-write heads must travel the entire surface of the disk just to find one file.

Finding a file is much faster if its component clusters are consecutive. SPEEDISK optimizes, or defragments, your hard disk, placing the clusters of each file next to one another and moving all files toward the beginning of the disk.

- **UPGRADE INFORMATION** SPEEDISK 7 contains all of the functions found in SPEEDISK 6 and relocates a few options.

To Defragment/Optimize a Hard Disk

1. In the dialog box that appears, select the drive you want to defragment.

2. In the Recommendation dialog box, select an optimization method and then select **Optimize**, or select **Cancel** to configure the program. In version 6, select **Optimize** to run SPEEDISK as it is currently configured, or select **Configure** to reconfigure the program. If you select Optimize (in either version), skip to step 11. If you configure the program, continue with steps 3 through 10.

238 SPEEDISK

3. Optionally specify the order in which directories are written to disk during optimization. (See "To Specify Directory Order.")

4. Optionally specify the order in which files are to be listed within directories. (See "To Specify File Sort Order.")

5. Optionally specify files that should be placed at the beginning of the disk during optimization. (See "To Place Files at the Beginning of a Disk.")

6. Optionally specify files that are not to be moved during optimization. (See "To Specify Unmovable Files.")

7. Optionally specify the method of optimization. (See "To Select an Optimization Method.")

8. Optionally set miscellaneous options. (See "To Set Miscellaneous SPEEDISK Options.")

9. Save the new configuration. Pull down the Configure menu, and select the **Save Options to Disk** option.

10. Pull down the Optimize menu and select the **Begin Optimization** option, or press **Alt-B**. The optimization process may take some time to finish.

11. Select **OK** to acknowledge completion of the operation.

12. In the dialog box that appears, select **Another Drive** to defragment another drive, select **Configure** to change program configuration, or select **Exit Speed Disk** if you are finished. If you select Another Drive, go back to step 1. If you select Configure, go back to step 3.

In step 2, for an explanation of the optimization methods, see "To Select an Optimization Method."

To Place Files at the Beginning of a Disk

1. Pull down the Configure menu, and select the **Files To Place First** option.

2. In the Files To Place First dialog box, optionally add a filespec to the file list. Select **Insert** and type a filespec. Repeat as necessary.

3. Optionally remove a filespec from the file list by highlighting the filespec and selecting **Delete**. Repeat as necessary.
4. Optionally rearrange the order of the files. Highlight a filespec you want to relocate, select **Move** to tag the filespec, use ↑ and ↓ or the mouse to relocate it, and select **Move** again to untag it. Repeat as necessary.
5. Select **OK**.

As a general rule, you get an increase in hard-disk performance if frequently accessed files (those that will not change in size, such as .COM or .EXE files) are placed at the beginning of the disk, thus minimizing the distance the read-write heads must go to find them. This function allows you to specify the files to be placed at the beginning of the disk.

To Save the Current Configuration

- Pull down the Configure menu, and select the **Save Options to Disk** option.

Saved settings remain in effect in the current session and in future sessions until they are changed again.

To Select a Different Drive to Defragment/Optimize

1. Pull down the Optimize menu, and select the **Drive** option.
2. In the dialog box that appears, select the drive to defragment or optimize.
3. Go to step 2 in "To Defragment/Optimize a Hard Disk."

Use this function if, during configuration (steps 3 through 9), you want to defragment or optimize a different drive from the one you initially chose.

To Select an Optimization Method

1. Pull down the Optimize menu and select the **Optimization Method** option.
2. In the Select Optimization Method dialog box, select from five available options.
3. Select **OK**.

In step 2, the options are as follows:

- Full Optimization defragments all files and moves them toward the beginning of the disk, closing all gaps.
- Full with Directories First defragments all files, closes all gaps, and moves directories to the very beginning of the disk.
- Full with File Reorder defragments all files, closes all gaps, moves directories to the very beginning of the disk and sorts files. This is the most comprehensive optimization option.
- Unfragment Files Only defragments all files but does not close gaps.
- Unfragment Free Space fills empty space by moving files toward the beginning of the disk without unfragmenting them.

To Set Miscellaneous SPEEDISK Options

1. Pull down the Configure menu, and select **Other Options**.
2. Toggle any of three available options.
3. Select **OK**.

In step 2, the options are as follows:

- Read-after-Write checks that data was properly written to a new location on disk.

- Clear Unused Space overwrites all unused space as data is relocated.
- Beep When Done enables or disables beep upon completion of optimization.

To Specify Directory Order

1. Pull down the Configure menu, and select the **Directory Order** option.

2. In the Select Directory Order dialog box, optionally highlight a directory in the Directory list box and select **Add** to add it to the Directory Order box. Repeat as necessary.

3. Version 6 only. Optionally highlight a directory in the Directory Order box, and select **Delete** to remove it. Repeat as necessary.

4. Optionally rearrange files in the Directory Order box. Highlight the directory you want to relocate, select **Move** to tag it, use ↑ and ↓ or the mouse to reposition the directory, and select **Move** again to untag it. Repeat as necessary.

5. Select **OK**.

Use this function to specify the order in which directories are written on the disk during Full Optimization or Directory Optimization. (See "To Select an Optimization Method.") As a general rule, the best performance results from placing the most frequently accessed directories first. Directories are placed as they are listed in the Directory Order box in the Select Directory Order dialog box.

In step 2, you can move the highlight quickly by using built-in Speed Search. To use Speed Search, simply type the first letter or letters of the directory you want to highlight. Each time you type a letter, the highlight bar jumps to the next directory name beginning with the letter typed. Pressing Ctrl-↵ cycles the highlight bar through all directories that match the current search string.

In step 4, some rearranging is usually necessary, because directories added to the Directory Order box are placed at the top of the list.

To Specify File Sort Order

1. Pull down the Configure menu, and select the **File Sort** option. The File Sort dialog box appears.
2. In the Sort Criterion box, select how files are to be sorted.
3. In the Sort Order box, specify whether files are to be sorted in Ascending or Descending order.
4. Select **OK**.

Use this function to specify the order in which files will be listed in their directories. This sorting can be accomplished by a file sort or by any kind of optimization. (See "To Select an Optimization Method.")

In step 2, there are five options from which to choose:

- Name, to sort files by file name
- Extension, to sort files by file extension
- Date & Time, to sort files by file date and time
- Size, to sort files in order of their size
- Unsorted, to leave files in whatever order they may be in

In step 3, the Ascending and Descending options have no effect if the sort order is set to Unsorted in step 2.

To Specify Unmovable Files

1. Pull down the Configure menu, and select the **Unmovable Files** option.
2. In the Unmovable Files dialog box, type the complete name of a file that is not to be moved and press ↓. Repeat as necessary.
3. Optionally remove files from the list by highlighting them and selecting **Delete**.
4. Select **OK** when finished.

Some files, such as those employed by certain copy-protection schemes, should not be repositioned on the disk. SPEEDISK is good at identifying such files. This function allows for manual editing of the unmovable file list.

To View a File Fragmentation Report

1. Pull down the Information menu, and select the **Fragmentation Report** option.
2. In the directory tree in the File Fragmentation Report dialog box, highlight a directory whose files you want to detail. Repeat as necessary.
3. Select **OK** when finished.

In step 2, you can move the highlight quickly by using built-in Speed Search. To use Speed Search, simply type the first letter or letters of the directory you want to highlight. Each time you type a letter, the highlight bar jumps to the next directory name beginning with the letter typed. Pressing Ctrl-↵ cycles the highlight bar through all directories that match the current search string.

The report details the name of each file in the highlighted directory, the percentage of the file that is unfragmented, the total number of fragments that make up the file, and the number of clusters the file occupies.

Files that are moderately fragmented are shown in yellow on a color display and are bulleted on a monochrome display. Files that are highly fragmented are shown in red on a color display and are bulleted on a monochrome display. Files that are 100 percent unfragmented are displayed normally.

To View the Map Legend

1. Pull down the Information menu, and select the **Map Legend** option.
2. Select **OK** when you are finished reading.

A partial legend appears on the screen with the disk map. Use this option to display a complete legend.

To View Relevant Disk Information

1. Pull down the Information menu, and select the **Disk Statistics** option.
2. Select **OK** when you are finished reading.

This function provides information such as disk size, percentage of disk space that is occupied and free, number of files on the disk, number of clusters allocated to files and directories, and number of unused clusters.

To View a Static File List

1. Pull down the Information menu, and select the **Show Static Files** option.
2. Select **OK** when finished.

This function lists files deemed unmovable by SPEEDISK, as well as those specified as unmovable by the user. (See "To Specify Unmovable Files.")

To Walk the Disk Map

1. Pull down the Information menu, and select the **Walk Map** option.
2. Move the flashing block to the cluster whose contents you want to detail.
3. Select **OK** when you're finished reading the Contents of Map Block dialog box.
4. Repeat steps 2 and 3 as necessary.

This function details the contents of cluster blocks as they appear on the SPEEDISK disk map. Specifically, it shows which clusters are represented by the block, which files belong to the clusters, and whether the clusters are optimized or fragmented.

SPEEDISK **245**

In step 2, you can move the flashing block with the mouse or the cursor keys. When using the mouse, drag the flashing block or simply click on the target cluster. When using the arrow keys, press ↵ to detail the target cluster.

After step 3, you can detail other blocks. When finished, if you have been using the arrow keys and the flashing block is still visible, press the Esc key. If you have been using the mouse, simply select the next function you want to perform.

• SYNTAX

SPEEDISK [*drive*:] [*/options*]

drive: specifies the drive to defragment/optimize. If you specify *drive:* on the command line, omit step 1 in "To Defragment/Optimize a Hard Disk."

The options are the following:

/B reboots the computer after defragmentation/optimization.

/F specifies Full Optimization. (See "To Select an Optimization Method.")

/FD specifies Full With DIR's First optimization. (See "To Select an Optimization Method.")

/FF specifies Full With File Reorder optimization. (See "To Select an Optimization Method.")

/Q specifies Unfragment Free Space. (See "To Select an Optimization Method.")

/SD[-] sorts files by date and time. Append the optional minus sign to sort in descending order.

/SE[-] sorts files by extension. Append the optional minus sign to sort in descending order.

/SKIPHIGH tells SPEEDISK to use only conventional memory, rather than High Memory, as workspace.

/SN[-] sorts files by file name. Append the optional minus sign to sort in descending order.

/SS[-] sorts files by file size. Append the optional minus sign to sort in descending order.

/U specifies Unfragment Files Only. (See "To Select an Optimization Method.")

/V toggles the Read-after-Write option on. (See "To Set Miscellaneous SPEEDISK Options.")

- **NOTES** SPEEDISK will unfragment compressed drives such as those created by DOS 6's DoubleSpace.

SYSINFO
System Information

SYSINFO provides 24 screens of information (21 in version 6) about most aspects of your computer. It details system configuration, gives complete characteristics of installed drives, details memory usage, and provides CPU and hard-disk benchmarks.

- **UPGRADE INFORMATION** SYSINFO 7 can display all of the information screens found in SYSINFO 6 and adds three more, which display your NDOS.INI, SYSTEM.INI, and WIN.INI files.

To Cycle through Information Screens Consecutively

- At the bottom of any information screen, select **Next** to see the next screen in sequence. Select **Previous** to see the previous one.

The order in which information screens appear corresponds to the order of options on the pull-down menus. The first screen (System Summary) is the first option on the first menu, the second screen is the second option, and so on.

To Print a Complete System Summary Report (Version 7)

1. Pull down the File menu and select the **Print Report** option.
2. In the Topics list, select the screens you want to include in the report.
3. If you want to run the same report again in the future, select **Save** and enter a file name in the Save Report Options dialog box that appears.
4. Select a destination for the report from the Destination drop down list.

248 SYSINFO

5. Select **OK**.

This function allows you to print multiple information screens in one report.

In step 2, if you have previously saved a set of screens for a report, you may load it here instead of selecting the screens all over again. To do so, select Load and then the name of the set from the Load Report Options dialog box.

In step 3, you can save the set of screens you selected in step 2, thereby simplifying future runs of the same report.

To Print a Complete System Summary Report (Version 6)

1. Pull down the Report menu, and select **Print Report**.
2. In the Report Options dialog box, select the information screens you want to include in the report.
3. In the User Text box, optionally toggle the **Report Header** option to include a header in the report.
4. Optionally toggle the **Notes at End of Report** option to append comments at the end of the report.
5. Select **Printer** to send the report to your printer. Select **File** to send the report to a file.
6. If you are printing to a file, type the path and file name and select **OK**.
7. If you are printing to a file, select **OK** to acknowledge completion.

This function allows you to print the contents of multiple information screens in one report. The Report Options dialog box has an option for every information screen in SYSINFO.

Toggling the Report Header option on in step 3 adds an additional step to the sequence between steps 6 and 7: In the Report Header dialog box, type your header and select OK.

SYSINFO **249**

Toggling the Notes at End of Report option on in step 4 also adds an additional step between steps 6 and 7: In the User Notes dialog box, type your comments and select OK. Comments can occupy a maximum of ten lines. Move the cursor between lines by using ↑ and ↓ only. Pressing ↵ terminates input and is equivalent to selecting OK.

To Print an Information Screen

1. Select the **Print** option at the bottom of the information screen.

2. In the Print Current Information dialog box, select **Printer** to send the output to your printer. Select **File** to send output to a file.

3. If you are printing to a file, type the path and file name to which you want output sent, and select **OK**.

4. Select **OK** to acknowledge completion.

Omit step 3 if you are printing to the printer and not to a file.

To View a Particular Information Screen

Each information screen can be accessed by selecting one option on one menu. (See Table 3 for details.) The screens show the following information:

- *CONFIG.SYS:* display of CONFIG.SYS file.
- *AUTOEXEC.BAT:* display of AUTOEXEC.BAT file.
- *NDOS.INI:* display of NDOS.INI file. Version 7 only.
- *WIN.INI:* display of WIN.INI file. Version 7 only.
- *SYSTEM.INI:* display of SYSTEM.INI file. Version 7 only.
- *System Summary:* type of main processor, math coprocessor, BIOS, video standard, mouse, keyboard, bus, amount of memory installed, number and types of drives, number of ports, and type of operating system running.

- *Video Summary:* kind of card installed, kind of monitor installed, current video mode, character size, maximum number of on-screen scan lines, amount of video memory, video page size, and address of first segment of video memory.
- *Hardware Interrupts:* hardware interrupt usage.
- *Software Interrupts:* software interrupt usage.
- *Network:* current user and type of network (SYSINFO is only compatible with Novell Netware networks).
- *CMOS Values:* status and contents of CMOS, including type and number of installed drives and amount and kind of memory installed.
- *Disk Summary:* number of drives installed, drive letters assigned to them, and their type, capacity, and current default directory.
- *Disk Characteristics:* logical and physical characteristics of any drive on your system (select the drive in the drive list box in the upper-right corner of the Disk Characteristics screen).
- *Partition Tables:* location and contents of partition table.
- *Memory Summary:* kind and amount of memory installed, how much is used, and how much is free.
- *Expanded Memory (EMS):* display of technical information about any expanded memory (amount used and available), LIM driver version, etc.
- *Extended Memory (XMS):* display of technical information about any extended memory (amount used and available), driver version, etc.
- *DOS Memory Blocks:* details on first 640K of memory, listing what applications are loaded, the starting address and size of each application, and to what each belongs.
- *TSR programs:* name, location in memory, and size of TSRs loaded.
- *Device Drivers:* devices loaded, the starting memory address, and description of each.

Table 3: Information Screens in SYSINFO

SCREEN	MENU	OPTION
System Summary	System	System Summary
Video Summary	System	Video Summary
Hardware Interrupts	System	Hardware Interrupts
Software Interrupts	System	Software Interrupts
Network	System	Network Information
CMOS Values	System	CMOS Status
Disk Summary	Disks	Disk summary
Disk characteristics	Disks	Disk Characteristics
Partition Tables	Disks	Partition Tables
Memory Summary	Memory	Memory Usage Summary
Expanded Memory (EMS)	Memory	Expanded Memory (EMS)
Extended Memory (XMS)	Memory	eXtended Memory (XMS)
TSR Programs	Memory	TSR Programs
DOS Memory Blocks	Memory	Memory Block List
Device Drivers	Memory	Device Drivers
CPU Speed	Benchmarks	CPU Speed
Hard-Disk Speed	Benchmarks	Hard-Disk Speed
Overall Performance Index	Benchmarks	Overall Performance Index
Network Speed	Benchmarks	Network Performance Speed
CONFIG.SYS File	File (v7) or Report (v6)	View CONFIG.SYS File
AUTOEXEC.BAT File	File (v7) or Report (v6)	View AUTOEXEC.BAT File

- *CPU Speed:* speed of CPU relative to Compaq 486/33 (386/33 in version 6), IBM PC/AT (8 MHz), and IBM PC/XT (4.77 MHz).

- *Hard-Disk Speed:* speed of hard disk relative to hard disks that come standard with Compaq 486/33 (386/33 in version 6), IBM PC/AT (8 MHz), and IBM PC/XT (4.77 MHz); average access times commonly used for comparing hard disks.

- *Overall Performance Index:* combination of CPU speed and hard-disk speed tests, comparing overall speed with Compaq 486/33 (386/33 in version 6), IBM PC/AT (8 MHz), and IBM PC/XT (4.77 MHz).

- *Network Speed:* read and write tests of network server's hard disk, measuring throughput in kilobytes per second.

• SYNTAX

SYSINFO [/options]

The options are the following:

/AUTO:# cycles continuously through all information screens at intervals of # seconds. Press Esc to stop and return to DOS.

/DEMO cycles continuously through the System Summary screen and Benchmark screens at 5-second intervals. Press Esc to stop and return to DOS.

/DI displays technical information about the current drive.

/N starts SYSINFO without memory scan.

/NOHDM prevents SYSINFO from detecting the hard drive model.

/REP:*filename* prints a report to *filename*.

/SOUND sounds a beep after each test of the CPU when you run the Benchmarks CPU Speed option.

/SPEC:*filename* prints a report containing the set of information screens saved as filename. Use with the /REP option.

/SUMMARY displays the System Summary screen without loading the SYSINFO program shell.

/TSR displays a list of loaded TSRs.

TS
Text Search

The TS program looks for a specified text string in any of three places: on an entire disk, in a specified group of files, or in the erased portion of a disk.

- **UPGRADE INFORMATION**   TS 7 contains all of the functions found in TS 6 and adds one, which allows you to copy found data to a file.

To Search for Text in Files

1. Start TS.
2. Press **F**.
3. Enter the filespec for the files you wish to search.
4. Enter the text you wish to search for.
5. If any text is found, press Y to continue the search, or press N to stop.

In step 3, use wildcards, such as *.DOC or *.* to indicate which files you want TS to look through.

In step 5, if TS finds the text you are looking for, it is displayed on screen along with surrounding text. Pressing **Y** causes TS to look for another occurrence of this text; pressing **N** returns you to DOS.

To Search for Text on Disk

1. Start TS.
2. Press **D** to search an entire disk; press **E** to search only the erased portion of a disk.
3. Enter the drive letter of the disk you wish to search.

4. Optionally enter the name of a file into which any found text will be copied.

5. Enter the text you wish to search for.

6. If any text is found, press **Y** to copy it to the file specified in step 5; press **N** not to copy it.

7. Press **Y** to continue searching for the text; press **N** to stop.

In step 2, pressing D will search for text on the entire disk, beginning to end. Pressing E searches only the erased or "empty" portion of the disk, the part that does not contain files.

Steps 4 and 5 occur in reverse order in version 6.

Step 5 is optional. Enter a file name here if you wish to make a copy of any text that is found. Note that the file you enter here must be located on a drive other than the one being searched. If you skip step 5, skip step 6 as well.

Found text is displayed on screen along with any surrounding text.

● **SYNTAX**

TS *filespec* "*text*" [*/options*]

filespec is the drive, path, or file name you want to search. Specify a drive letter if you want to search an entire disk or the erased portion of a disk (otherwise, the current disk is assumed). Specify a file name if you want to search within files. If you do not, you will be prompted to do so.

text is the text to search for. Make sure to enclose it in quotes. If *text* is omitted, you are prompted for it.

The options are as follows:

/A makes search automatic and returns you to DOS when complete.

/C# starts the search at cluster number #. Use when searching entire disks or erased portions of disks.

/CS makes the search case sensitive.

/D searches an entire disk.

/E searches only the erased portion of a disk.

/EBCDIC enables TS to search through files in EBCDIC format. This format is often used on IBM mainframes.

/F:*filename* allows you to copy found data to *filename* when searching for text on disk.

/LOG formats found text neatly for output to a printer or file.

/S searches for *text* in all subdirectories of the directory specified in *filespec*. Use when searching for text in files.

/T displays only the names of the directories and files in which *text* was found, and does not display *text* itself.

/WS enables TS to search through files in WordStar format. Use this option when searching through files.

See Also FILEFIND

UNERASE

UNERASE enables you to recover all or parts of erased files. When a file is erased, its entry is removed from the directory structure and the FAT (file allocation table). The file's data, however, remains on the disk, making unerasure possible. If an erased file's data is not overwritten by another file that uses the same disk space, UNERASE can recover the erased file in its entirety. If erased data is partially overwritten, UNERASE allows you to reassemble the remaining parts manually.

- **UPGRADE INFORMATION**   UNERASE 7 is nearly identical to UNERASE 6, but it adds more flexibility to the manual unerasing of files.

To Add Data to an Existing File

1. Highlight the file to which you want to add data.
2. Pull down the File menu, and select the **Append To** option.
3. Go to step 4 in "To Unerase a File Manually."

This function allows you to add clusters manually to a file that already exists or has been unerased. It is only available if you highlight an existing file. Therefore, you may have to toggle the Include Non-Erased Files option on. To find out how to do this, see "To Include Existing Files on the File List."

To Change the Current Directory

1. Pull down the File menu and select the **Change Directory** option, or press **Alt-R**.
2. In the Change Directory dialog box, highlight the directory to which you want to change, and select **OK**.

In step 2, you can move the highlight quickly by using built-in Speed Search. To use Speed Search, simply type the first letter or letters of the directory you want to highlight. Each time you type a letter, the highlight bar jumps to the next directory name beginning with the letter typed. Pressing Ctrl-↵ cycles the highlight bar through all directories that match the current search string.

Because directories always appear on the file list, some directory navigation is also possible from the file list itself. Double-clicking or pressing ↵ when a directory is highlighted makes that directory the current one.

To Change the Current Drive

1. Pull down the File menu and select the **Change Drive** option, or press **Alt-D**.
2. In the Change Drive dialog box, select a drive.

To Include Existing Files on the File List

- Pull down the Options menu, and select the **Include Non-Erased Files** option.

This option is a toggle. When toggled on, both erased and existing files appear on the file list. When toggled off, only erased files appear. This option is not available when the file list displays the results of a search (see "To Search for Erased Files in Erased Directories," "To Search Erased Disk Space for Specific Text," and "To Search for Deleted Data Fragments").

To List All Files on the Current Drive

- Pull down the File menu and select the **View All Directories** option, or press **Alt-A**.

Use this function to display all files on the current drive. You can list all files or only erased files (see "To Include Existing Files on the File List").

To List Files in the Current Directory Only

- Pull down the File menu and select the **View Current Directory** option, or press **Alt-C**.

Use this function to display only the current directory on the file list. You can list all files or only erased files (see "To Include Existing Files on the File List").

To Rename a File

1. Highlight the file you want to rename.
2. Pull down the File menu and select the **Rename** option.
3. In the Rename dialog box, type the new file name and select **OK**.

This function is only available if the highlighted file already exists or has been recovered. (See "To Include Existing Files on the File List" if you want existing files on the file list.)

To Resume a Discontinued Search

- Pull down the Search menu, and select the **Continue Search** option.

Use this function to resume a search (for lost names, text, or data types) that you have interrupted.

To Search for Deleted Data Fragments

1. Pull down the Search menu, and select the **For Data Types** option.
2. In the Search for Data Types dialog box, select the data types for which you want to search.
3. Select **OK**.

This function searches the erased portion of the disk for specific kinds of data. In step 2, select one of the following options:

- Normal Text, to search for ASCII text
- Lotus 1-2-3 and Symphony, to search for Lotus and compatible spreadsheet data and Symphony data
- dBASE, to search for database data
- Other Data, to search for anything else

When a match is found, the cluster or clusters containing the selected data type are given a file name and appear on the file list, available for unerasure (see "To Unerase a File or Group of Files Automatically"). File names begin with FILE0000; subsequent file names are numbered sequentially. The appended extensions depend on the kind of data contained in the file.

To Search Erased Disk Space for Specific Text

1. Pull down the Search menu, and select the **For Text** option.

2. In the Search for Text dialog box, type the string for which you want to search.

3. Optionally toggle the **Ignore Case** option off for a case-sensitive search.

4. Select **OK**.

This function searches erased disk space for text you specify. When a match is found, the cluster or clusters containing the search string are given a file name and appear on the file list, available for unerasure (see "To Unerase a File or Group of Files Automatically"). File names begin with FILE0000; subsequent file names are numbered sequentially.

In step 3, the Ignore Case switch toggles case-sensitive searches on or off. If it is turned on (the default), then the search is not case-sensitive. Searching for *Linda* will find every consecutive occurrence of the letters *l-i-n-d-a* without regard to case: *Linda, LINDA, LiNdA*, etc. If it is turned off, then the search will only find exact matches of the search string. Searching for *Linda* will only find *Linda*, and not *LINDA, linda, lInDa*, etc.

To Search for Erased Files in Erased Directories

- Pull down the Search menu, and select the **For Lost Names** option.

The names of erased files are kept in existing directories and are listed for unerasure on the file list. When a directory is deleted, however, the names of deleted files contained in the directory cannot be so easily accessed. This function searches the disk for the names of erased files in erased directories—lost names. When found, the lost files can be unerased, completely or partially, depending on how much of their data has been overwritten (see "To Unerase a File or Group of Files Automatically" and "To Unerase a File Manually").

To Sort the File List

1. Pull down the Options menu.
2. Select one of the six available sort options.

In step 2, select one of the following options:

- Sort by Name, to sort the file list by name
- Sort by Extension, to sort by file extension
- Sort by Time, to sort by file date and time—only available when viewing files in the current directory (see "To List Files in the Current Directory Only")
- Sort by Size, to sort by file size
- Sort by Directory, to sort alphabetically by directory—available when viewing all files on the current drive (see "To List All Files on the Current Drive")
- Sort by Prognosis, to sort by prognosis for successful recovery

To Specify the Range of a Search

1. Pull down the Search menu, and select the **Set Search Range** option.
2. In the Search Range dialog box and at the **Starting Cluster:** prompt, type the number of the first cluster of the range you want to search.
3. At the **Ending Cluster:** prompt, type the number of the last cluster in the range you want to search.
4. Select **OK**.

When you start a search, UNERASE, by default, searches the entire current disk. Use this function if you want to limit searches to particular parts of the current disk.

To Tag a File for Unerasure

1. Highlight the file you want to tag.
2. Pull down the File menu and select the **Select** option, or press the spacebar, or click the right mouse button.

The Select option is only available when an untagged file is highlighted.

To Tag a Group of Files for Unerasure

1. Pull down the File menu and select the **Select Group** option or press the gray plus key on the numeric keypad.
2. In the Select dialog box, type a filespec for the files you want to tag (*.TXT, *.DOC, *.*, etc.), and select **OK**.

To Unerase a File or Group of Files Automatically

1. Highlight or tag the file(s) you want to unerase.
2. Select **Unerase** on the file list.

262 UNERASE

3. In the Unerase dialog box, if you are unerasing more than one file, optionally toggle the **Prompt for Missing 1st Letters** option off and select **Unerase**.
4. Enter the first letter of the file name.

UNERASE makes the automatic unerasure of files simple and straightforward. It is merely a matter of manipulating the file list to show the file you want to unerase.

In step 1, see "To Tag a File for Unerasure" and "To Tag a Group of Files for Unerasure" if necessary.

In step 3, an erased file loses the first letter of its file name. When unerasing a file, therefore, the first letter of the file name must be supplied. If you are unerasing more than one file, toggle the Prompt for Missing 1st Letters option off if you do not want to supply the first letter for each file. This causes UNERASE to make *a* the first letter of each unerased file. Omit step 3 if you are unerasing only one highlighted file, that is, if you have not actually tagged any files.

Omit step 4 if the Prompt for Missing 1st Letters option is toggled off in step 3.

To Unerase a File Manually

1. Highlight the file you want to unerase.
2. Pull down the File menu and select the **Manual Unerase** option, or press **Alt-M**.
3. In the Unerase dialog box, enter the first letter of the erased file's name.
4. In the Manual Unerase dialog box, select **Add Cluster**.
5. In the Add Clusters dialog box, select one of the options for adding a cluster or group of clusters to the file.
6. Optionally select **View File** to see the contents of the clusters assembled so far. Select **OK** in the View File dialog box when you're finished.

7. Optionally select **View Map** to see the area(s) on the disk map used by the assembled clusters. Select **OK** in the View Map dialog box when you're finished.

8. Repeat steps 4 through 7 as necessary.

9. Select **Save** to save the unerased file.

Unerasing a file manually requires that you assemble (steps 4 and 5) and save (step 9) a file's component clusters. So that you can keep track, all assembled clusters are listed by number in the Added Clusters box in the Manual Unerase dialog box. You can unerase only one file at a time, even if more than one file on the file list is tagged.

In step 5, select one of the following options:

- All Clusters, to have UNERASE assemble all the clusters likely to belong to the file
- Next Probable, to have UNERASE add only the next most probable cluster
- Data Search, to add clusters by searching for specific data
- Browse, to add clusters one at a time after viewing each individually. Version 7 only.
- Cluster Number, to assemble a specific cluster or range of clusters

If you select Data Search, follow these steps before going to step 6:

1. In the Data Search dialog box, enter a search string in ASCII characters at the **ASCII** prompt or in hex characters at the **Hex** prompt.

2. Optionally toggle the **Ignore Case** option off for a case-sensitive search.

3. Optionally toggle the **Search a Specified Sector Offset** option and type an offset number to limit the search to particular offsets on the disk.

4. Select **Find**.

264 UNERASE

5. When a match is found, it appears in the View File dialog box. Select **Hex** to view the data as hex characters or **Text** to view the data as ASCII characters.
6. Select **Add Cluster** if you want to add the cluster containing the match to the list of assembled clusters.
7. Select **Find Next** to search for the next occurrence of the search string.
8. Repeat the fifth, sixth, and seventh steps if necessary.
9. Select **Done** when you are finished searching and have gathered the clusters you want to add to the file.

Version 7 only. If you select Browse, follow these steps before going to step 6:

1. Select **Hex** to view the displayed cluster as hex characters or **Text** to view it in ASCII.
2. Select **Add** if you want to add the displayed cluster to the list of assembled clusters.
3. Select **Next** to view the next cluster in sequence, **Prev** to view the previous cluster, or **Go To** to view a particular cluster.
4. Repeat the above steps as necessary.
5. Select **Done** when you have added all the clusters you want to add to the list.

If you select Cluster Number, follow these steps before going to step 6:

1. In the Cluster Number dialog box and at the **Starting Cluster:** prompt, type the number of the first cluster in the range of clusters you want to add to the file.
2. At the **Ending Cluster:** prompt, type the name of the last cluster in the range of clusters.
3. Select **OK**.

In step 9, the clusters you have assembled or added will be recovered as one file. If, however, the clusters you have assembled are, taken together, smaller than the original file, there is one extra step: In the Confirm Save dialog box, select Save Anyway to save what you have, or select Resume to go back to step 4.

To Unerase a File to a New File Name Manually

1. Highlight the file you want to unerase.
2. Pull down the File menu, and select the **Create File** option.
3. In the UnErase dialog box, type the new file name and select **OK**.
4. Go to step 4 in "To Unerase a File Manually."

This function allows you to erase a file manually and to give the file a new name.

To Unerase a File to a New Location Automatically

1. Highlight the file you want to unerase.
2. Pull down the File menu, and select the **Unerase To** option.
3. In the Unerase To dialog box, select a new drive for the unerased file.
4. Edit the suggested path and file name as needed, and select **OK**.

In step 4, you have to edit the suggested path if you want to place the unerased file in a subdirectory of the drive you specified in step 3, or if you want to supply the correct first letter of the file name. Erased files lose the first characters of their file names, so UN-ERASE automatically attaches an *a* during this procedure.

To Untag a Group of Files

1. Pull down the File menu and select the **Unselect Group** option or press the gray minus key on the numeric keypad.

2. In the Unselect dialog box, type the filespec for the files you want to untag (*.DOC, *.*, etc.), and select **OK**.

The Unselect Group option is only available when one or more files are tagged.

To Untag a Single File

1. Highlight the tagged file you want to untag.
2. Pull down the File menu and select the **Unselect** option, or press the spacebar, or click the right mouse button.

The Unselect option will be available only when a tagged file is highlighted.

To View the Contents of a File on the File List

1. Highlight the file whose contents you want to view.
2. Select the **View** option at the bottom of the file list.
3. In the View File dialog box, select **OK** when finished.

In step 3, the View File dialog box has other options. If the file is presented in text mode, select Hex to view the file in hex characters. If the file is presented in hex mode, select Text to view the file in ASCII characters. Select Next to view the next file on the file list, and select Prev to view the previous file on the file list.

To View Pertinent Information about a File on the File List

1. Highlight the file about which you want information.
2. Select the **Info** option at the bottom of the file list.
3. In the Information dialog box, select **OK** when finished.

This function shows the erased file's name, date, time, size, attributes, prognosis for unerasure, the number of its starting cluster, and the number of clusters that make up the file.

UNERASE **267**

In step 3, the Information dialog box has two other options. Select Next to view information about the next file on the file list. Select Prev to view information about the previous file.

● **SYNTAX**

UNERASE [*filespec*] [*/options*]

filespec specifies the name of the file or group of files you want to unerase. If *filespec* is just a file name, *filespec* is unerased automatically, and the program returns you to the DOS prompt. If, however, *filespec* uses wildcards, the unerase program comes up with all files matching *filespec* tagged. You must then take appropriate steps to unerase these files. (See "To Unerase a File or Group of Files Automatically" and "To Unerase a File Manually.")

The options are as follows:

/IMAGE causes UNERASE to use data from the IMAGE program to unerase files and not use data from DOS's MIRROR program.

/MIRROR causes UNERASE to use data from DOS's MIRROR program to unerase files and not use data from the IMAGE program.

/NOINFO causes UNERASE not to use data from IMAGE or DOS's MIRROR program to unerase files. (Version 7 only.)

/NOPROTECTED prevents UNERASE from unerasing files protected by SmartCan or DOS's Delete Sentry program. (Version 7 only.)

/NOTRACK causes UNERASE not to use data from DOS's Delete Tracking program.

/PROTECTED causes UNERASE to unerase only files protecteed by SmartCan or DOS's Delete Sentry Program. (Version 7 only.)

/SKIPHIGH causes UNERASE to use only conventional memory. (Version 7 only.)

● **NOTES** Unerase can recover files from compressed drives such as those created by DOS 6's DoubleSpace.

UNFORMAT

UNFORMAT recovers data on disks that have been formatted accidentally. UNFORMAT works best when critical system information (the boot record, root directory, and file allocation table, or FAT) has been saved with IMAGE or SFORMAT (Safe Format). Data can also be recovered when critical system information is not saved, though files will be placed in generically named directories (DIR0, DIR1, etc.). UNFORMAT will not work on disks that are completely overwritten when formatted. UNFORMAT can also be used to reconstruct some severely damaged disks.

- **UPGRADE INFORMATION** UNFORMAT 7 is identical to UNFORMAT 6.

To Unformat a Disk

1. In the Unformat dialog box, select **Continue**.
2. In the dialog box that appears, select the drive you want to unformat.
3. When asked whether you saved IMAGE (critical system) information on the drive to be unformatted, select the appropriate response, **Yes** or **No**.
4. Select **Yes** in the confirmation box that appears.
5. The next few steps differ depending on your selection in step 3:

    - If you selected **Yes** in step 3 and IMAGE information has been saved on the disk to be unformatted, then select **OK** or **Recent** in the Image Info Found dialog box to unformat the disk using IMAGE information. Select **Yes** in the Absolutely Sure confirmation box. Select **Full** in the Full or Partial Restore dialog box.

    - If you selected **Yes** in step 3 and IMAGE information has not been saved, select **Yes** in the dialog box to unformat the disk without the IMAGE information.

- If you selected **No** in step 3, go to step 6.

6. Select **OK**, twice if necessary, to acknowledge completion of unformatting.

In the Full or Partial Restore dialog box, you can select Partial to restore all or only some of the disk's critical system information. Toggle any of the system areas you want to restore: Boot Record, File Allocation Table, or Root Directory. Then select OK.

In step 3, do not attempt to unformat the host drive, which contains a compressed volume, if IMAGE information has not been saved (i.e., the answer to the question you are asked in this step is no).

In step 6, selecting OK a second time is necessary when a disk without IMAGE information is unformatted. The second OK acknowledges the generic directories (DIR0, DIR1) into which recovered files are placed.

• SYNTAX

UNFORMAT [*drive*:] [*/options*]

drive: specifies the drive to be unformatted. If you specify a drive on the command line, you can skip steps 1 and 2 in "To Unformat a Disk."

The options are as follows:

/IMAGE causes UNFORMAT to use data from the IMAGE program to unformat disks and not use data from DOS's MIRROR program.

/MIRROR causes UNFORMAT to use data from DOS's MIRROR program to unformat disks and not use data from the IMAGE program.

See Also IMAGE, SFORMAT

WIPEINFO
The Secure Deletion Program

WIPEINFO allows you to dispose of private data securely. When you delete a file from a disk, it is removed from the directory and the file allocation table (FAT), but its data remains on the disk, making it possible to unerase an erased file. When you use WIPEINFO, however, the data is completely overwritten, making recovery impossible. WIPEINFO can expunge entire disks or files that you specify.

- **UPGRADE INFORMATION**   WIPEINFO 7 is identical to WIPEINFO 6, but for a few cosmetic changes.

To Configure WIPEINFO

1. In the WipeInfo dialog box, select **Configure**.
2. In the Wipe Configuration dialog box, select a wipe method.
3. Select a concomitant wipe value.
4. At the **Repeat Count**: prompt, enter the number of times you want to repeat the wipe.
5. Select **OK** to set these options for the current WIPEINFO session only, or select **Save Settings** to set options for both current and future sessions.

In step 2, there are two wipe methods available: Select Fast Wipe: simply to overwrite data (this is sufficient protection against all but the most sophisticated electronic snoops), or select Government Wipe: if you work for the Department of Defense or have a security clearance.

In step 3, select the character that WIPEINFO uses to overwrite data by typing its numeric value. For a Fast Wipe, the default is 0. For a Government wipe, you also select the number of times WIPEINFO overwrites with 1's and 0's before it writes with the character you specify. The defaults for this option are 3 and ASCII character 246, respectively.

To Overwrite the Contents of an Entire Disk

1. In the WipeInfo dialog box, select **Drives**. The Wipe Drives dialog box appears.
2. In the Drives box, select the drive or drives to be overwritten.
3. In the Wiping Method box, select the areas of the disk(s) to be overwritten.
4. Select **Wipe**.
5. In the Warning dialog box, select **Wipe**.
6. Select **OK** to acknowledge completion.

In step 2, every drive installed on your system appears in the Drives box. Toggle the drive or drives you want to delete.

In step 3, select Wipe Entire Drive if you want to overwrite all of a disk. Select Wipe Unused Areas Only to overwrite disk space not containing data. This option allows you to preserve data currently on a disk while destroying data from earlier erasures using the DEL command in DOS.

To Wipe Files from a Disk

1. In the WipeInfo dialog box, select **Files**. The Wipe Files dialog box appears.
2. In the File Name box, enter a filespec indicating the file or group of files to be wiped. Preface the filespec with a new path if necessary.

3. Optionally toggle any or all of four file options: **Include Subdirs**, **Confirm Each File**, **Hidden Files**, or **Read-Only Files**.
4. In the Wiping Method box, specify the areas to be wiped and the method to be used.
5. Select **Wipe**.
6. In the Warning dialog box, select **Wipe**. If **Confirm Each File** is toggled on, select **Wipe**, **Skip**, or **Auto** in the Wiping Files dialog box.
7. Select **OK** to acknowledge completion.

In step 2, the current directory is supplied as a path. To change this path, type a new one or select the Directory option at the bottom of the Wipe Files dialog box. In the Change Directory dialog box that appears, type a new default directory or select it from the Drive drop down list and the Subdirectories list (version 7) or from the Sub-directories and Drives list boxes (version 6). You must enter a filespec (*.DOC, *.*, FILE.EXT, etc.) in addition to the path.

In step 3, there are four options you can toggle:

- Include Subdirs, to wipe files matching the filespec supplied in step 2 that are in subdirectories beneath the specified path.

- Confirm Each File, to selectively wipe out or keep each file matching the specified filespec.

- Hidden Files, to overwrite hidden files matching the filespec supplied in step 2. Hidden files will not be wiped unless this option is toggled on.

- Read-Only Files, to overwrite read-only files matching the filespec supplied in step 2. Read-only files will not be wiped unless this option is toggled on.

In step 4, select one of three options:

- Wipe Files, to overwrite the specified files.
- Delete Files Only, Don't Wipe, to *delete*, not wipe, files. This is equivalent to using the DEL command in DOS; the file name is removed from the directory structure and the

FAT, but the data remains on disk (thus, you can still recover the files by using Unerase).

- Wipe Unused File Slack Only, to keep files intact on disk but to overwrite each file's slack area.

The *slack* is unused space assigned to a file. If, for example, the cluster size on a hard disk is 2K (2048 bytes) and a file called EXAMPLE is 3100 bytes large, the file occupies one entire cluster and part of a second. Both clusters, including the unused part of the second cluster—the slack—are assigned to EXAMPLE in the FAT. As files change size and are deleted, slack areas fill up with data.

If you toggle Confirm Each File on, select Wipe to overwrite a file, Skip to keep the file intact on disk, or Auto to wipe automatically all remaining files matching the supplied filespec.

● **SYNTAX**

WIPEINFO [*drive:*] [*/options*]

drive: specifies the drive to be wiped.

OR

WIPEINFO [*filespec*] [*/options*]

filespec specifies the file or files to be wiped.

The options are the following:

/BATCH wipes specified drive or files without pausing for confirmation and automatically returns to DOS when finished.

/E overwrites unoccupied or erased disk space, leaving data intact. Use this option when you specify a drive, not a file.

/G# uses Government Wipe, repeating wipe # times. The default = 3. (Version 6 only.)

/GOV# uses Government Wipe, repeating wipe # times. The default = 3. (Version 7 only.)

/K overwrites file slack, leaving files intact. Use this option when you specify a file, not a drive.

/N deletes files; it works like the DEL command in DOS. Use this option when you specify a file, not a drive.

/R# repeats the wipe a specified number of times. The default = 1.

/S wipes files in all subdirectories below the default directory. Use this option when you specify a file, not a drive.

/V# overwrites data with the specified ASCII value. The default = 1.

INDEX

Numbers
1st FAT (Object menu), 21
2nd FAT (Object menu), 23
16550A test, 152

A
"Access denied" message, 36
active windows, 33, 35–36
Add Menu Item (Menu menu), 203, 204
Adjust Size (Disk menu), 50
Advanced Recovery Mode (DISKEDIT), 45
Advanced Search (Search menu), 99
ALIAS command (NDOS), 156
aliases
 deleting, 199
 editing, 171
 feeding program keystrokes from, 181
 memory for, 184, 217
 saving to memory, 196
Allow Floppy Access, for Disk Protect, 48
Alt key
 current state of, 8–9
 for pull-down menus, xviii
Alternate Names (Configuration menu), 211
ANSI.SYS driver, 2, 8, 126, 195
Append To (File menu), 256
archive file attribute, 42, 91, 157
 changing with FILEFIND, 105
 and copying files, 162
 and FOR command, 172
archive files, search for, 100
ASCII characters
 converting, 39
 in hex view, 20
ASCII files
 copying, 162
 printing, 209
 screen display of, 199
ASCII table (Tools menu), 38–39
ASCII text
 locating, 94
 search for deleted, 259
 view for, 35, 182
ASK (Batch Enhancer), 1–2, 12
ASSIGN command (DOS), and CALIBRAT, 16
ATTRIB command (NDOS), 157
attributes. *See* file attributes
audit information, for NDisks, 54, 69
auto-close timeouts, 51, 60, 74
AUTOEXEC.BAT file, 212
 displaying, 249
 loading NDD with, 217
 storing on rescue disk, 226
Auto View setting, for DISKEDIT, 35, 38
Auto-Repair, by Norton Disk Doctor, 143
average access time, 252
Average Seek test, 14

B
background color, 2, 7, 8, 126, 160–161
 after clearing screen, 4
 of box, 4
 of window, 10
Backspace key, xxi
BACKUP command (DOS), 89
backup copies, 104. *See also* rescue disk
backup programs, archive attribute for, 42, 91
bad clusters, 22
 locating, 15
 marking, 29
 repairing, 82
batch files, 1–12
 alias for, 156
 conditional branching in, 5–6
 creating in FILEFIND, 96–98
 custom menus or prompts in, 1–2
 displaying mulitiple lines of text in, 197–198

feeding program keystrokes from, 181
IF statements in, 176–178
IFF statement in, 178–179
loading in memory, 183
pauses in, 4–5
setting time for executing, 9
stopping, 158
subroutine completion, 190
subroutines in, 174
terminating, 188
battery, and CMOS information, 82
baud rate, 128
BE (Batch Enhancer), 1–12
BEEP (Batch Enhancer), 3, 12
BEEP command (NDOS), 158
beeps
by NDOS, 217
at optimization completion, 241
binary files
copying, 162
view for, 35
BIOS, 249
BIOS Seek Overhead test, 14
Black and White option, 128, 131, 206
blanking screen display, 51, 58–59, 64–65
blinking box, 167
blinking horizontal line, 168
blinking text, 160, 161
blinking vertical line, 169
blocks, marking, 29–30
boot record
cluster for, 22
editing, 18–19
restoring, 81
saving on IMAGE.DAT file, 116
storing on rescue disk, 78, 226
testing and repairing, 142–149
view, 35
write-protecting, 48
Boot Record (Object menu), 18
bootable disks, 232
creating, 79
system files on, 41, 91
booting, partition for, 24
border for box, 167
border of screen, color of, 8, 160, 161
BOX (Batch Enhancer), 3–4, 10
boxes
in batch files, 1
drawing on screen, 167–168
branching, conditional, 1, 2, 5–6
buffer, size for undo, 31
bus, 249
buttons
in dialog boxes, xx
radio, xx–xxi

C

Calculator (Tools menu), 44
CALIBRAT, 13–16, 153
CANCEL command (NDOS), 158
case sensitivity
in data searches, 39–40
in FILEFIND, 102, 103, 105
of text search, 254
in text searches, 259
CD (Change Directory) command (NDOS), 158–159
CDD (Change Drive and Directory), 159–160
CGA color mode, 206
Change Directory (File menu), 256
Change Drive (File menu), 257
Character Filters setting, in DISKEDIT, 38
characters. *See also* text
color of, 7
printing multiple to screen, 6–7
CHDIR (Change Directory) command (NDOS), 159
clearing screen display, 4, 8, 160, 195
clipboard, 17–18
editing, 19
limitations of, 32
Clipboard (Object menu), 19
Clipper, fixing database files, 107–110
Close All (Disk menu), 53–54
closing
all open NDisks, 53–54, 66–67
NDisks, 54, 67
windows, 32
CLS (Batch Enhancer), 4, 10
CLS command (NDOS), 160
Cluster (Object menu), 19
clusters
editing, 19–20

filling, 28–29
information on, 36
link commands for, 29
marking, 79–80
number of sectors on, 18
reassembling in UNERASE, 263
statistics on, 244
use when saving files, 237
CMOS
skipping testing, 144, 145
testing, 153
CMOS information
changing date and time, 127
information screen, 250
restoring, 81
storing on rescue disk, 78, 226
cold reboot, 189
color, 8, 222
of background, 2, 7, 8, 161
in batch files, 1
of border, 8, 160, 161
of box, 167–168
changing for DOS, 125–126
of character, 7
after clearing screen, 4, 160
of foreground text, 8
of horizontal line, 168
in Norton Utilities Shell, 205
of palette, 126–127
of prompt, from ASK, 2
testing, 153
of text, 8, 126, 160–161
of vertical line, 169
of window, 10
COLOR command (NDOS), 160–161
.COM file name extensions, placement on disk, 239
COMMAND.COM file. *See also* NDOS program
protecting, 48
transferring, 79
command prompt, modifying, 186–187
command stack
displaying, 175
memory for, 184
command-line help, xxiii, xxiv
commands
assigning alias to, 156

executing on selected group of files, 192–194
executing on directories and subdirectories, 173–174
file exception for, 171–172
log of, 183
repeating, 172–173
running from NORTON, 220
Commands menu
➤ Set Attributes, 94
➤ Set Date/Time, 95
➤ Target Fit, 102
Compare Windows (Tools menu), 33
comparing windows, 33
comprehensive memory test, 153, 154
compressed drives, xvii
NCACHE AND, 124
NDD test of, 149
omitting testing, 149
SPEEDISK defragmentation of, 246
compressed format, Norton Utilities installed in, 211
compression tests, skipping, 144
computer
information about, 247
rebooting, 7
concatenation of files, 161
conditional branching
in batch files, 1, 5–6
by ASK, 2
CONFIG.SYS file, 212
COUNTRY parameter in, 127
DISKREET.SYS driver in, 50, 55, 64
displaying, 249
loading NDOS.COM command shell with, 216
NCACHE2 driver in, 121
storing on rescue disk, 226
configuration
of DISKEDIT, 37
of DISKMON, 212–213
of mouse, 206, 222–223
of NCACHE2, 214–216
of NCD (Norton Change Directory), 134
of NDIAGS (Norton Diagnostics), 150
of NDOS, 195–196, 217–218

of Norton Disk Doctor, 142, 216–217
of Norton Utilities, 222–225
of screen display, 206, 222–223
of serial ports, 128–129
Configuration (Tools menu), 37
Configuration menu
➤ Alternate Names, 211
➤ AUTOEXEC.BAT, 217
➤ CONFIG.SYS, 216
➤ Expand Programs, 211
➤ Menu Editing, 210–211
➤ Passwords, 219
➤ Printer Setup, 208–209
➤ Startup Programs, 212
➤ Video and Mouse, 205, 206
Configure (Directory menu), 134
Configure menu
➤ Directory Order, 241
➤ File Sort, 242
➤ Files To Place First, 238
➤ Floppy Types, 231
➤ Hard Disks, 229
➤ Unmovable Files, 242
context-sensitive help, xxiii, xxiv
Continue Search (Search menu), 258
control box, for dialog boxes, xxii
conventional memory, 184
 for disk cache, 122
 NCACHE in, 215
 for NDD, 149
converting, numeric bases, 39
Copy (Edit menu), 17, 32
COPY command (DOS), 86, 87
COPY command (NDOS), 161–162
copy protection schemes, and hidden files, 42, 91
Copy Tree (Directory menu), 134–135
copying
 ASCII files, 162
 binary files, 162
 data to clipboard, 19
 directories, 134–135
 floppy disks exactly, 86–87
 group of files, 97
 hidden files, 162
 marked data, 17
Country Info, changing, 127
CPU speed, 252
Create Batch (List menu), 96

Create File (File menu), 265
Ctrl key, current state of, 8–9
current drive, information about, 36
current objects, information about, 36
cursor
 control in batch files, 1
 position, 7, 191
 size of, 125, 131, 196, 208
custom colors, 206
custom menus, in batch files, 1–2

D

damaged disks
 Advanced Recovery Mode for, 45
 fixing, 80–81, 82
damaged files, reconstructing, 107–113
data, searches for, 39–40. *See also* searches
data bits, 128
Data Encoding Testing, 14
data fill, 28–29
data loss, head crash and, 47
database files, fixing, 107–110
data-read errors, 82
date of system, changing, 127
dates
 checking before copying, 162
 in printed files, 119
 setting for file, 42–43, 93, 95
 sorting, 84–85
 specifying for file search, 99, 260
day of the month, 6
day of the week, 9
dBASE
 fixing database files, 107–110, 113
 search for deleted files, 259
decimal code, for ASCII characters, 39
decimal numbers, converting, 39
decrypting files, 56–57, 69–70
default directory
 changing, 101
 searches of, 99
default drive, searching, 98
default settings
 for colors, 127
 for formatting floppies, 231–232
 resetting original for DISKREET, 51

defragmenting
  disks, 237–246
  hard disks, 237–238
  selecting drive for, 239
DEL command (NDOS), 162–163
DELAY (Batch Enhancer), 4–5, 10
DELAY command (NDOS), 163
Delete (Directory menu), 135–136
Delete key, xxi
Delete Menu Item (Menu menu), 210
Delete Sentry (DOS), 267
Delete Tracking program, 267
deleted files, search for fragments, 258–259
deleting
  aliases, 199
  after copying directory, 135
  data protection after, 88–90
  directories, 135–136
  environment variables, 200
  group of files, 97
  NDisks, 57, 70
  from program list, 210
  protecting file data after, 234
  secure, 270
  volume labels, 134
DES encryption method, 55, 61, 69, 75
descending sort order, 85
DESCRIBE command (NDOS), 164
DESCRIPT.ION hidden file, 164
device drivers
  for DISKREET, 50, 55, 64, 213
  information screen, 250
  for NCACHE2, 121
Diagnose Disk, in NDD, 146–148
diagnostic tests, running batch, 151–152
dialog boxes
  buttons in, xx
  color of, 205
  moving, xxii
  navigating within, xxi–xxii
DIR command (NDOS), 164–166
directories
  adding descriptions of, 164
  changing, 101, 133, 159–160, 256
  command execution on, 173–174
  copying, 134–135
  creating, 137
  damaged, 81
  deleting, 135–136
  displaying structure, 21
  editing, 20–21
  link commands for, 29
  locating, 94
  moving files between, 184–185
  order for SPEEDISK, 241
  removing, 188
  renaming, 139, 189–190
  saving variables to memory, 196
  searching default, 99
  searching for files in erased, 260
  selecting, 21
  setting order in optimizing, 238, 240
  size information about, 136
  sorting, 84–85, 260
  for swap files, 225
  viewing files in current, 258
Directory (File menu), 99
Directory (Object menu), 20
directory attributes, NDOS command for, 157
Directory menu
  ▶ Configure, 134
  ▶ Copy Tree, 134–135
  ▶ Delete, 135–136
  ▶ File List, 136
  ▶ Make, 137
  ▶ Print Tree, 137
  ▶ Prune & Graft, 138
  ▶ Remove Tree, 135–136
  ▶ Rename, 139
  ▶ Tree Size, 136
directory stack, 166, 185, 187
directory tree
  printing, 137–138
  rearranging, 138
  testing and repairing, 142–149
Directory view, 34
DIRS command (NDOS), 166–167
disk caches, 121–124
  and CALIBRAT, 16

flushing, 122
disk drives, saving variables to memory, 196
disk light, turning off and on, 47
disk map, 244-245
Disk menu
- ➤ Adjust Size, 50
- ➤ Change Disk, 133
- ➤ Change Disk Password, 52
- ➤ Close All, 53-54
- ➤ Delete, 57
- ➤ Free Space, 139-140
- ➤ Print Tree, 137
- ➤ Rescan Disk, 139
- ➤ Search Floppies, 60
- ➤ Volume Label, 134

Disk Monitor dialog box
  Disk Light, 47
  Disk Park, 47
  Disk Protect, 48
disk space
  statistics on, 244
  viewing information on, 139-140
Disk Statistics (Information menu), 244
Disk Tools, Create Rescue Diskette, 78
disk writes, time dalay for, 122
DISKCOPY command (DOS), 86
DISKEDIT, 17-46
  configuring, 37
  edit/object functions, 17-32
  info functions, 36-37
  tools functions, 37-46
  window functions, 32-36
diskettes. *See* floppy disks
DISKMON, 47-49, 212-213
  configuring, 212-213
DISKREET 6, 50-63
DISKREET 7, 64-77
DISKREET device driver, loading, 213
DISKREET.INI file, 51
disks. *See also* damaged disks
  defragmenting, 237-246
  formatting, 229-232
  information about, 244, 250
  overwriting contents, 271
  physical layout of, 18
  placing files at beginning of, 238-239
  printing to, 118, 209
  rescanning, 139
  searching for text in, 253-254
  testing and repairing, 146-148
  unformatting, 268-269
  used and unused space on, 37
DISKTOOL, 78-83
  Create Rescue Diskette, 78
  Make a Disk Bootable, 79
  Mark a Cluster, 79-80
  Recover from DOS's Recover, 80
  Restore Rescue Diskette, 81-82
  Revive a Defective Diskette, 82
displaying
  command stack, 175
  file contents, 266
  information screen, 249
  volume labels, 200-201
Do Not Load the NDisk Manager option, 53
DOS
  help for, 175
  Shell to, 46
  version of disk formatting, 18
DOS colors, changing, 125-126
DOS commands
  ASSIGN, 16
  BACKUP, 89
  COPY, 86, 87
  DISKCOPY, 86
  FASTOPEN, 124
  FDISK, 24
  JOIN, 199
  MIRROR, 267
  and NDOS, 155
  RECOVER, 80-81
  SUBST, 16, 199
  XCOPY, 87
DOS environment
  size of, 184
  in upper memory, 218
DOS ERRORLEVEL code
  from ASK, 2
  for JUMP, 6
  for SHIFTSTATE, 9

DOS files, NDisks as, 55
DOS format, 230, 232
  renaming command, 233
DOS memory blocks, 250
DOS prompt
  returning to, from Batch Enhancer, 5
  temporary exit to, 46
DOS system files. *See* system files
double-clicking, links and, 38
double-density disks, formatting, 232
DoubleSpace (MS DOS 6), xvii
  NDD testing of, 148
  and NDisk, 77
DR DOS 6's SuperStore, xvii
DRAWBOX command (NDOS), 167–168
DRAWHLINE command (NDOS), 168–169
DRAWVLINE command (NDOS), 169
Drive (Object menu), 31
Drive Info (Info menu), 36
drive letters, for NDisks, 69, 72, 73–74
Driver (Options menu), 64, 66, 73–74
drives, 249
  changing, 133, 159–160, 257
  checking for space on, 115
  compressed, xvii
  displaying directory tree for, 140
  excluding from DISKEDIT, 46
  free space on, 173
  information about current, 36
  listing all files on, 257
  NDD test of specific, 145
  searching multiple, 99
  selecting, 31
  selecting for defragmentation, 239
  testing file list for fit, 102
drop down lists, xix–xx
drop shadow, for box, 168
DS (Directory Sort), 84–85
dumping memory, 18
DUPDISK (Disk Duplicator), 86–87

E

EBCDIC format, printing files in, 119, 209

ECHOS command (NDOS), 170
Edit (NDisks menu), 72–73
Edit menu
  ➤ Copy, 17
  ➤ Fill, 28
  ➤ Mark, 30
  ➤ Paste Over, 17
  ➤ Undo, 31
  ➤ Write Changes, 17
Edit Menu Item (Menu menu), 210
editing. *See also* DISKEDIT
  alias, 171
  boot record, 18–19
  clipboard, 19
  clusters, 19–20
  directories, 20–21
  disabling in DISKEDIT, 37
  environment variable, 171
  FATs (file allocation tables) (1st copy), 21–22
  FATs (file allocation tables) (2nd copy), 23
  files, 23
  menus, 223
  NDisks, 57
  partition table, 24–26
  physical sectors, 26–27
  saving after, 17
  sectors, 27
  undoing, 31
EGA color mode, 126, 206
encrypted disks, selecting, 31
encrypted drives. *See also* NDisks
encrypting files, 58, 60–61, 70–71
encryption method, for NDisks, 54, 55, 69
End key, xix, xxi
ending, batch files, 188
ENDLOCAL command (NDOS), 170
End-of-File marks, 29
ENDTEXT command (NDOS), 197–198
environment variable, editing, 171
environment variables, 194
  deleting, 200
  memory for, 217
  saving to memory, 196
<EOF> (End-of-File) in cluster, 22, 29

EP (Erase Protect), 88–90, 218. *See also* SmartCan
ERASE command (NDOS), 171
erased files, recovering, 256–267
error messages, customizing for NDD, 143–144
errors, data-read, 82
Escape character, 195
ESET command (NDOS), 171
Excel, reconstructing damaged files, 107, 111, 113
EXCEPT command (NDOS), 171
exclude drives, from CALIBRAT, 16
.EXE file name extensions, placement on disk, 239
EXIT (Batch Enhancer), 5, 10
EXIT command (NDOS), 172
Exit Prompt setting, in DISKEDIT, 38
exiting
  from NDOS, 172
  programs, xxii–xxiii
  temporary to DOS, 46
Expand Programs (Configuration menu), 211
expanded memory, 184, 250
  for disk cache, 122
  NDOS in, 197
  testing, 153
expanding files for Norton programs, 211, 223–224
exploding window, 10
extended memory, 184, 250
  for disk cache, 122
  NDOS in, 197
  testing, 153

F

FA (File Attributes), 91–92, 94
Fast Mouse Reset option, 208
Fast proprietary method, 55, 61, 69, 75
Fast Wipe, 270
FASTOPEN command (DOS), 124
FAT view, 35
FATs (file allocation tables)
  CALIBRAT testing of, 14
  editing 1st copy, 21–22
  editing 2nd copy, 23
  information on, 36
  link commands for, 29
  number of sectors on, 18
  saving on IMAGE.DAT file, 116
  testing and repairing, 142
  using 2nd copy, 43
FD (File Date and Time), 93
FDISK command (DOS), 24
File (Object menu), 23
file attributes, 91–92
  and DIR command (NDOS), 164
  NDOS command for, 157
  setting, 41, 94–95
file encryption, setting options, 60–61, 75
file header, for database, 108, 109
file list
  all files on drive, 257
  configuring, 96
  including existing files on, 257
  printing, 101–102
  sorting, 193, 260
  static, 244
File List (Directory menu), 136
File menu
  ➤ Append To, 256
  ➤ Change Directory, 256
  ➤ Change Drive, 257
  ➤ Create File, 265
  ➤ Decrypt, 56–57, 69–70
  ➤ Directory, 99
  ➤ Encrypt, 58, 70–71
  ➤ File Options, 60–61
  ➤ Hardware Configuration, 151
  ➤ Load Settings, 129
  ➤ Manual Unerase, 262
  ➤ Options, 150
  ➤ Print Report, 247
  ➤ Rename, 258
  ➤ Report, 151–152
  ➤ Save Settings, 129
  ➤ Select, 261
  ➤ Select Group, 261
  ➤ Unselect, 266
  ➤ Unselect Group, 265
  ➤ View All Directories, 257
  ➤ View Current Directory, 258
file name extensions
  .@#!, 55

erase-protection of files by, 89
files sorted by, 84–85, 136, 260
write-protection of files by, 48
file names
  changing, 189–190, 258
  new for unerased file, 265
  in printed header, 119
  repairing, 149
  sorting directory by, 84–85, 136
File Options (File menu), 60–61
file protection
  activating, 88–89, 234–235
  deactivating, 89, 235
file servers, and CALIBRAT, 16
file size
  sorting by, 260
  specifying for file search, 99
FILEFIND, 94–106
FILEFIX, 107–113
files
  adding descriptions of, 164
  decrypting, 56–57, 69–70
  deleting original after encryption, 71, 75
  for disk information, 139
  editing, 23
  encrypting, 58, 70–71
  as exception in command execution, 171–172
  expanding for Norton programs, 211, 223–224
  fragmentation report on, 243
  going to specific, 101
  information about, 266
  link commands for, 29
  listing, 136
  locating, 98, 114
  manually purging, 90, 235–236
  moving between directories, 184–185
  printing directory tree to, 137
  printing to, 118, 209
  renaming, 189–190
  repositioning on disk directory, 84
  saving, 237
  searching for text in, 253
  setting date and time of, 42–43, 93, 95
  setting order in optimizing, 238, 240
  sort order of, in SPEEDISK, 242
  tagging for Unerase, 261
  temporary, 225
  UNERASE to add data to, 256
  unmovable, 242–243, 244
  untagging single, 266
  viewing, 104–105
  viewing contents, 266
  wiping, 271–274
  write-protecting, 48
Files To Place First (Configure menu), 238
Fill (Edit menu), 28
Find (Tools menu), 39
Find Object (Tools menu), 40
FL (File Locate), 114
floppy disks
  caching, 215
  and CALIBRAT, 16
  copying exactly, 86–87
  formatting, 48, 231–232
  protecting against accidental format, 116
  searching for NDisks, 60
  selecting, 31
  storing hard disk information on, 226–228
  testing, 153
Floppy Types (Configure menu), 231
flushing, disk caches, 122
FOR command (NDOS), 172–173
foreground color
  of box, 4
  after clearing screen, 4
  intensity of, 8
  of text, 8
formatting
  disks, 229–232
  floppy disks, 48, 230
  low-level, by CALIBRAT, 15
  recovering data after, 116, 268–269
formatting disk
  without data destruction, 82
  with DUPDISK, 86–87
Fragmentation Report (Information menu), 243
FREE command (NDOS), 173

Free Space (Disk menu), 139–140
free space on drives, 173
    defragmenting, 240
FS (File Size), 115
full optimization, 240
Full Stroke tests, 14

G

Global (Options menu), 76
GLOBAL command (NDOS), 173–174
GOSUB command (NDOS), 174–175
GOTO (Batch Enhancer), 5–6, 12
Government Standard (DES) encryption method, 55, 61, 69, 75
Government Wipe, 76, 270
graphical controls, 207
greyscale color mode, 206
group of files
    acting on, 97
    executing command on, 192–194
    tagging for UNERASE, 261
    totalling size of, 115
    untagging, 265–266
Grow Window (View menu), 34

H

hard disk controller, CALIBRAT testing, 14
hard disk interleave, 13, 14–15
hard disks
    decision to allow formatting, 229
    defragmenting, 237–238
    optimization, 13
    parking, 47
    protecting against accidental format, 116
    speed of, 252
    storing information about, 226–228
    testing, 153
Hard Disks (Configure menu), 229
Hardware Configuration (File menu), 151
hardware interrupts, information screen, 250
headers, for printed files, 119, 209

Help
    for NDOS and DOS, 175
    for Norton Utilities version 6, xxiv
    for Norton Utilities version 7, xxiii
hex code, for ASCII characters, 39
Hex Converter (Tools menu), 39
hex string, search and replace for, 103
hex view, 34, 35
    for editing clusters, 20
    for editing files, 23–24
    editing sectors in, 28
hidden file attribute, 42, 91, 157
    changing with FILEFIND, 106
    and FOR command, 172
hidden files
    copying, 162
    DUPDISK copying of, 86
    encrypted files as, 75, 77
    overwriting, 272
    preventing addition of, 48
    search for, 100
High Memory
    for DISKEDIT, 46
    for DISKREET, 63, 77
    NCACHE in, 215
    NCACHE2 in, 124
HISTORY command (NDOS), 175–176, 184, 217
Home key, xix, xxi
horizontal line, drawing, 168–169
host drive tests, skipping, 144
hot keys
    to close NDisks, 67
    color of, 205
    for keyboard lock and screen blanking, 59, 64

I

IBMBIO.COM file, 41, 48, 91
IBMDOS.COM file, 41, 48, 91
IDE controllers, and CALIBRAT, 16
IF command (NDOS), 176–178
IFF command (NDOS), 178–179
Ignore Case option, in data searhes, 39–40
IMAGE.DAT file, 116
IMAGE program, 116, 212–213, 267, 268

importing, database file structure, 110
inactive windows, 33, 35–36
Include NonErased Files (Options menu), 257
info functions, 36–37
Info menu
- ► Drive Info, 36
- ► Map of Object, 37
- ► Object Info, 36

Information menu
- ► Disk Statistics, 244
- ► Fragmentation Report, 243
- ► Map Legend, 243
- ► Show Static Files, 244
- ► Walk Map, 244–245

information screen
printing, 249
viewing, 249
INKEY command (NDOS), 179–180
INPUT command (NDOS), 180
installing Norton Utilities, 117, 211
INSTDOS, 117
integrity of hard disk, testing, 13
IntelliWrites, 122, 124, 125, 215
intensity, of foreground text, 8
interactive interface, xviii–xxii
interleave, for hard disk, 13, 14–15
IO.SYS file, 41, 91
transferring, 79
write-protecting, 48

J

JOIN command (DOS), 199
JUMP command (Batch Enhancer), 5–6, 10

K

keyboard, 151, 249
input character from, 179–180
input multiple characters from, 180
password for locking, 51, 58–59, 64–65
Keyboard & Screen Lock (Options menu), 53
keyboard lights, testing, 153

keyboard repeat rate, 129–130, 131
KEYSTACK command (NDOS), 181, 216

L

landscape orientation, 209
laptop computers, video mode for, 206
left-handed mouse, 208
LH command (NDOS), 181–182
line
drawing horizontal, 168–169
drawing vertical, 169
line editing, in NDOS, 196
line numbers
in printed files, 119, 120
for screen display of file, 199
line spacing
for printed file, 119, 120
when printing, 209
Link menu, 29
- ► Window, 33–34

linking
in DISKEDIT, 38
windows, 33–34
list boxes, xix
LIST command (NDOS), 182
List menu
- ► Create Batch, 96
- ► Print List, 101
- ► Set List Display, 96

Load Settings (File menu), 129
LOADBTM command (NDOS), 183
LOADHIGH command (NDOS), 183
loading
batch files in memory, 183
EP (Erase Protect), 218
IMAGE, 212–213
NDOS, 217–218
SMARTCAN, 218
terminate-and-stay resident programs in Upper Memory, 181–182
locking keyboard, password for, 51, 58–59, 64–65
LOG command (NDOS), 183
logical disks, NDisks as, 68

logical drives, 20, 31
logical operators, for IF statement, 177
logical sectors, vs. physical sectors, 27
loopback plugs, 150
lost files, locating, 94–106
Lotus 1-2-3
   reconstructing damaged files, 107, 111, 113
   search for deleted files, 259
low-level format, by CALIBRAT, 15
LP (Line Print), 118–120

M

Maintenance mode, for DISKEDIT, 45, 46
Make (Directory menu), 137
map, of objects, 37
map legend, 243
Map Legend (Information menu), 243
Map of Object (Info menu), 37
margins, for printed files, 118, 119, 120, 208
Mark (Edit menu), 30
marked data, copying, 17
marking
   blocks, 29–30
   clusters, 79–80
master password, changing, 66
math coprocessor, 249
memory
   amount installed, 249, 250
   CALIBRAT testing of, 14
   loading batch files in, 183
   testing, 153
   for video, 250
memory buffer, for data from disk, 121
MEMORY command (NDOS), 184
Memory Dump (Object menu), 18
Menu Editing (Configuration menu), 210–211
Menu menu
   ➤ Add Menu Item, 203, 204
   ➤ Delete Menu Item, 210
   ➤ Edit Menu Item, 210
   ➤ Sort by Name, 220
menus
   editing, 223
   pull-down, xviii
messages
   "Access denied," 36
   displaying, 170
   from NCACHE2, 123
   for NDIAGS, 150
microprocessor, 249
MIRROR program (DOS), 267
monitor, 250
monochrome color mode, 206
MONTHDAY (Batch Enhancer), 6
mouse, 249
   configuring, 206, 222–223
   left-handed, 208
   setting sensitivity of, 130
   testing of, 153
   using, with lists, xx
   using, to resize split windows, 34
   using, with pull-down menus, xviii
MOVE command (NDOS), 184–185
moving
   dialog boxes, xxii
   files between directories, 184–185
moving computers, head parking before, 47
MSDOS.SYS file, 41, 91
   transferring, 79
   write-protecting, 48
multitasking, NCACHE2 write ability, 123

N

names
   changing for directories, 139
   of Norton programs, 211–212, 224
NCACHE, 121–124
NCACHE2, 121–124, 214–216
NCACHE.INI file, 123, 214
NCC (Norton Control Center), 125–132
   restoring saved settings, 129
   saving settings, 129

NCD (Norton Change Directory), 133–141
 configuring, 134
NDD (Norton Disk Doctor), 142–149
 configuring, 142, 216
 customizing error message in, 143–144
 Diagnose Disk, 146–148
 setting auto-repair options in, 143
 skipping tests in, 144, 145
 undoing changes in, 147, 148
NDDUNDO.DAT file, 148
NDIAGS (Norton Diagnostics), 150–154
 configuring, 150
 printing results of one test in, 152
 running specific test in, 152–154
 running tests consecutively in, 154
NDisks
 adjusting size of, 50–51, 72
 closing, 54, 67
 closing all open, 53–54, 66
 creating, 54–56, 67
 deleting, 57, 70
 drive letters for, 69, 72, 73–74
 editing, 57
 modifying, 72–73
 opening, 59, 73
 opening automatically, 62
 options for data after deleting, 61
 password for, 50, 51, 52, 55, 65, 68
 read-only, 73
 searches for, 74
 searching floppy disks for, 60
 setting options, 76
NDisks menu
 ➤ Close All, 66
 ➤ Create, 67
 ➤ Delete, 70
 ➤ Edit, 72–73
 ➤ Open, 73
 ➤ Search, 74
NDOS.INI file, displaying, 249
NDOS program, 155–202
 configuring, 195–196
 exiting from, 172
 help for, 175
 loading and configuring, 217–218
 in upper memory, 218
network
 DISKREET on, 77
 information screen, 250
 speed, 252
network drives
 activity indicator for, 47
 and CALIBRAT, 16
neutral state, for file attributes, 42
NLSFUNC program, COUNTRY parameter in, 127
NOCLOBBER, 196
nondestructive low-level format, by CALIBRAT, 15
Norton Change Directory. *See* NCD (Norton Change Directory)
Norton Control Center. *See* NCC (Norton Control Center)
Norton Diagnostics. *See* NDIAGS (Norton Diagnostics)
Norton Disk Doctor. *See* NDD (Norton Disk Doctor)
Norton programs
 expanding files, 211, 223–224
 length of names for, 211–212, 224
 quitting, xxii–xxiii
 startup, 212
Norton Utilities
 configuring, 222–225
 installing, 117
 new features of, version 7, xvii
 password for, 219–220, 225
NORTON Utilities Shell, 203–221
 color in, 205
 running programs from, 220
NUCONFIG, 118, 222–225
numeric bases, converting, 39

O

Object Info (Info menu), 36
Object menu
 ➤ 1st FAT, 21
 ➤ 2nd FAT, 23
 ➤ Boot Record, 18
 ➤ Clipboard, 19

- Cluster, 19
- Directory, 20
- Drive, 31
- File, 23
- Memory Dump, 18
- Partition Table, 24
- Physical Sector, 26
- Sector, 27–28

objects
 information about current, 36
 map of, 37
 writing, 32
opening, NDisks, 59, 73
operating system, 24, 249
optimal interleave, 14
optimization method, 240
Optimize menu, ▶ Drive, 239
optimizing. *See* defragmenting
Options (File menu), 150
Options menu
- Auto-Close Timeouts, 60
- Change Main Password, 51
- Driver, 64, 66, 73
- File, 75
- Global, 76
- Include NonErased files, 257
- Keyboard & Screen Lock, 53
- Master Password, 66
- Security, 61
- Startup Disks, 62
- System Settings, 52

output redirection, 197
overall performance index, 252
overwriting
 deleted files, 76
 encrypted data, 61
 unused space, 241

P

page numbers, for printed files, 120
page size
 for printing, 208
 video, 250
Palette Colors, 126–127
parallel ports, testing, 150, 153
parity setting, 128
parking, hard disk, 47

partition table
 cluster for, 22
 editing, 24–26
 information screen, 250
 restoring, 81
 skipping testing, 144, 145
 storing on rescue disk, 78, 226
 testing and repairing, 142–149
 write-protecting, 48
Partition Table (Object menu), 24
Partition Table view, 35
partitions
 selecting, 31
 valid system entries in, 25
passwords
 changing master, 66
 for encrypted files, 58
 for Norton Utilities, 219–220, 225
passwords for NDisks, 50, 51, 52, 55, 65, 68
Paste Over (Edit menu), 17, 32
path, 97, 198–199
Pattern Testing, 15
pause in execution, 4–5, 163
performance index, 252
physical drives, 20, 31
physical errors, testing disk for, 147
Physical Sector (Object menu), 26–27
physical sectors
 editing, 26–27
 for partition, 24–25
 vs. logical sectors, 27
POPD command (NDOS), 166, 185
portrait orientation, 209
ports, 249
 configuring, 151
 for printer, 209
PostScript format, 120
prefix, repairing for WordPerfect file, 112–113
Print List (List menu), 101
Print Object As (Tools menu), 30
Print Report (File menu), 247
Print Report (Report menu), 248
PRINTCHAR (Batch Enhancer), 6–7, 12
printer configuration files, 118, 208–209, 223

printer control codes, 119, 120
Printer Setup (Configuration menu), 208–209
printers
  selecting, 208
  specifying type, 119
printing
  CALIBRAT report, 13
  directory tree, 137–138
  in DISKEDIT, 30
  to disks, 118, 209
  file list, 101–102
  information screen, 249
  one NDIAGS test result, 152
  system summary report, 151–152, 247–249
  text files, 118–120
prognosis, UNERASE sort by, 260
program list (Norton)
  adding program to, 203–204
  adding topic to, 204
  deleting program from, 210
  editing program entry on, 210
  editing topic entry on, 210
  sorting, 220
programs, running from NORTON, 220
PROMPT command (NDOS), 186–187
prompts
  in batch files, 1–2
  from CALIBRAT, 15
  color of, 2
  for missing 1st letter in UNERASE, 262
  for NDD disk repairs, 143
  for NDisk password, 54
  for surface error repairs, 148
prompts, xxi. *See also* DOS prompt
Prune & Graft (Directory menu), 134, 138
pull-down menus, xviii
purging files manually, 90, 235–236
PUSHD command (NDOS), 166, 187

Q

Quattro Pro, reconstructing damaged files, 107, 111
Quick format, 230, 232
Quick Links setting, in DISKEDIT, 38
Quick Move setting, for DISKEDIT, 22, 37
Quick option, for changing password, 65–66
QUIT command (NDOS), 188
Quit menu, ➤ Shell to DOS, 46
quitting, Norton programs, xxii–xxiii

R

radio buttons, xx–xxi
RAM. *See* memory
RAM disks
  activity indicator for, 47
  and CALIBRAT, 16
  and DISKREET.SYS driver in CONFIG.SYS, 63, 77
  FAT for, 22
  selecting, 31
  for temporary files, 225
RD (Remove Directory) command (NDOS), 188
Read-after-Write option, for SPEEDISK, 240
read-ahead buffer, 215
read-ahead sectors, 123–124
read-only file attribute, 42, 91, 157
  changing with FILEFIND, 106
  and FOR command, 172
read-only files
  NDisks as, 73, 75
  overwriting, 272
  search for, 100
Read Only setting, in DISKEDIT, 37
read/write heads, positioning, 47
REBOOT (Batch Enhancer), 7, 12
REBOOT command (NDOS), 188–189
rebooting
  in batch files, 1, 7, 12
  and drive letters for NDisks, 74

Recalculate Partition (Tools menu), 26
records in database, fixing, 109
RECOVER command (DOS), 80–81
redirecting output, 197
relative sectors, for partition, 26
Remove Tree (Directory menu), 134, 135–136
REN command (NDOS), 189–190
Rename (Directory menu), 139
Rename (File menu), 258
RENAME command (NDOS), 190
repairing. *See also* NDD (Norton Disk Doctor)
   disks, 146–148
   file names, 149
repeat delay for keyboard, 129–130
replace. *See* search and replace
report
   on file fragmentation, 243
   system summary, 247–249
Report (File menu), 151–152
Report menu, ➤ Print Report, 248
reports
   from CALIBRAT, 13
   from NCACHE2, 124
   from NDD, 147
   on file repairs, 107
   on surface testing, 146
   on system summary, 151–152
   writing CALIBRAT to file, 16
Rescan Disk (Disk menu), 139
RESCUE, 226–228
rescue disk
   creating, 78–79, 226–227
   restoring, 81–82, 227
resizing
   partitions, 24
   split windows, 34
restoring, rescue disk, 81–82
RETURN command (NDOS), 190
RMDIR command (NDOS), 190
root directory, IMAGE.DAT file in, 116
ROWCOL (Batch Enhancer), 7, 10
running, group of files, 97

S

SA command (Batch Enhancer), 8, 12
Safe Format, 116, 229–233, 268
Save Settings (File menu), 129
saving
   editing changes, 17
   SFORMAT settings, 231
scan lines, 250
Screen Attributes (SA) command, 8, 12
SCREEN command (NDOS), 191
screen coordinates
   for cursor, 191
   for drawing box, 4, 167–168
   for window, 10
screen display
   of ASCII files, 199
   blanking, 51, 58–59, 64–65
   of characters, 6–7
   clearing, 4, 160
   clearing by NDOS, 195
   color of, 8
   configuring, 206, 222–223
   cursor position on, 7
   drawing horizontal line on, 168–169
   drawing vertical line on, 169
   drawing window on, 9–10
   number of lines on, 131, 133–134, 207
   prompt appearance on, 186–187
   of text, 170
   text written to by batch file, 7
   turning off during Pattern Testing, 15
   writing text to, 191–192
scroll bars, color of, 205
SCRPUT command (NDOS), 191
SCSI controllers, and CALIBRAT, 16
Search (NDisks menu), 74
search and replace, text string, 102–103
Search menu
   ➤ Advanced Search, 99
   ➤ Continue Search, 258
   ➤ For Data Types, 258–259
   ➤ For Lost Names, 260

- ▶ For Text, 259
- ▶ Set Search Range, 261

searches
- for data, 39–40
- of default directory, 99
- of default drive, 98
- for deleted data fragments, 258–259
- of disks for text, 253–254
- of erased disk space for text, 259
- for files, 98, 114
- for files in erased directories, 260
- of floppy disks for NDisks, 60
- of multiple drives, 99
- for NDisks, 74
- resuming discontinued, 258
- for System Area objects, 40–41
- for text in files, 253

Sector (Object menu), 27–28
sector boundaries, 31
sector on hard disk, checking, 15
sector translation, and CALIBRAT, 16
sectors, 18
- editing, 27
- information on, 36
- number of, in partition, 26
- read-ahead, 123–124

Secure option, for changing password, 65–66
Security (Options menu), 61
Security Wipe, 61
Seek Testing, 13, 14, 16
Select (File menu), 261
SELECT command (NDOS), 192–194
Select Group (File menu), 261
selecting, xviii–xxii
- directories, 21
- drives, 31
- files for editing, 23
- from list, xix

serial ports
- configuring, 128–129
- testing, 150, 152, 153

Set Attributes (Tools menu), 41
SET command (NDOS), 194
Set Date/Time (Tools menu), 43
Set List Display (List menu), 96

Set Search Range (Search menu), 261
SETDOS command (NDOS), 195–196
SETLOCAL command (NDOS), 170, 196
SFORMAT command, 116, 229–233, 268

shadow
- for box, 168
- for window, 10

shell. *See* NORTON Utilities Shell
Shell to DOS, 46
Shift key, current state of, 8–9
SHIFTSTATE (Batch Enhancer), 8–9
Show Static Files (Information menu), 244
Shrink Window (View menu), 34
slack, 273
SmartCan, 218, 234–236, 267. *See also* EP (Erase Protect)
software interrupts, information screen, 250
Sort by Name (Menu menu), 220

sorting
- directories, 84–85, 165, 260
- file list, 193, 260
- in FILEFIND, 96
- program list (Norton), 220

sound, in batch files, 1, 3
speaker, testing, 150, 153

Speed Search
- for directories, 21, 133
- in Prune & Graft option, 138
- in SPEEDISK, 241, 243
- in UNERASE, 256–257

SPEEDISK, 237–246
- directory order in, 241
- file fragmentation report from, 243
- file sort order in, 242
- for hard disk, 237–238
- map legend, 243
- optimization method, 240
- options, 240–241
- placing files at disk beginning, 238–239
- unmovable files in, 242–243

Split Window (View menu), 35
split windows
- closing, 32

creating, 35
spreadsheet files, fixing, 111
Stacker, xvii
Startup Disks (Options menu), 62
start-up options, password for, 51
startup programs, 224
Startup Programs (Configuration menu), 212
static file list, 244
status bar, of windows, 32
stop bits, 128
stopping batch files, 158
stopwatches, 130–131, 132, 198
strings. *See* text
subdirectories. *See also* directories
   copying with directory, 135
   and FOR command, 172
   wiping files from, 272
subroutines, in batch files, 174
SUBST command (DOS), 16, 199
SuperStore, xvii
SuperStore Pro, xvii
surface testing, 142–143
   running only, 145–146
   setting options, 144
   skipping, 145
swap files, 225
SWAPPING command (NDOS), 197
Switch Windows (View menu), 35–36
Symphony
   reconstructing damaged files, 107, 111, 113
   search for deleted files, 259
SYSINFO, 247–252
system, information about, 247
system area
   checking and repairing, 142–149
   search for objects, 40–41
   write-protecting, 48
system board, testing, 153
system date, changing, 127
system file attribute, 41, 91, 157, 172
system files
   DUPDISK copying of, 86
   leaving disk space for, 232
   search for, 100
   transferring, 79
   when formatting, 230
SYSTEM.INI file, displaying, 249
System Integrity Testing, 13, 14
system settings, for DISKREET, 52–53
System Settings (Options menu), 52
system summary
   information screen, 249
   printing report, 151–152, 247–249
system time, changing, 127

T

Tab key, in dialog boxes, xxi
target fit, 102
TEE command (NDOS), 197
temporary files, location of, 225
terminate-and-stay resident programs
   DISKMON as, 49
   EP (Erase Protect) as, 89
   information screen, 250
   loading in Upper Memory, 181–182
terminating batch files, 188
testing disks, 146–148
text
   color of, 8, 126, 160–161
   displaying in vertical column, 201–202
   entering at prompt, xxi
   printing files, 118–120
   screen display of, 170
   searching erased disk space for, 259
   searching files for, 253
   writing to screen, 7, 191–192
TEXT command (NDOS), 197–198
text string
   search and replace, 102–104
   search for file containing, 100
Text view, 34
time
   in printed files, 119
   running batch file at specified, 9
   setting for file, 42–43, 93, 95
   sorting, 84–85, 260
time of system, changing, 127
timed delays, in batch files, 1

timed execution, in batch files, 1
timeouts, auto-close, 51, 60, 74
TIMER command (NDOS), 198
timers, 130–131
toggle options, xx–xxi
tools functions, 37–46
Tools menu
  ▶ Advanced Recovery Mode, 45
  ▶ ASCII table, 38–39
  ▶ Calculator, 44
  ▶ Compare Windows, 33
  ▶ Configuration, 37
  ▶ Find, 39
  ▶ Find Object, 40
  ▶ Hex Converter, 39
  ▶ Print Object As, 30
  ▶ Recalculate Partition, 26
  ▶ Set Attributes, 41
  ▶ Set Date/Time, 43
  ▶ Use 2nd FAT Table, 43
  ▶ Write Object To, 32
track, number of sectors on, 18
Track-to-Track test, 14
TRASHCAN subdirectory, 89
Tree Size (Directory menu), 136
TREEINFO.NCD file, 139, 140, 141
TRIGGER (Batch Enhancer), 9
TRUENAME command (NDOS), 198–199
TS (Text Search), 253–255
TYPE command (NDOS), 199

U

UNALIAS command (NDOS), 199
Undo (Edit menu), 31
undoing
  for edits, 31
  NDD changes, 147, 148
UNERASE, 116, 256–267
  adding data to file, 256
  manual operation, 262–265
  new file name for, 265
  preventing use of, 270–274
  tagging file for, 261
UNFORMAT, 116, 268–269
unmovable files, in SPEEDISK, 242–243, 244
Unselect (File menu), 266
UNSET command (NDOS), 200
Unsplit Window (View menu), 32
unused clusters, marking, 29
unused space
  defragmenting, 240
  overwriting, 241
  wiping, 273
Upper Memory
  DISKREET loaded into, 63, 77
  loading terminate-and-stay resident programs in, 181–182
  NCACHE2 in, 124
  NDOS and DOS environment in, 218
Use 2nd FAT Table (Tools menu), 43

V

variables, assigning keyboard input to, 179–180
VDISK, and DISKREET.SYS driver in CONFIG.SYS, 63
vertical column, displaying text in, 201–202
vertical line, drawing, 169
VGA color mode, 126, 206
video, 249, 250
Video and Mouse (Configuration menu), 205, 206
video grid, testing, 153
video memory, testing, 153
video mode
  changing, 128
  testing, 154
view
  for DISKEDIT, 38
  of files, 104–105
View All Directories (File menu), 257
View Current Directory (File menu), 258
View menu, 34–35, 133–134
  ▶ Grow Window, 34
  ▶ Shrink Window, 34
  ▶ Split Window, 35
  ▶ Switch Windows, 35–36
  ▶ Unsplit Window, 32
viewing. *See* displaying; screen display
views, changing, 34–35

viruses, write-protection against, 48
VOL command (NDOS), 200–201
volume labels, 140
    adding to disk, 230, 232
    changing or deleting, 134
    displaying, 200–201
VSCRPUT command (NDOS), 201

W

Walk Map (Information menu), 244–245
warm boot, 189
WEEKDAY (Batch Enhancer), 9, 10
WIN.INI file, displaying, 249
WINDOW (Batch Enhancer), 9–10, 12
Window (Link menu), 33–34
windows
    in batch files, 1
    closing, 32
    color of, 10
    comparing, 33
    DISKEDIT functions for, 32–36
    exploding, 10
    linking, 33–34
    resizing, 34
    shadow for, 10
    splitting, 35
    zooming, 10

Windows (Microsoft)
    and DISKREET, 63
    and expanded memory for NCACHE2, 122
    installing Norton Utilities under, 117
WIPEINFO, 270–274
WordPerfect files, fixing, 111–113
WordStar format
    displaying files in, 38
    printing in, 119, 120, 209
    searching text in, 255
Write Changes, (Edit menu), 17
Write Object To (Tools menu), 32
write-back buffer, 215
write-protection
    of files, 48
    of NDisks, 57
writing objects, 32

X

XCOPY command (DOS), 87
XXFORMAT command, 233

Z

Zenith DOS, excluding drives from CALIBRAT, 16
zooming boxes, 207
zooming window, 10

Help Yourself with Another Quality Sybex Book

Understanding Presentation Graphics
Michael Talman

A must for anyone using a computer to produce business graphics, reports, and presentations, whether on a Macintosh or a PC, and regardless of software used. It's an in-depth guide to effective communication, with guidelines for planning and organization; graphic design do's and don'ts; ways to use color to best advantage; and proven techniques for conveying a clear message.

382pp; 7 1/2" x 9"
ISBN: 0-7821-1023-1

Available at Better Bookstores Everywhere

Sybex Inc.
2021 Challenger Drive
Alameda, CA 94501
Telephone (800) 227-2346
Fax (510) 523-2373

Sybex. Help Yourself.

NDOS COMMANDS IN COMMON WITH DOS

APPEND	ASSIGN	BACKUP
CHKDSK	CHOICE (DOS 6 only)	COMMAND
COMP	DEBUG	DEFRAG (DOS 6 only)
DELTREE (DOS 6 only)	DISKCOMP	DISKCOPY
DOSKEY	DOSSHELL	EDIT
EDLIN	EMM386	EXE2BIN
EXPAND	FASTOPEN	FC
FDISK	FIND	FORMAT